MATTERS OF GRAVITY

MATTERS OF GRAVITY

Special Effects

and

Supermen

in the

20th Century

SCOTT BUKATMAN

DUKE UNIVERSITY PRESS *Durham & London 2003*

©2003 Duke University Press   All rights reserved
Printed in the United States of America on acid-free paper ∞
Typeset in Cycles by Tseng Information Systems, Inc.
Library of Congress Cataloging-in-Publication Data appear
on the last printed page of this book.

FOR VIVIAN

Hence, the work proceeds by conceptual infatuations,
successive enthusiasms, perishable manias.
Roland Barthes

Ah-h - Sky so kopless, so jailless
Oh - Sky so full of universe.
Ignatz
Krazy Kat, George Harriman

CONTENTS

PREFACE

"Somehow we know by instinct that outsize buildings cast the shadow of their own destruction before them, and are designed from the first with an eye to their later existence as ruins," wrote the late W. G. Sebald in his novel *Austerlitz*.[1] The September 11 attack on the World Trade Center literalized these words as few could have imagined in their waking lives. The terror born of the attack, the eloquence of the towers' wreckage, and the horrifying sense that we had seen it before (in movies, in dreams) but had never seen anything like it, all combine to produce a palpable gulf between the author of this preface and the author of the explorations of weightlessness and urban utopianism contained in this book.

As I write this, 2001 is over, and we are comfortably cocooned in 2002, a year that, precisely because it lacks the mythic resonance of "2000" or "2001," places us firmly, finally and indisputably, in the future. But nothing will ever represent the future as strongly, to me, as Stanley Kubrick's *2001: A Space Odyssey*. It was the first film, I remember so vividly, that I ever attended alone, the friends and family of this nerdy eleven year old having little interest in either science fiction or experimental cinema. The 2001 that Kubrick and his collaborator Arthur C. Clarke offered us, back in 1968, introduced us to the future through the movements of giant space stations cartwheeling through space, as precisely piloted shuttle craft waltzed in graceful tandem toward an ultimate and strangely loving rendezvous. The real 2001 was not so benign, as precision flying now turned airliners into massive missiles plowing through the monolithic towers. The excavation site of the alien anomaly on the moon—with its bathtub walls and diminutive, central, artifact of a lost past—casts its shadow startlingly upon its appalling real-world double: ground zero. If *2001* rehearsed an aesthetic of immersive weightlessness, as Annette Michelson has demonstrated, then the events of September 11 restored the awesome power of gravity.[2]

In the immediate aftermath of September 11, my fascination with the fantasied liberation represented by weightlessness, the cessation of "gravity's dull lure" upon my body and being, made me ashamed.[3] I had returned to New York only two weeks earlier, back in my home town thanks to a sabbatical leave from my "home" university. My partner and I had a startlingly clear panoramic view of the first tower's collapse from the roof of our Brooklyn row house. It fell in silence—the endless rumble followed—and disappeared into that sickening white and yellow cloud. I finally came to know something of the terror, as opposed to the exaltation, of the sublime. The impossibility of unfettered existence slammed home.

As Slavoj Žižek pointed out, our national nightmare was also, discomfitingly, our national fantasy, endlessly rehearsed in one super-heated Hollywood blockbuster after another.[4] Superheroes, science fiction, and special effects were too easily aligned with what we had seen, while the rooftop romances of the musical comedy were obviously too naïve to speak to this experience. These were toys—I'd called them that myself—and had to be put away.

But not forever.

Michael Chabon's splendid novel, *The Amazing Adventures of Kavalier and Clay*, concerns two cousins, Sam, a young New Yorker, and Joseph, smuggled out of Prague in the late 1930s, who create a comic book superhero called The Escapist. Years later, Joe reflects upon what the comics have meant to him: "The usual charge leveled against comic books, that they offered merely an easy escape from reality, seemed to Joe actually to be a powerful argument on their behalf."[5]

Joe identifies the desire "to slip, like the Escapist, free of the entangling chain of reality and the straitjacket of physical laws . . . if only for one instant; to poke his head through the borders of this world, with its harsh physics, into the mysterious spirit world that lay beyond."[6] A similar desire drives the protagonist of a Steven Millhauser novella about a comics creator and animator (modelled on Winsor McCay): "It was desperately important to smash through the constriction of the actual, to unhinge the universe and let the impossible stream in."[7] We are implored by these writers, through their mouthpieces, to smash or poke through these "harsh physics," to encounter alternatives to the weighty structures of the real.[8]

All the fantasied escapes from gravity that dominate the pages of this volume—the bodiless exultation of cyberspace, the dances on the ceiling in *Royal Wedding* and *2001*, the amusement park rides, the cinema itself, and, of course, Superman's flight across the skies of Metropolis, recall our bodies to us by momentarily allowing us to feel them differently. It is a momentary effect, a temporary high: we are always returned to ourselves. These escapes, however, are more than retreats from an intolerable existence, they are escapes *into* worlds of renewed possibility. "Reality" is at least partly a function of our habitual behaviors and conceptual schema, so we should never underestimate the power of a good daydream.

All of this matters to me because academic discourse tends to slight these media and those aspirations. It so often mistrusts the pleasures of illusion, dismissed as illusions of pleasure. A colleague of mine once remarked, or so I heard it told, that I might lack the necessary *gravitas* for higher academia. Meant slightingly, I suppose, yet as G. K. Chesterton once observed of Coney Island, "If a child saw these coloured lights, he would dance with as much delight as at any other coloured toys; and it is the duty of every poet, and even of every critic, to dance in respectful imitation of the child."[9] In reviewing and selecting material for this collection, I found an endless return to weightlessness, to levitation and levity (*levitas*). The heroic spectator in these essays soars in fantasies of unrestricted flight. But they are more than fantasies, hysterical responses to, or denials of a world of heavy machinery and stolid meaning. These popular media and genres produce some of that very mobility and ubiquity for us. Their lightness, their triviality, and even their delicacy are the very things that give them worth. The dialogue that these adventures introduce between body and perception can be complex, deeply pleasurable, and indeed, *real*. This book, then, is offered in defiance of the spirit of gravity, but with a new cognizance of gravity's irresistible pull.

ACKNOWLEDGMENTS

I am deeply indebted to Ken Wissoker, a true friend at Duke University Press, for giving me the opportunity to gather together these pieces, with their different voices, from their disparate corners. I also want to thank him for keeping *Terminal Identity* in print and me out of limbo.

Vivian Sobchack and I have shared, over more than a decade, interests, ideas, and laughs promiscuously. This splendid friendship has been essential to my life and work, and her writing continues to dazzle me. Thomas Elsaesser chaired the 1990 Society for Cinema Studies conference panel at which I "premiered" my Tomorrowland stuff; he has been overly generous ever since. Everyone should have a Dana Polan for support, dialogue, and cameraderie. And Annette Michelson's inspiration cuts across everything in this book. If it were not for her, I surely would have gone into some other line of work.

Reading over these essays, the person I was and the people I knew have been recalled to vivid life. I've moved too often in these ten years, each time with its own joys and difficulties and in the end, I fell away from too many of those I treasured. This makes me unutterably sad, but I take some solace in remembering them now.

Many of these chapters have benefited from gifted and sympathetic editors: Vivian Sobchack, Mark Dery, Rodney Sappington, and Tyler Stallings were especially superb collaborators. Students at the University of New Mexico, der Freie Universität, and Stanford University have responded to my energy and ideas with plenty of their own. The input and feedback that I received from, in no particular order, Alex Nemerov, Caitlin Kelch, Sandy Rubin, Istvan Csiscery-Ronay Jr., David Chen, Jon Lewis, Alex Juhasz, Henry Breitrose, Oksana Bulgakowa, Karin Elsaesser, Nancy Graham, Alan Labb, Tom Gunning, Karen Voss, Anne Friedberg, Brian Kelly, and Susana Sosa made everything here better. Workshops and lectures were indispensable to putting my whims and notions to the test: I am grateful to Stanford's Film History Workshop and audiences in Berkeley, Cologne, Antwerp, Berlin, Skövde, and Las Cruces. Randy Scott at Michigan State University Library's Comic Art Collection was a gracious and helpful host. Thanks to Alison Tarnovsky of Astralwerks Records. Jill Dawsey, Alan Labb, and Daniel Hoffman-Schwartz were supremely helpful in the preparation of the manuscript. And to the kids at the malt shop, really, this one's for you.

And let's not skip the kitties: the greatly missed Pook and Bama, Ellis, and the dream team, archy and Cleo.

Finally, Lela Graybill. She won't dance—don't ask her—yet she has been the most wondrous dance partner of my life. I got lost, but look what I found.

These chapters first appeared in the following journals and anthologies. "There's Always . . . Tomorrowland" was originally published in *October 57* (summer 1991). "Gibson's Typewriter" was published in *South Atlantic Quarterly* (fall 1993), a special cyberculture issue edited by Mark Dery that was later reprinted as *Flame Wars: The Discourse of Cyberculture* (Durham: Duke University Press, 1994). "X-Bodies" first appeared in *Uncontrollable Bodies: Testimonies of Identity and Culture*, edited by Rodney Sappington and Tyler Stallings (Seattle: Bay Press, 1994). "The Artificial Infinite" was included in *Visual Displays: Culture beyond Appearances*, edited by Lynne Cook and Peter Wollen (Seattle: Bay Press, 1995). "The Ultimate Trip" was published in *IRIS* 25 (spring 1998), a special issue on film theory and the digital image. "Taking Shape" first appeared in *Meta-Morphing*, edited by Vivian Sobchack (Minneapolis: University of Minnesota Press, 2000). "Syncopated City" was published in *The Spectator* 18.1 (fall/winter 1998), edited by Karen Voss. An extremely rough version of "The Boys in the Hoods" appeared in *Iconics* (spring 2000), a journal published by the Japan Society of Image Arts and Sciences.

I have tried to eliminate the most glaring redundancies, bring some sources up to date, and tweak the prose, but I thought it best not to tinker too much with these deeply present tense essays. Some additional comments have been added to the notes.

INTRODUCTION

The music video for Fat Boy Slim's "Weapon of Choice" begins with Christopher Walken sitting, dozing, in an anonymous hotel lobby. The video's full effect depends on our recognizing Walken, who not only exudes eccentric menace but combines catatonia with explosive violence.[1] A sampled trumpet riff rises in volume; a cut to a boom box on a stray cleaning cart confirms its source. Walken glowers sideways at this sonic intrusion, yet his limbs and neck respond to these rhythms with a will of their own. He stands, his intentions unclear. As the music builds to a crescendo, he moves dramatically into an exaggerated rock dancer's pose. And when the driving bass track thrums into existence, his face still locked in impassivity, Walken's body explodes into terpsichorean action.

Choreography, camera movement, and montage encompass the deserted space of the lobby, transgressing its hushed banality and turning it into a space of increasingly exuberant performance. Meanwhile the p-funk familiar voice of Bootsy Collins, he of the audible smile, turns a stray line from *Dune* into a funk mantra. Walken's face remains ambiguously blank but occasionally betrays a goofy glee. He glides on a luggage cart, tap dances across the cold marble floors, go-go dances on escalators and tables, spins onto an elevator, and finally sails over a railing and into the void.

Walken's body, once leaden with exhaustion, is now lighter than air, swooping through a weightless space that seems to exist only to permit his motion. The null space of the atrium is invested with drama as Walken flies from wall to wall and floor to floor, like Spiderman or Peter Pan (or should that be Linda Blair or Fred Astaire?). His delight at this physical liberation is matched by the spectator's own: these are familiar fantasies, not only of flight but of film. Above the lobby he hovers before a space-filling vertical panel of painted sky, "halfway between the gutter and the stars," everything now transcendent bliss.

This superb video, directed by Spike Jonze, gracefully enunciates much of what occupies the following chapters. *Matters of Gravity* concentrates on the experience of technological spectacle in popular American culture, primarily in the century just passed. It moves across a set of diverse objects that includes theme parks, cinematic special effects, superhero comics, and musical sequences in order to track the lived experience of technology presented in mass cultural forms. The popular genres and media explored in this volume invoke heightened, even exaggerated, bodily awareness in relation to highly technologized environments. "Weapon of Choice" certainly does. The hermetic environment of a corporate hotel, a transient habitat both uninhabited and uninhabitable, is rewritten as a space to be danced on. The camera plays a strong part in undermining the instrumental rationality of corporate space; closed spaces suddenly open as Walken's dancing body finds and exploits new places to move. This sterile space is possessed through a tactics of movement that exaggerates the incursive power that de Certeau ascribed to the walker in the city.[2]

Technology is made marvelous in "Weapon of Choice" by the special effects that permit Walken to soar, free of gravity's determinism. *Matters of Gravity* is about such flights as this, flights that are not only made possible by (frequently developing) technology but showcase that technology prominently. Space becomes delirious in the video through dance, through a camera following the body's trajectory through space, and through a final special effect that resonates with a thousand other fanciful flights. There is sublimity (he floats transcendent) and exuberance (he dances with his tongue sticking out). And at the center of all this there is the "attraction" of Christopher Walken himself: musical star, special effect, and superhero all in one.

"Weapon of Choice" reveals alienation within late capitalism and its transient spaces, the anxious status of the body under the terms of a disembodied globalism. But alienation yields to kinetic response: the bricolage of sampled tracks, acts of fantastic mobility, and perceptual surprise (with the merest touch of shock). The video provides a musical tactics of inhabitation and trespassing, a fantasy of repossessing both one's space and one's body, almost a jumping out of one's skin. The phenomenologic of these tactics constitutes an embodied, kinetic incursion, a means of remapping the subject (as a trajectory) onto the spaces of industrial and electronic capitalism. This interplay of controlled space and the evocation of weightless escape was often condensed by means of popular recreations throughout the twentieth century and is the focus of *Matters of Gravity*.

The sociocultural and phenomenological shifts that marked the period from the later nineteenth century through at least the end of the twentieth certainly depended on the rapid, constant development and dissemination of advanced technologies that restructured the landscape, regulated time, and concentrated citizens into new configurations of strangers. What Schivelbusch called "panoramic perception" corresponded to such upheavals in lived experience. The world of panoramic perception was already a world in motion, but it was a steady, lateral motion, a movement that "obliterated" the heretofore normative measures of space and time. If more of the world was now offered up to vision, this was concomitant with a deemphasis on the proximate. The gaze was forced to shift from foreground to mid- or background as the world slid past our enframed, glassed-in gaze. A continuum of views replaced "the" view, as our bodies no longer belonged to the world we saw.

Small wonder, then, that popular recreations have historically put the body back in the picture. Simulated railway travel, for example, emphasized the rocking motion and smoke as much as the panoramic views. Panoramic perception was accompanied by what I have called kaleidoscopic perception, which was more frenetic and corporeal. Kaleidoscopic perception—which operated through a combination of delirium, kinesis, and immersion—distilled the "experiential milieu" of urban modernity.[3] The spectator was no longer at a safe remove but was plunged into a jagged discontinuum of views. If the lateral glide characterized the panoramic, the kaleidoscopic was the headlong rush, the rapid montage, and the bodily address.[4]

Kaleidoscopic perception was fundamental to the rhetorics that surrounded the modern metropolis, and it was endemic to such urban entertainments as phantasmagoria, amusement park rides, and, perhaps most paradigmatically, the cinema. The city was presented as a chaotic tumult of activity and sensory bombardment, sometimes to damn it, other times to celebrate it, but always to heighten its transformative power. Kaleidoscopic perception served to turn the fear of instability into the thrill of topsy-turveydom.

The result was something different from modernity's random stimuli or controlled shocks; it permitted the body an existence apart from function or quantification and a pleasurable, playful renewal of perception itself.[5]

In this scenario, it should be evident that spectacular experience—the experience of spectacle—is something more than a virtual, illusory, engagement with a not so real world. Media do not simply (or pretend to) mediate a preexistent real. Our experience of media is a real experience, not just the idea of one (as Steven Shaviro succinctly states, "Cinematic images are not representations, but *events*"[6]). Understanding media as a legitimate rather than a surrogate phenomenon means understanding media as providing a set of tactics for negotiating modernity.

This is a somewhat different claim from those made by what has been called the "modernity thesis."[7] In its broadest outline, the modernity thesis understands the sensational entertainments of modern culture to produce "a general reconditioning or recalibration of the individual's proclivities to correspond to the greater intensity and rapidity of stimuli."[8] This thesis, which owes much to Georg Simmel's 1903 essay, "The Metropolis and Mental Life," variously holds that sensational entertainments produce a "perceptual conditioning" that alternatively sustains the restlessness and nervousness of modern citizens by providing ongoing novelty and stimulation or yields a "momentary artificial invigoration" of exhausted and deadened nerves; prepares citizens for, and innures them to, the shocks of modernity; or serves as a "compensatory response to the impoverishment of experience" under the conditions of modern life.[9] It's difficult to miss the suspicion of mass culture that undergirds the modernity thesis in all of its variants, a suspicion rooted in more thoroughgoing European critiques of the expanding domains of capital. Kracauer, for example, values the mass medium of the cinema primarily as a vulgar signpost pointing to the crisis in social relations provoked by industrial modernity. Otherwise, mass culture remains complicit with (and somewhat constitutive of) dominant ideological structures, keeping citizens in their place and allowing them to, as the great industrial metaphor has it, "let off steam."

Much critical discourse continues to focus on the strategies of control whereby amusement parks and world's fairs are defined as "tamed" and institutionally managed versions of carnival. Roller coasters, Ferris wheels, and carousels are thus ultimately defined by the *limitations* they place upon movement. White Cities are more overtly pedagogical, imparting valuable lessons in civic possibility while inscribing a telos of racial and social progress. I would hardly deny such assertions, but is this the whole story, is this the *only* story? I doubt it. There has to be *something* between the carnival and the panopticon.

The suspicion of mass culture permeates other modes of scholarly engagement. It is blazingly evident that to varying degrees theme parks, science fiction, Hollywood blockbusters, and superhero comic books constitute a rather blunt form of ideological interpellation: reactionary, masculinist, and driven to mastery.[10] However, critical studies of visual or time-based media all too frequently fail to consider issues of *form* with the sophistication routinely brought to bear on literary objects. Hence, differences among media are elided through a reliance on (or faith in) highly linear narrative structures as the overriding, deterministic, and teleological locus of "meaning." Objects involving multisemic forms of address are routinely reduced to their narrative "functions" or, worse, the stasis of narrative "closure." While it is acknowledged that there is something *more* in these entertainments, that "something" has frequently been tarred or celebrated under the rubric of "excess." The term is misapplied. These entertainments do not exceed *themselves* but rather the arbitrary conditions of narrative's hierarchical dominance (or, similarly, the bounds of linguistically based signification). And so the chapters that follow strenuously avoid considerations of narrative, not to invalidate the claims of narratology but to displace its centrality in the analysis of visual or movement-based media.

Robert Warshow, writing in the mid-1950s, offered an alternative to the distanced view of the modernity thesis with regard to analyzing popular cultural forms. In an essay on the movies, Warshow indicated the problems inherent in what have remained the two dominant tendencies in the analysis of popular cultural forms, which he referred to as the "sociological" and "aesthetic" approaches. The validity of his elegant declaration of principles extends beyond cinema (and did for Warshow as well). He notes that

> out of that work has emerged the general outline within which all future discussion must find its place. I think it may be said nevertheless that both these approaches, in their separate ways, have tended to slight the fundamental *fact* of the movies, a fact at once aesthetic and sociological but also something more. This is the actual, immediate experience of seeing and responding to the movies as most of us see them and respond to them. A critic may extend his frame of reference as far as it will bear extension, but it seems to me almost self-evident that he should start with

the simple acknowledgment of his own relation to the object he criti-
cizes; at the center of all truly successful criticism there is always a man
reading a book, a man looking at a picture, a man watching a movie.[11]

Before any objection can be lodged against that philosophically suspect
phrase "immediate experience," it should be noted that Warshow does not
aspire to a prelinguistic, Brakhagian innocence. "The man" at the center of
this passage is already defined by prior experience and knowledge of the
world. Warshow's essays are historically grounded, most notably in the crisis
of the American Left in the Stalinist era. But he remains alert to sensation—it
informs his superb descriptions, his musings on the materiality of the filmic
medium, and his willingness to let Krazy Kat be Krazy Kat.

Warshow advocates beginning with the critic's response as a prelude to
any more extensive interrogation, which has great relevance to the studies
that comprise *Matters of Gravity*. There is no getting rid of me in the following pages—my initial or ongoing fascination guides my writing, and I write
primarily out of respect for that fascination. It seems clear to me that, be-
side the sociological or aesthetic frames of reference that might explicate the
critic's experience of a work or medium, a phenomenological approach, con-
centrating on perceptual experience and embodied response, can easily find
a place, and without abdicating broader social perspectives.

Lewis Mumford wrote in 1934 that "In order to reconquer the machine
and subdue it to human purposes, one must first understand it and assimilate it. So far, we have embraced the machine without fully understanding
it, or, like the weaker romantics, we have rejected the machine without first
seeing how much of it we could intelligently assimilate."[12] One argument in
Matters of Gravity is that a bodily assimilation (what Barbara Stafford calls a
"sensationalized knowledge") of the machine might serve as prelude to the
intellectual assimilation invoked by Mumford. Thinking through the body
becomes a way of thinking through technology, of inscribing ourselves within
rapidly changing conditions of existence. Media and rides mediate the fact of
technology by translating it into the terms of human perception and bodily
cognition. In *Terminal Identity* I tried to demonstrate how technologies of representation or simulation permitted an embodied perspective on electronic
technology.[13] *Matters of Gravity* extends this thesis historically and conceptually.

The essays in *Matters of Gravity* themselves move from a consideration of
the body as constructed by spectacular experience to an emphasis on the per-

forming body moving within the built environment of the American city. The attention to the embodied sensibility tracking through space is supplemented by a perceptual and kinetic identification with the highly visible bodies on display, virtuostic bodies that morph, that sing, that fly. This shift in emphasis stems, in part, from the (presumably temporary) exhaustion of science fiction as a vehicle for technological and urban imaginations. The final chapters indulge the more ludic approaches to urban inhabitation presented in urban musicals and superhero comics. The city is refigured as a playground in the two genres that permit the most strikingly unfettered access to urban space, genres that license the suspension of the physical laws that govern time and space. These are also the genres that depend the most on a public gaze, as opposed to those genres (such as film noir) that occupy the city's most interstitial locations. Here are performative bodies that posture and pretend in public, before the public eye, bodies that literalize and externalize the American mythology of remaking the self. "In the city one can make and remake one's self at will," Simmel told us—the city has long been a place for imposters. We are asked to accept these marvelous beings (stars and superheroes) as fictions, as artifice, but even their imposture is only another aspect of their overall virtuosity.

The book is divided into three sections, which follow, not coincidentally, the order of the essays' initial publication. "Remembering Cyberspace" reprises and historicizes some key notions developed in *Terminal Identity,* which proposed a phenomenology of electronic culture. Digital technological process operated beyond the perceptual horizon of the human sensorium, and as a consequence, anxieties regarding the place of the human subject, now a potentially "virtual" subject, returned to the foreground. *Terminal Identity* tracked these anxieties into and through the bodily reformations, deformations, and dissolutions that characterized not only science fiction but other discourses, including critical theory, that borrowed from the rhetorics of the genre.

The essays in this first section are similarly concerned with the metaphoric, and often hyperbolic, return of the body as a site of continuing coherence in the face of disembodied technology. The technology was almost secondary to the rhetorical and conceptual possibilities unleashed by the mere possibility of such machinery, and so all discourse became science fiction, thought experiments backed by synthesizers. In the age of "cyberculture," artists, writers, technologists, and scholars saw in electronic technology the promise of remaking the world and all its reified conceptual categories (hence Donna Haraway's proclamation, "I would rather be a cyborg than a goddess"). Chapter 1, "There's Always . . . Tomorrowland," presents itself as a ride—the writings of cyberculture *are* rides, high-tech, hip rides into the future, filled with an intellectual excitement licensed, perhaps even dictated, by the gleaming newness of it all. Like the futures promised by Futurama or Tomorrowland, though, that particular future is already a slightly musty part of our past. And when we disembark, blinking our way back into the glaring light of the present, we might look at each other with a slight hesitation, a little embarrassed by our own credulity. But what a great ride. Step right up.

Section Two, "Kaleidoscopic Perceptions," concentrates on the technological sublime presented by special effects technologies. In these chapters, cinema returns to a pride of place. While the implications of technologically supplemented bodily movement and the gaze mobilized through a range of media dominate the essays in *Matters of Gravity*, they are most fully theorized in chapters 4 and 5, "The Artificial Infinite" and "The Ultimate Trip." Kinesis, even of the virtual kind, recalls the body into being to serve as the ground for all the conceptual and sensual flights provided by wide-screen special effects, theme park attractions (including ride films and Hale's Tours), superhero comics, and dance sequences. As interface designers and media scholars both came to admit, the cinematic experience was always as embodying as most virtual reality systems (which came as no surprise to theorists of early cinema).[14]

The final section, "The Grace of Beings," emphasizes utopian bodily performance within and against rapidly changing relations to technological culture. Morphing, musicals, and superheroes all embody the fantasies and agonies of metamorphosis; all negotiate bodily limits via virtuostic and graceful movements of transformation. In quest of alternatives to cyberspaces and cyberbodies, I've been drawn to musicals and superhero comics: kaleidoscopic perceptions presenting bodies of virtuostic grace, performative bodies exuberantly riding the axiomatic technological space of the city. In her sprawling study of "mongrel Manhattan" in the 1920s, Ann Douglas describes a moment when American culture, "led by New York," promoted "something like an egalitarian popular and mass culture aggressively appropriating forms across race, class, and gender lines."[15] Urban musical comedies exemplify this heterogeneous cultural mix within an innately pluralist and antihierarchical Manhattan. Superheroes are also inscribed in the discourse of urban modernity. They dwell in the highest regions and the lowest depths, and grasp the city in unprecedented ways. These genres give us extraordinary characters who glide through the complexities of urban space, emerging in bursts of flamboyance into public view, then disappearing into the anonymity of the crowd. These fabulous negotiations of body, self, and space contrast sharply with electronic fantasies of abandoning the body, becoming a cyborg, becoming virtual.

These days, I would rather be a mongrel than a cyborg.

REMEMBERING CYBERSPACE

ONE

REMEMBERING CYBERSPACE

Figure 1. Tomorrow's drivers—today!

There's Always . . . Tomorrowland:
Disney and the Hypercinematic Experience

The various attempts to integrate modern science into
new myths remain inadequate.

Ivan Chtcheglov

There's nothing so loathsome as a sentimental surrealist.

Thomas Pynchon

1. Skyway to Tomorrowland

One Tomorrowland attraction in the early days of Disneyland was the Autopia, where youngsters could drive actual, though miniature, automobiles. It was Walt Disney's intent that these young citizens-to-be would thereby learn traffic safety at an early age and hence would be prepared to enter the LA freeway system. Unfortunately, the children took "demented delight" in crashing the cars, and the ride had to be put on tracks.[1] One can't blame the kids for resisting the immaculately conceived guidance that dominated the park at all turns, but the Disney ethos could hardly tolerate these signs of technological breakdown.

Disneyland began as a park where Walt could extend his miniature train set within surroundings of realistic landscape effects. A fascination with Americana further informed the project from an early stage, and dioramas depicting historical events and eras (much like the tableaux of early film history) were placed along the train's route in a "coherent sequence." Finally, the design was founded in a desire to construct a safe and clean environment, thoroughly distinct from the chaos and boorishness of the traditional amusement park. The end result was an America reduced, frozen, and sanitized—a fortress against the dis-ease of 1950s' society. Walt announced that, "Disneyland is going to be a place where you can't get lost."[2]

Such tendencies are exaggerated at Walt Disney World, whose acreage is twice that of Manhattan. The Magic Kingdom and EPCOT Center are now supplemented by Typhoon Lagoon (a water theme park), Pleasure Island (which features discos and other "entertainment"), Fort Wilderness Camp-ground, the Disney/MGM Studio Theme Park,[3] numerous hotels, and a convention center. It is no longer possible to "do" the entire facility during a week-long vacation, although many families frantically try. In the "panic" terminology of Arthur Kroker ("Between ecstasy and fear, between delirium and anxiety"), Disney World has become a "panic vacation."[4]

Tomorrowland grows more wonderful with the passage of every year, as its parabolic, populuxe stylings give a full and nostalgic voice to the aspirations of the new frontiers of the 1964 New York World's Fair (although its concrete expanses also suggest a down-at-heels airport). The extroversion of its boomerang-inflected balustrades stands in contrast to the imploded and anonymous mall structures of EPCOT's Future World. EPCOT Center was Walt's dream of an Experimental Prototype Community of Tomorrow: real futures, brought to you by real corporations. This latter-day ode to tomorrow could as well be any corporate plaza on the outskirts of any urban area. Its immaculate commons, mirrored facades, and soaring fountains stand in proud affirmation of nothing in particular, while in Tomorrowland each aerodynamically turned, turquoise and white detail enshrines a visible yearning for flight, a thrusting beyond limits, and the hope and confidence in an unambivalently better tomorrow. It unintentionally becomes the most charming of retro-futures.[5]

Tomorrowland—the very name carries a casual colloquialism. Tomorrow is, after all, not so far away, while *land* suggests the whimsicality of the fairy tale (it is an all important suffix in conveying a childlike innocence or nostalgia). Its extension at EPCOT, however, is something more than an exercise in self-similarity—Future World is a state of mind rather than a spatial location, a corporate symbol of monadic inclusiveness.[6] The future is indefinite and permanent; the world is inescapable and boundless. Tomorrowland holds promise; Future World sounds like a threat. The expansiveness of the missions to Mars and exploration among the stars is replaced by the imploded concern with the cybernetic spaces of information management.

These Disney worlds bear an interesting relation to works of contemporary science fiction (SF) literature and cinema, in which ontologies of space and narrative combine and often contradict one another. Science fiction can be said to provide the referential dimension that is absent from the disembodied spaces of the electronic realm: the function of the genre, then, is to compensate for the loss of the human in the labyrinths of blip culture by transforming it into an arena susceptible to human control. Recent SF frequently posits a reconception of the human and the ability to interface with the new terminal paraspace. What occurs is a simultaneous grounding and dislocating of human bodily experience.

Referring to the 1939 World's Fair, H. Bruce Franklin has correctly noted that, "A fair billing itself as the World of Tomorrow may be considered just as much a work of science fiction as a short story or a novel, a comic book or a movie."[7] This is surely also true of exhibitions billed as Tomorrowland or Future World, exhibitions that carry the visitor into an ambivalently defined future.[8] The Disney futures are simultaneously reactionary and progressive, nostalgic and challenging. They are also richly imbricated with the shifting experiences and metaphors of postmodern urbanism, electronic culture, and pervasive redefinitions of space and subjectivity, as the subsequent analyses will demonstrate. Please keep your hands inside the vehicle at all times.

2. Retro-Futures

The pervasive fear that underlies the decade just past is a consequence of recognizing that we already inhabit the future. No longer is "the future" a harmless fiction, a utopian era that, by its very definition, will never arrive; it is instead upon us with a vengeance. Our presence in the future has thus initiated an obsessive recycling of the past, a seemingly inexhaustible period of meganostalgia; a return to a period of (imaginary) mastery; and an attempt to answer the question "How did I get here?" when cause and effect have vanished within the random intricacies of quantum reality. Even futures past are exhumed and aired, their quaint fantasies simultaneously mocked and yearned for. A collection of *Popular Mechanics* articles and illustrations entitled "Wasn't the Future Wonderful?" demonstrates the promise of an abundant, machine-aided existence, as the satisfied citizen calmly smokes his pipe amid an array of vacuum-tubed Rube Goldberg devices that tirelessly service his every desire. Scott McCloud's comic book character Zot lives in a wonderfully bulbous city that could have been designed by Frank R. Paul for the cover of any issue of *Amazing Stories*. These are reveries of progress based on visibility.

William Gibson's science fiction short story "The Gernsback Continuum" is about the end of the future. A photographer engaged to capture images of the utopian architectures of Frank Lloyd Wright and other 1930s and 1940s futurists enters one of those zones endemic to postmodern fiction ("Ever so gently, I went over the Edge"). In a giant ontological shift, he finds himself within this imaged, imagined, but never created retro-future. Gibson's description perfectly evokes the aspirations of another age, but it also sounds like a trip to Disneyland.

> They were white, blond, and they probably had blue eyes. They were American. Dialta had said that the Future had come to America first, but had finally passed it by. But not here, in the heart of the Dream. Here, we'd gone on and on, in a dream logic that knew nothing of pollution, the finite bounds of fossil fuel, of foreign wars it was possible to lose. They were smug, happy, and utterly content with themselves and their world. And in the Dream, it was *their* world. Behind me, the illuminated city: Searchlights swept the sky for the sheer joy of it. I imagined them thronging the plazas of white marble, orderly and alert, their bright eyes shining with enthusiasm for their floodlit avenues and silver cars.[9]

To exorcise these "semiotic ghosts," the narrator watches television until they go away.

If the retro-futures are based in externalization and visibility, then one notices in the architecture of Future World the very erosion of the visible and the dataist implosion behind the mirrors of anonymous technocultural interfaces. The rides behind these facades, however, are relentlessly, reassuringly, *human*, thanks to the simulations technologies of audioanimatronics™. The Horizons pavilion at EPCOT Center (presented by General Electric), for example, contains an exemplary retro-future exhibit entitled "Looking Back at Tomorrow." "People had some pretty mixed up ideas about the future," the narrator says (smugly), as "guests" are treated to the sweetly simulated futures of Jules Verne, Georges Méliès, Fritz Lang, Buck Rogers, Hugo Gernsback, and the Jetsons. The return to the retro-futures of the 1920s through the 1950s speaks to a perceived loss of subjective comprehension of, or control over, the invisible cyberhistories and cyberspaces of the present. This is the Dataist Era: the disembodying spaces of the terminal era exist independent of direct human experience or control.

3. Narrative Strategies

Disneyland, notes Thomas Hine in *Populuxe*, "was the first place ever conceived simultaneously with a TV series," and the park is assuredly notable for its overall narrative character. The Magic Kingdom was designed not by architects but by filmmakers, Hine continues, not as a group of buildings but as an experience. It was "a movie that could be walked into."[10] One is led along Main Street USA toward the pinnacle of Fantasyland's castles. At the central square, towering starjets lead to Tomorrowland, while other monuments lead to further adventures. Phillip Johnson stated that the park's architecture was dedicated not to the design of space but to "the organization of procession."[11] A general telos operates whether one concentrates on the overall structure of the entire park, the features of the various lands, or the details on each of the buildings—as Hine says, the experience is of a sequence of establishing shots, medium shots, and close-ups. Several writers have observed how the rides mimic the proairetic and hermeneutic structures of narrative: "Each car is wired for stereophonic sound and turns electronically so that the occupant sees only what the designer has intended . . . exactly the way the movie camera sees" (King, 120).

The topics of these rides are intensely narrative as well; Peter Pan's Flight recapitulates the entire narrative of the film, encounters with giant plastic sea creatures in 20,000 Leagues under the Sea are narrated by an ersatz James Mason, and the famed Jungle Cruise provides a human guide pretending to steer the vessel while interacting with the real flora and pseudofauna. Even the roller coaster, whose raison d'etre is purely kinetic sensation, is narrativized in the Magic Kingdom. Space Mountain and Thunder Mountain are geographically specific, simulated experiences (a space flight, a runaway train) that arguably add little to the basic pleasures of gravity.

Narrative provides a comforting and teleological paradigm for the physical experience. It is not a startling innovation, this commingling of kinesis and narrative. As Raymond Fielding pointed out in 1957, Disney's Trip to the Moon is only an update of the Hale's Tours exhibits that were popular between 1904 and 1906.[12] Audiences for Hale's Tours boarded a mock train carriage, and while a film of exotic locales played up ahead the coach would be rocked and a breeze might even play over them. Now retitled Mission to Mars, the Disney attraction features a preflight area, seats that move in a simulacrum of gravitational effects, a film view of the exotic Martian landscape through upper and lower "windows," and even a fictitious crisis for dramatic effect. This combination of simulation and transportation, as noted, was a fundament of the parks' conception. The WEDway (as in Walter E. Disney) People Mover has the distinction of being a ride with no purpose beyond demonstrating its own transport technology (it remains one of the most relaxing attractions at the park). The implications carried by the rides of Tomorrowland bear upon the ontological status of the subject in an era defined by an implosive and disembodying proliferation of electronic technologies (as will be shown).

4. Futurama

Seemingly opposed to the banality of the Disney narrative experience is the tough posturing of cyberpunk science fiction, a popular subgenre in the 1980s. John Clute, a science fiction editor and critic, describes a crisis in science fiction representation that is grounded in the passage from the thrusting promise of the Space Age to the invisible circulations and movements of the Electronic Age.

> No longer has information any tangible, kinetic analogue in the world of the senses, or in the imaginations of writers of fiction. Gone are the great arrays of vacuum tubes, the thousands of toggles that heroes of space fiction would flick *almost* faster than the eye could see as they dodged space "torpedoes," outflanked alien "battle lines," steered through asteroid "storms"; gone, more importantly, is any sustained sense of the autonomy, in space and time, of gross visible individual human actions. And if "actions" are now invisible, then our fates are likewise beyond our grasp. We no longer feel that we penetrate the future; futures penetrate us.[13]

Technological change has moved into the terminal spaces of the computer, the video screen, and the fiber optic cable. Through its surreal yet plausible spatialization of electronic culture, cyberpunk science fiction achieved real importance. The invisible spaces of the computer are metaphorically "entered" by the physiologically enhanced "cyberspace cowboys" of William Gibson's *Neuromancer* (1984), for example, reinstating the possibility of "visible individual human actions."

Cyberpunk stages a rejection of the white towers of technocracy in favor of a street-level science fiction exemplified in cinema by the retrofitted urbanism of *Blade Runner* (Ridley Scott, 1982). Cyberpunk polemicist Bruce Sterling writes that science fiction "has always been about the impact of technology. But times have changed since the comfortable era of Hugo Gernsback, when Science was safely enshrined—and confined—in an ivory tower. The careless technophilia of those days belongs to a vanished, sluggish era, when authority still had a comfortable margin of control."[14] The measured forms of instrumental reason no longer dominate the technosphere, which has now slipped, as Baudrillard continually notes, into a self-regulating and implosive state.

Cyberpunk is notorious for its repudiation of this ivory-towered confidence, this faith in a future that works:[15] this is not quite true of Disney's

Horizons. Following its reactionary retrospective of retro-futures, Horizons presents its own set of prognostications based upon the by this time dubious premise of technological progress devoid of social implications. Improved urbanism, undersea farming (a Disney mania), colonies in outer space— nothing disturbs the stability of the white, heterosexual, middle class, extended nuclear family (and, speaking of nuclear, how *is* all this powered?). Indeed, tranquility is improved, as holographic videophones permit instantaneous communication (reach out and touch someone).

The simple but unavoidable irony of this audioanimated™ diorama is that there isn't even the gesture toward a social reality that can be found in Lang's *Metropolis* and the poetry of his *Frau du Mond* or in Méliès's *Voyage dans la lune*. The outmoded futures retain a special vibrancy: the Disney version is at once more utopian, more banal, and more ignorant. Only the citizens, in their homogenized glory, are revealed and encountered, their lives conveniently (and conventionally) narrativized. The central planning apparatus (corporate? governmental?) remains invisible, functioning as the omniscient narrator of this future world and its successes. Bruce Franklin has written of Futurama that "It is the corporation that plans and builds, while the people are purely passive, comfortably watching the creation in motion as mere spectators."[16]

5. Situationist Cities

Of course, Disneyland and Disney World exemplify the future vision that they propose better than any other site on Spaceship Earth. Disney's contemporary future is dominated by a benign corporate sponsorship providing effective population control, abundant consumer goods, and the guarantee of technological infallibility.[17] These "theme parks" have long aroused admiration for their skillfully designed spaces. City planner James Rouse declared that "The greatest piece of urban design in the US today is Disneyland. Think of its performance in relation to its purpose."[18] Margaret King argues that Disneyland and Disney World humanize their technology through architecture: "The Disney town is a kind of stage based on architectural symbols for romanticized, stylized human interaction. . . . The example of the parks may provide an alternative vision of what people seek in urban environments: everyday life as an art form, with entertainment, fantasy, play-acting, role-playing and the reinstatement of some of the values which have been lost in the megalopolis."[19]

Guy Debord's projection of the ideal situationist city anticipates the divi-

Figure 2. "A place where you can't get lost"

sion of the theme parks into separate monadic "lands" or "worlds": "In each of its experimental cities unitary urbanism will act by way of a certain number of force fields, which we can designate by the classic term 'quarter.' Each quarter will tend toward a specific harmony, divided off from neighboring harmonies; or else will play on a maximum breaking up of internal harmony."[20] The situationist's division of the city also echoes the psychologist's topology of the brain. "The districts . . . could correspond to the whole spectrum of diverse feelings that one encounters *by chance* in everyday life," Ivan Chtcheglov proposes, listing the Bizarre and Happy Quarters as examples.[21] Souvenir maps of Disneyland in fact suggest such a model: the different-colored lands echo the diagrams of cerebral lobes, while Main Street mimics the stalk of the central nervous system, leading into the central hub (the *corpus calossum*), which links these different regions. One might take this idea further—it's surely interesting that the rough and ready macho pragmatism represented by Frontierland and Adventureland is located in the "left brain," while the whimsy of Fantasyland and the fantastic science fiction of Tomorrowland are strictly right-brain "functions."[22]

The situationists demanded a revolution in everyday life; the dual commu-

nist/capitalist reliance on labor was refused in favor of a more total liberation of the individual from the repressive reason of the state. Situations were
designed to provoke a recognition of alienation and permit the perception
of the reifications of spectacle. The division of urban space would produce
maximal harmonies and disharmonies, a notion exploited in science fiction
(Samuel Delany's *Triton* features an anarchic, libidinal, "unlicensed zone."
Theater groups roam the zone, abruptly performing for "microaudiences"
of one). Can one perceive in these situationist texts of 1953–58 (Disneyland
opened in 1955) an impulse toward a politicized Disneyland, the theme park
as situation and unitary urban field? "That which changes our way of seeing
the streets is more important than what changes our way of seeing painting.
. . . It is necessary to throw new forces into the *battle of leisure.*"[23]

6. Imploded Fields

The "guests" circulate through the "lands" of the Magic Kingdom or the
"worlds" of EPCOT Center. When Disneyland first opened, there was no
analogue for this aimless travel, this *dérive*, but now the shopping mall endows these environments with phenomenological and sociological familiarity. Malls aspire to the same monadism as the Disney worlds, and their
designs echo that of the parks with varying explicitness.[24] Parking is relegated
to vast outside areas, leaving the "real world" invisible beyond the boundaries of the commercial kingdoms (and one must note Baudrillard's wonderful caveat that the real world only *seems* real against the background of Disneyland's explicit simulations). Perhaps, as in the hypermall in Edmonton,
Alberta, there is an amusement park. The spectacle has even come full circle:
the national shopping pavilions and restaurants of EPCOT's World Showcase
(opened in 1982) recall the kiosks and "food courts" of countless suburban
malls, while the malls incorporate the rides and themes of the Disney parks.
The World Showcase represents a peculiar implosion of American tourism:
foreign lands are further reduced and domesticated, rendered safe while remaining absurdly picturesque (with actual natives[25]). Welcome—with apolo-
gies to Professor McLuhan—to the global mall.

William Kowinski proposes that strolling through a mall is a visual, blip
culture experience: "It's TV that you walk around in."[26] One chooses from
among an abundance of selections (stores::channels), solicited by an array of
colorful enticements and standardized slickness, overwhelmed by the overall electronic buzz. Arthur Kroker makes the same comparison, but in postcyberpunk language: "Shopping malls are liquid TVs for the end of the twen-

tieth century. . . . Shopping malls call forth the same psychological position as TV watching: voyeurism . . . Rather than flicking the dial, you take a walk from channel to channel as the neon stores slick by. And not just watching either, but shopping malls have this big advantage over TV, they play every sense. . . . A whole image-repertoire which, when successful, splays the body into a multiplicity of organs, all demanding to be filled."[27] The body implodes within the cyberspace of the shopping mall in yet another manifestation of terminal identity. Kowinski: "It's worth noting that Disneyland and the first enclosed malls were being built at about the same time."[28]

Here history demands the recognition of Disney's achievement in the 1950s as the first film producer to exploit the medium of television. The TV series *Disneyland* was a gigantic promotional piece for this new park: the behind the scenes footage, old films, and new productions (e.g., *Davy Crockett*) were all geared toward selling the new attraction (Richard Schickel even argues that Disneyland represented a uniquely new medium). The ABC network financed the new park by buying more than one-third of the shares of Disneyland, Inc.[29] If William Thompson, calling the park a "technological cathedral," noted in 1971 that "Disneyland itself is a kind of television set," then it is worth stressing that the mutually reinforcing symbiosis of the Disneyland/world/mall and the implosive reality of television is not coincidental, but designed.[30]

6A. Great Moments with Mr. Lincoln

The opening ceremonies of Disneyland were telecast live; among the hosts was Ronald Reagan, who would one day be represented by a simulacrum therein.[31]

7. Terminal Tactics

From Michel de Certeau's *The Practice of Everyday Life:* "I call a *strategy* the calculation (or manipulation) of power relationships that becomes possible as soon as a subject with will and power (a business, an army, a city, a scientific institution) can be isolated. It postulates a *place* that can be delimited as its *own* and serve as the base from which relations with an *exteriority* composed of targets or threats . . . can be managed."[32] De Certeau's researches are pertinent to the strategic spaces of Disney World and Disneyland ("a business, an army, a city, a scientific institution"[33]). As Robert Venturi has noted of all utopias, the Disney spaces exist in relation to the hostile environments lying beyond their gates. These are protected environments, sustained only by a massive infusion of capital on a daily basis. Citizenship in the Magic

Kingdom costs over forty dollars per day per park. The populist, apolitical, futuristic perfection is thus an illusion dependent on the commodity's denial of its exchange value and its pretense to a pure use value (EPCOT becomes an educational experience rather than a gimmicky amusement park). The forty-three-dollar "passport" purchased at the gate permits the visitor to circulate "freely" through this delimited, manageable world.

For de Certeau, *tactics* refers to the set of practices performed by subjects upon and within these controlled fields: "I call a 'tactic,' on the other hand, a calculus which cannot count on a 'proper' (a spatial or institutional localiza-tion), nor thus on a borderline distinguishing the other as a visible totality. The place of a tactic belongs to the other. A tactic insinuates itself into the other's place, fragmentarily, without taking it over in its entirety, without being able to keep it at a distance."[34] A tactic is equivalent to a speech act, which "is at the same time a use *of* language and an operation performed *on* it."[35] It is temporal, a trajectory across the spaces of strategic control. If the Disney empire is a strategic space, then it is one that seems particularly susceptible to the trickster tactics of its visitors. When Disneyland opened, its designers waited to see where people actually walked before the layout of paths and park areas was finalized. The parks actually assimilate the tactical trajectories of its visitors, returning them in the form of strategies. Walking across the grass loses its subversive appeal—it's easier and more efficient to keep to the walkways. Subversion is rendered pointless or even, as in the case of the infamous Autopia, impossible.

Thus, what one finds at Disneyland, or Disney World, are *simulations of tactics:* simulations of the dérive, that aimless passage across the complexities of urban space so cherished by the situationists; and simulations of walk-ing, in the specific sense of inscribing oneself upon the territories of strategic power. There is no discovery that one is not led to, no resolution that has not already occurred, no possibility of revealing "that man behind the curtain," the Wonderful Wizard of O(rlando) Z(one). This space is unique within de Certeau's terms in that it impedes the tactical enunciations characteristic of everyday life while remaining an unfailingly popular vacation destination.

8. Radiant Cities

The World of Motion ride at EPCOT Center (presented by General Motors) concludes with a large model of a future city replete with gleaming white spires, pneumatic transport, hovercars, and an overall expansiveness that never, ever sprawls. The resemblance of this metropolis to GM's Futurama, that delightful city of the future (1960!) from the 1939 World's Fair, is obvious. A vision of the future still survives at EPCOT Center, then, based on central management, urban planning, and continuing technological progress. Disney World becomes a final haven for a purely technocratic projection of the future—the last bastion of instrumental reason (a "Futurama-induced administrative competence," as novelist Richard Powers put it).[36]

Perhaps Disneyland/World is Radiant City. Le Corbusier's urban dreamscape represented the apotheosis of his concern with centralized management. The corporation was unfit to organize the public realm on its own, as was government; the "hierarchy of administration has replaced the state" (Fishman, 228). The zones of Radiant City constitute a geometry of instrumental reason—the rationality of design transcending the competing economic ideologies of capitalism and communism. Like Disneyland, Radiant City enshrined a "value neutral" dedication to the technologies of rationalism. Robert Fishman uses terms that strongly suggest the now mythic role of Walt Disney himself: "Le Corbusier's concept of the planner combines two distinct images. One is the planner as scientist, surgeon, 'technician'—the man of reason, a disinterested lover of humanity who studies the problems of the city, formulates clear solutions, and carries them out with an unswerving will. The second is the planner as artist, the isolated man of vision whose insights are the most profound record of his nation's spiritual life" (210).

In the comic book *Mr. X*, the designer of Somnopolis, a.k.a. Radiant City, returns to destroy his corrupted creation. The city had been designed through *psychetecture* (an appropriation of the situationists' *psychogeography?*), but his utopian vision has been altered. The flat, dark artwork illustrates an urbanism of competing anachronisms where no two clocks agree, figures fling themselves to the ground below, and humans and robots coexist in a perpetual ennui. The architect, Walter Eichmann, is devastated, but others criticize his obsession: "You became one of those robots that you hated. You became a machine. . . . You became the city, Walter!" (Umberto Eco called Disneyland an "immense robot").[37] Central planning is advanced as an outmoded vehicle of megalomaniacal control, a misguided attempt to impose order on a chaotic, surreal existence. Radiant City is the dream, but Somnopolis represents the worst nightmares of Le Corbusier and *Walter E. Disney*. Postmodernism, in all manifestations, rejects these master narratives of centralized power.[38]

9. Cyberpunks and Hippie/Hackers

Cyberpunk's resistance to the authoritarian mythos of Radiant City has been noted. Bodies in cyberpunk fiction and performance are invested in technology at street/skin level. "For the cyberpunks," author/editor Bruce Sterling writes, "Technology is visceral. . . . it is pervasive, utterly intimate. . . . Under our skin; often, inside our minds" (xi). In gentler language, cyberpunk is "about how our increasingly intimate feedback relationship with the technosphere we are creating has been, is, and will be, altering our definition of what it means to be human itself" (Spinrad, 186). The body is inscribed and defined, paradoxically extended and delimited by these pervasive, invasive technologies. It is a matter of interface.

Drawing on the work of Xerox's Palo Alto Research Center, Steven Jobs and the engineers at Apple Computer designed their Macintosh for maximum user friendliness. Alienating keyboard commands were replaced with an intuitively based system: point, click, access.[39] The goal was to empower the individual faced with the forces of central control. Their 1984 commercial, directed by Ridley Scott, featured a most spectacular projection of the Orwellian vision, but now the proles were controlled by Big Blue, IBM (which was unnamed). Personal computing with a friendly interface was "why 1984 won't be like 1984." Alvin Toffler: "Instead of merely receiving our mental model of reality, we are now compelled to invent it and continually reinvent it. This places an enormous burden on us. But it also leads toward greater individuality, a demassification of personality as well as culture."[40] Telematic power would be anticorporate, decentralized, personal: such was the mythos.

Thus, in the 1980s two technomyths arose: cyberpunk and hippie/hacker.[41] Both are opposed to technocratic mythologies of centralized control, but while hippie/hacker substitutes an ethos of personal control and individual empowerment, cyberpunk enacts the end of controls in its depiction of a world where technology circulates more or less freely and even (as in *Neuromancer*) has its own agenda. Baudrillard, whose prose aspires to the condition of science fiction, is quintessential cyberpunk, while the Media Lab at MIT preserves the hippie-hacker ambition. Both acknowledge our inevitable imbrication in the new state of things, what Toffler has called blip culture. The comforts of Disneyland and Disney World reveal a paradox of control by presenting the highest degree of user friendliness in a human-technology interface, while situating it within a massively centralized apparatus.

10. Terminal Theme Park

Scientific American describes the cutting edge of new interface technologies in terms familiar to students of cinema—as a quest for realism. *Brainstorm* notwithstanding, however, cinema has nothing with which to rival the virtual reality systems of contemporary electronics. One NASA system, designed by

VPL Laboratories, features a head-mounted apparatus using two color monitors (Eyephones) to create an analogue of depth perception through a simulated parallax. Sensors respond to head (and even eye) movement and "the user can enjoy the illusion of scanning an artificial panorama as he turns his head."[42] With the addition of the Dataglove, which translates hand movements into electric signals, the user can grasp and manipulate the objects in the virtual environment.[43] Voice recognition completes the interface, and the user can thus handle "objects" in the computer-generated environment. For Timothy Leary, this virtual realm is the ultimate way to "tune in"—a developer notes, "The computer literally knows where your head's at."[44] To be installed into such an apparatus would be to exist on two planes simultaneously; while one's objective body would remain in the real world, one's *phenomenal body* would be projected into the terminal reality. Sterling observes: "Eighties tech sticks to the skin."[45] *To* the skin and *under* the skin— Marvin Minsky, cofounder of MIT's Artificial Intelligence Laboratory, muses that wires inserted into the nerves will allow Dataglove users the sensation of touch.

The narrative strategies of the Disney worlds constitute another kind of virtual reality system, one that is largely conditioned by the narrative strategies that move guests through a technologically informed yet fundamentally conservative and historically bound vision of "the future." At the same time, however, the theme parks are remarkably effective, albeit less explicit, visible projections of terminal space. Disneyland/World is a retro-future, a narrative, Radiant City, but it is also a gigantic piece of installation art that spatializes the structures of a computer system.

Each of the rides and attractions—files—are gathered into the subdivisions of the different lands—folders. "Utilities" punctuate the array in the form of food and service kiosks. The pervasive transportation systems (monorail, horse-drawn carriage, railroad, paddleboat, double-decker bus, WED-way People Mover) shuttle guests/users from function to function, constituting an extremely efficient operating system. All the technology remains hidden behind the tropical plants and architectural facades of the attractions, just as the ubiquitous beige shell of the personal computer disguises the microcircuitry within. Finally, the blips being processed and circulated within this cybernetic paraspace—are us. The computer becomes a site of bodily habitation and experience in the theme parks—a technological interface so effective that most users are unaware of the interface at all.

In its structure and geography EPCOT easily suggests a spatialization of its own computerized functions, while cyberpunk's defining trope has been its own representation of the nonphysical, electronic spaces of the terminal realm, as prefigured by the 1982 film *TRON* (Steven Lisberger, a Disney production). *TRON* used vector and raster graphic programs to dramatize its cybernetic arenas, as designed by Syd (*Blade Runner*) Mead and the comic book artist Moebius (Jean Giraud). In this saga of an evil corporate takeover of a small individualistic computer company, a battle fought largely in terminal space, one sees a collision of cyberpunk and hippie/hacker formations.[46] The film also extends the historical relationship between cinema and emergent technology.

The motion picture camera has been invariably attached to subjective vision, but equally pervasive has been the linking of cinematic vision to new technologies.[47] In Clair's *Paris Qui Dort*, the camera, mounted on the elevator of the Eiffel Tower, demonstrates the intricacy of that monument to modernity as nothing else could, while Eisenstein's appropriation of a factory conveyor in *Strike* (1925) creates a space at once phenomenal and polemical. The cinema has thus produced coincident analogues of subjective interiority and technological exteriority. Cinema is a cyborg apparatus—part human, part machine. When Metz declares that the fundamental identification that the spectator has is "with the camera," the historical significance of this ought to be understood: the "double movement" of projection and introjection, presented by Metz in primarily phenomenological terms, can clearly be seen in terms of the *projection* of a purposive human consciousness, but the *introjection* is of a particularly technologized space, a space the camera mediates and assimilates to the terms of human vision.[48] The crisis of the subject in postmodern electronic space, then, is a crisis frequently represented in terms of an ambiguous and shifting vision, which may or may not be subjective.[49]

The movie *TRON* oscillates between the familiar, character-oriented subjectivity of "classical" Hollywood cinema and the terminal identity generated by the hyperbolic trajectories of a computer-simulated camera position. Here there are no literal point of view structures. "Camera" movement, simulated by the computer's graphics capability, is partly tied to vehicular movement, but it is also somewhat autonomous, swinging from high angles to low in a giddy display of its own cybernetic power. *TRON* not only constitutes an early narrative about virtual reality (VR); it also provides a taste of the VR experience in which the camera finally serves to give the viewer *a place* in this computerized world, a place defined almost solely in terms of spatial penetration and kinetic achievement.

Thus, while Margaret King argues that Disneyland presents "traditional values in a futuristic form," she has perhaps missed a more interesting aspect. The strategic narratives of the park prepare its guests for the future, and for the technologies to come, by grounding them in heavily traditional forms. The sophistication of the audioanimatrons™ is used to present singing bears and presidential simulacra; anthropomorphism is as prevalent as in any Disney film, and the narrative telos of the architecture and the rides further serves to acclimate the subjects to the technologies around them. The entrance to the park is a crucial part of this process: "Main Street is not an end in itself but the entryway into other less familiar realms."[50] Recalling the above discussion of Disneyworld as Disneymall, Anne Friedberg has noted that "The mall creates a nostalgic image of town center as a clean, legible, safe place," and this is an image fostered even more hyperbolically by Main Street, USA.[51] The narrative process of technological accommodation is heightened in Future World, where the rides narrate the histories of the technologies of communication, transportation, electricity, and energy. The "preshows" include tricked-up industrial films for such companies as United Technologies, Exxon, and General Electric (GE) (connections to the defense industry remain unstressed), while the shows feature the more traditionally entertaining audioanimatrons™ to illustrate the technological histories.

But the rides do more than narrate. The combination of simulation and transportation seems to be an urgent part of the agenda. The body is put in motion in Disneyland, where real movement of the subject's actual body occurs. Inevitably, however, this is supplemented by a further, simulated kinesis. The wraparound movie screens inevitably feature helicopter drops into the Grand Canyon (handrails are provided for queasy participants). The Carousel of Progress (sponsored by GE) rotates its audience around a series of audioanimated™ historical tableaux, a variation on the nineteenth-century form of the diorama: "The entire Diorama building became a machine for changing the spectator's view."[52] The Disney version, here and elsewhere, transforms the real spatial movement of the spectator into a simulated temporal trajectory. Further kinetic play is encountered in the narratively conservative Horizons, as the four-person vehicle moves laterally across an enormous IMAX screen. As a whirling molecular shape rotates outward to apparently engulf the visitors, the car tilts against the direction of the vortex. The kinesthesia is intense and effective, enhanced (as in Hale's Tours) by the "horizon" of the vehicle. The World of Motion propels its cars through a tunnel of frantically surging, projected images that includes the vertiginous passage into cyberspace originally used in *TRON*. In the meantime, artificial breezes, sounds, and even smells extend the sensory address (the Universe of Energy's dinosaur show includes a change in humidity). Paul Virilio, confronted with the hypercinematic experience of Omnimax, notes that "we can no longer separate film from auditorium."[53] How much more true at Disney World, as the "auditorium" of George Lucas's Star Tours bucks and tilts to augment the action on-screen (the audience is seated in a flight simulator)![54]

Tom Gunning has asserted that such prototypical technological attractions as Hale's Tours gave "a reassuring context to this experience. . . . The desire to provide a place for the spectator related to the movement within the spectacle reveals the enjoyable anxiety the audience felt before the illusion of motion."[55] Lynne Kirby notes that this anxiety is hardly innocent, and she has convincingly argued that Hale's Tours was a symptomatic response to an urban-induced "hysteria" and that the simulated transport served to equip its audience with an illusion of mastery over, or at least accommodation to, the mighty technological forces that were being increasingly deployed.[56]

Kirby refers to Walter Benjamin on the role of cinema in a dramatically technologized world: "The film is the art form that is in keeping with the increased threat to his life which modern man has to face. Man's need to expose himself to shock effects is his adjustment to the dangers threatening him. The film corresponds to profound changes in the apperceptive apparatus. . . ."[57] The same is true for the hypercinematic simulations of Tomorrowland and Future World.[58] A catharsis of technological breakdown is humorously, kinetically present in one of the most popular rides, Star Tours, in which your robot pilot malfunctions and sends you careening through space.

Kinesis is thus fundamentally bound to narrative, from Hale's Tours to Star Tours. The conjunction of space and story is similarly, though less evidently, played through in science fiction. Cyberpunk acknowledges the supercession of individual bodily experience in its hyperbolic, overdetermined prose, but ultimately the traditional operations of narrative firmly assert themselves. The decentering of the human subject performed by cyberpunk in its presentation of these *other spaces* existing beyond human intervention is undermined by the transformation of these spaces into arenas of dramatic action. Cyberspace is entered by the cyberspace cowboys, and thus human will and determination are brought to bear on this terminal realm. At its best, a symbiosis is proposed, but in practice the final *recentering* of the human subject within the cybernetic cosmology is beyond dispute.

12. Terminal Flesh

While Disney produces a simulation of tactical resistance, however, cyberpunk still engages in tactical warfare. Both theme park and cyberpunk are concerned with what de Certeau calls "the status of the individual in technical systems," as "the involvement of the subject diminishes in proportion to the technocratic expansion of these systems." The subject, increasingly unable to control these proliferating structures, "can henceforth only try to outwit them, to pull tricks on them, to rediscover, within an electronicized and computerized megalopolis, the 'art' of the hunters and rural folk of earlier days."[59] These are uncanny statements when juxtaposed with *Neuromancer*, a work quite evidently concerned with "the status of the individual *in* technical systems."

Cyberpunk is a narrative of tactics—corporations and military control the space of cyberspace, while outlaw c-space cowboys revel in their outsider status, becoming kinetic infiltrators, deceptors, and tricksters. At EPCOT Center the visitors are also kineticized outsiders but this time only as tourists who are, literally, just along for the ride.

What finally occurs through all of the intensification of sensory experience on the rides of Tomorrowland and Future World is nothing less than an inscription *of* the body *on* the body. These journeys into technologically complex zones ultimately serve to guarantee the continuing presence and relevance of the subject. You have a body, the rides announce, you exist. The body, and thus the subject, penetrates these impossible spaces, finally to merge with them in a state of kinetic, sensory pleasure. The visitor is thus projected into the datascape and is incorporated by the technology quite as fully as the cyberspace cowboys of *Neuromancer*. The inscription on the body announces the human-machine interface, and technology thereby creates the conditions for its own acceptance.

Merleau-Ponty has written of the complex interface between world and subject and of the fundamental physiognomic process whereby the "subject" is created at all: "the normal subject penetrates into the object by perception, assimilating its structure into his substance, and through this body the object directly regulates his movements. This subject-object dialogue, this drawing together, by the subject, of the meaning diffused through the object, and, by the object, of the subject's intentions—a process which is physiognomic perception—arranges round the subject *a world which speaks to him of himself, and gives his own thoughts their place in the world.*[60] What Disney and the cyberpunks permit, then, is nothing less than the process of "physiognomic perception" amid the previously inconceivable spaces of the telematic era. This engagement with a new world produces a new subjectivity, a new "terminal identity."

Despite its conservative narration of a benign, centralized technocracy, then, the Disney version is finally not so different from cyberpunk fiction in its presentation of a technological and overwhelming spatiality that is physically penetrated by the body of the subject. Future World dazzles its guests with dislocating other spaces in the manner of a science fiction text. And within such a narrativization, now augmented by a bodily address, these rides locate and center the human, further reifying the perceived power of the subject. The popularity of these theme parks bespeaks the massive need for reassurance and resituation that many continue to feel in the face of the invisible and hence unknowable spaces of terminal culture. The parks present technology with a Mouse's face.

All this occurs within the most protected, centralized, and technocratic of environments, complex spaces that raise pertinent questions for the understanding of technocultural formations, spaces that present both a traditionally grounded humanization of technology and the disembodying postmodern experience of a technological sublime, an installation that is the most extensive and explicit of strategic spaces but that assimilates visitor tactics in the process of building a technological interface. Here Baudrillard's most euphoric *and* despairing pronouncements both find continual figuration. Safely cocooned by the implosive architecture of the parks, the subject is itself assimilated and finally reconstituted by the extensive narrational telos, the evocation of a totalizing and benevolent urban experience, the hypercinematic engagement with a technologized phenomenology, the commodification of being, and the strategic usurpation of the everyday tactics of individual survival. In Future World, technology indeed seems to possess its own agenda and engages in an endless process of writing itself on the bodies of its "guests" while permitting them illusions of assimilation and mastery, illusions that are, at the same time, real bodily experiences. The enormous paraspatial and cybernetic realm of Walt Disney World constitutes a massive and self-regulating interface in which terminal space is rendered visible, malleable, and perhaps even adorable.

Gibson's Typewriter

Our writing materials contribute their part to our thinking.
Friedrich Nietzsche

Typewriter: It types *us*, encoding its own linear bias
across the free space of the imagination.
J. G. Ballard

That's Not Writing, That's Typing!

This is what we know about it: it's green (actually green and black), with celluloid keys of canary yellow. It's heavy; it's flammable; it's a "tough and elegant" Swiss machine from the shop of E. Paillard et Cie S.A., Yverdon. It was
once owned by a journalist, but it remained in the family. It was expensive.
It's a Hermes 2000. William Gibson wrote *Neuromancer* on it.

It is a tale often told in cybercultural enclaves and English departments:
William Gibson wrote *Neuromancer* on a manual typewriter. There is something charming about the anecdote, and it is not difficult to locate the source
of that charm. A simple bit of irony is at work in the apparently singular
fact that this novel all about computers, the novel that invented cyberspace
(sort of), the hippest, highest novel of the 1980s, should have been written
on such an antiquated device. That this primal work of electronic culture was
produced, not on a word processor or even an electric typewriter but on an
archaic piece of nineteenth-century technology, seems worthy of continual
note.

But there might be more at stake in the compulsive repetition of this
little cyberfable. Ironies are rarely simple, while we know that laughter or
amusement can mask anxieties that lurk only slightly beneath the surface.
In this instance, the anxieties center on contemporary relations to history,
technology, and language. In the telling of this story, two separate communities come into existence. The first, comprised of hackers and cyberdroolers,
share a dedication to the sheer coolness of new technologies. Come on, they

say, a *typewriter*?! The story enables those involved to position themselves as part of the new breed (what's a typewriter?). It's a funny story of personal idiosyncrasy, like finding out that Gibson rode a unicycle and wore pantaloons while he wrote. And then there is the more conservative community—English professors, let's say—that forms around the relief generated in linking this high-tech figure to the traditional world of letters (typewritten letters) and literature.

What our two anecdotal communities share is their regard of the typewriter as an obsolescent technology. For the more conservative group, *Neuromancer* is reinserted into canonical understandings of literature, as the terrors of the electronic age are displaced to a safe distance. The cyberheads become hacker undergrounders through the story: its telling constructs them as cyberspace cowboys with abilities superior to even those of cyberspace's architect. For this group, *Neuromancer* is situated as an instantiating text, as history is reduced to an ironic gloss. This very urgent history of mechanical technology becomes an absurd footnote within a cybercultural history that only believes in the newness of all phenomena, as though the world itself had been entirely reborn in the electronic era.

To an extent, I am sympathetic to (and complicit in) the construction of this ahistorical teleology. The ultimate effect of the electronic refiguring of the world remains indeterminate; the boundaries of new technological powers are still uncertain while all ontological categories are seemingly up

Figure 3. The Hermes 2000 typewriter.

for grabs. There is no question that *something* new is at work while we all slip into a state of terminal identity. But, despite this future-shocking onslaught, the discourse surrounding (and containing) electronic technology is somewhat surprisingly prefigured by the earlier technodiscourse of the machine age. Machines have become the metaphors that enable comprehension of postindustrial technological proliferation—even the high-tech, rust-proof sheen of *Mondo 2000* is just a seductive exercise in denial. Hence an examination of earlier technocultures is the movement of the moment (see Gibson and Sterling's novel *The Difference Engine* for Victorian era cyberpunk or "steampunk"). After all, the disappearance of history was proclaimed more than ten years ago by Jameson, Baudrillard, and their progeny. While a new "cultural dominant" has yet to emerge, many salient characteristics of postmodernity have waned or shifted terrain. Within this tumult, history can make—has been making—its necessary return. Perhaps its disappearance was little more than a trope of the postmodern text.

Some attention to the typewriter may therefore be warranted in order to type history back into *Neuromancer*. What emerges from a consideration of Gibson's typewriter, or at least what can be teased out of that consideration, are several overlapping tropes that tie cyberculture to its historical forebears. Reinstating the history of the typewriter indicates that *Neuromancer*'s disembodied informational cyberspaces are anticipated by the "obsolescent" rhetorics and technologies of what Mark Twain, the author of the first typewritten manuscript, once called "machine culture."

The Industrialization of Language in the Nineteenth Century

The history of the nineteenth century is, of course, marked by the pervasive spread of industrial technologies, which affect more than the conditions of production or even consumption. As the historical research of Wolfgang Schivelbusch demonstrates, industrialization resulted in a phenomenological reconfiguring of urban existence (through the introduction of new building materials, the impact of the railroad, and the adoption of the electric lighting of both interior and exterior spaces) as well as a pervasive reconception of spatiotemporal experience (through the convenient/marvelous/traumatic experience of railway travel and the related technologies of the telegraph and the cinema).[1] To these we might add that the telegraph, telephone, automated typesetting machine, and typewriter constitute a far-reaching industrialization of language in the nineteenth century. As Nietzsche remarked, in a typewritten letter from 1882, "Our writing materials contribute their part to our thinking."[2]

While Schivelbusch rejects technological determinism, he maintains that technological development so marks the nineteenth century that it must become the central issue for historians of that era. This same reasoning certainly also applies to the subsequent, and equally rapid and pervasive, developments of the Electronic Age.

The Typewriter and Its History: Improvements Wanted

The repression of the typewriter's historical significance in the *Neuromancer* anecdote has its analogue in the annals of technological history. No serious academic investigation of the typewriter has been published to my knowledge, and almost all curious writers seem to rely on the same two texts: *Typewriters and the Men Who Made Them* (hmm . . .) and, even better, *The Wonderful Writing Machine* (wow!), both highly positivist texts from the 1950s. The saga of the typewriter's development lacks a heroic central figure such as Edison, Whitney, or Bell (or Alan Turing, Steve Wozniak, or Bill Gates). In fact, the saga seems more of a case study of American manufacturing methods in the later nineteenth century, not exactly biopic material.[3]

There had been a number of attempts to construct writing machines in the eighteenth century. The first machines were developed for use by the blind and were designed to make a tactile impression on the page. The machine was to make it possible to process information despite a loss of visibility. A similar desire operates through the metaphor of Gibsonian cyberspace: a space in which the invisible processes of information circulation are recast in visual and tactile terms (the metaphor resides in the status of cyberspace as a narrated rather than an actual space). Typewriters accomplish their goals by spatializing information—the letters of the alphabet are dispersed in a standardized arrangement, each immediately available to the user. Information is rendered accessible, despite the lack of visual interaction: "Spatially designated and discrete signs—that, rather than increase in speed, was the real innovation of the typewriter."[4]

This arranged keyboard was the innovation of a Milwaukee newspaper editor, Christopher Latham Sholes (or the "father of the typewriter," as he is inevitably called). Earlier prototypes were usually characterized by a dial and a lever. Dial a letter, press the lever, and an impression is made on the paper (hidden from view). Release the lever, and the paper advances one space. The method was slow, and far removed from the flow of writing by hand. The machines were insufficient extensions of existing modes of human communication (to be McLuhanesque about it). Sholes had responded to a challenge published in *Scientific American* that exhorted its gadget-oriented readership to produce a writing machine that would improve on existing models (it was a 1987 *Scientific American* article that introduced virtual reality, or cyberspace, to a more general readership).[5] Inspired by the key of a telegraph sender, he constructed an array in which each piece of type was operated by a separate lever, all spread out before the user's gaze and hands.

Sholes was a colorful advocate of strange technological happenings. "Think of it!" he proclaimed in predicting the arrival of telegraph lines to Milwaukee. News from the East Coast would reach the city ten minutes after it was sent. "Language fails to convey anything like the sensations which the certainty of such an event must create." (This is not just a case of the technological sublime in action—Sholes was also interested in other forms of communication, as his active participation in midcentury spiritualist fads attests.)[6] We witness in Sholes's rhetoric a vested interest in an information revolution: his euphoria is a function of the speed and power of information technologies that would immediately empower the citizenry—a position espoused today by technoprophet Alvin Toffler. Late in his life he foresaw the obsolescence of his own medium, as news would be delivered to each home via little wireless teleprinters (this became a favorite fantasy of the twentieth century within the pages of *Popular Mechanics* and endless SF stories).

Advances in industrialism produced the enabling technologies that were fundamental to the execution of a reliable and durable typewriting mechanism (Hoke asserts that "The typewriter was the most complex mechanism mass produced by American industry, public or private, in the nineteenth century").[7] But a successful industrial invention equally implies successful economic exploitation. Newspaper publisher James Densmore worked with Sholes and his partners on simplifying the typewriter mechanism so that the device could be successfully and economically manufactured. Densmore then successfully marketed the invention to the Remington Firearms company, who, in the years following the Civil War, were retooling their munitions factories to produce sewing machines and other complex machines for American industry.[8]

A Typewriter Warmed in Hell: Typewriters Go to War

The juxtaposition between the technology of firearms and the machinery of the typewriter is provocative. In *Neuromancer*, a disassembled typewriter in Deane's office—Gibson's own machine making a cameo appearance—hides a weapon: "'It's on all the time,' Deane said mildly, taking a gun from behind the exposed works of his old mechanical typewriter and aiming it carefully

Figure 4. The typewriter goes to war. (Courtesy of the Library of Congress.)

at Case. It was a belly gun, a magnum revolver with the barrel sawn down to a nub."[9] And, from *The Wonderful Writing Machine:*

> In millions of homes the typewriter is really as important as the washing machine; it's just that the members of the family seldom think of mentioning that fact. A young man or woman would hardly consider going off to college without a portable (sometimes the same machine that Father used, with the tattered remnants of the school colors still sticking to the battered case). And—perhaps the ultimate test—when man goes into war he keeps his typewriter close by his side. The captain of a battleship insists that there be fifty-five typewriters on board before he feels fully equipped to meet the enemy. On the ground, as the army moves forward, there are more writing machines within four thousand yards of the front lines than medium and light artillery pieces combined.[10]

Learning to Type

Initial returns on the typewriter were surprisingly small. Businesses were originally loath to make the capital investment (machines and training) and were further concerned that typewritten correspondence would lack a "personal touch" and might prove offensive to clients. Journalists were surprisingly slow to adopt the new machine. Nietzsche procured an early machine to compensate for his failing eyesight, but he was unable to adapt to its rigors.

What rescued the machine from oblivion were the economic shifts that America underwent following the Civil War. In the move from an agrarian to an overwhelmingly industrial economy, businesses expanded enormously. The male office worker, traditionally a clerk who copied documents by hand, was simply unable to cope with the new volume of business-related paper-work. Of course, there was a vast, literate, potential work force available for employment at lower wages—middle-class women.[11] There was thus a major shift in the composition of the work force around the introduction of this new information-processing technology (cyborg fans will want to note that the women who worked on typewriters were themselves known as type-writers).

In his history, Richard Current stresses the increased output of informa-tion that resulted from the introduction of the typewriter: "the writing ma-chine swelled tremendously the output of recorded words." He further notes that once concise attorneys and businessmen, now dictating to a typist, re-vealed a tendency to wax loquacious. More documents, more words, more typewriters (the machine and the worker). As Current argues, "The multipli-cation of records not only measured but made possible a growing complexity of life. In particular, it facilitated the rise of both Big Business and Big Bureau-cracy."[12] Industrial culture and information culture arise together in a flood of typewritten symbols. Future shock and the overload of the Information Age here make their initial appearance. In the late twentieth century, com-puters developed into text-processing machines precisely in order to control the informational cyberblitz produced by all the typewriters in the world.

Information Overload in the Atomic Age

The Wonderful Writing Machine describes the rise of a profession that accom-panied the indisputable success of the typewriter in the twentieth century. As "the growing accumulation of old typewriting began to overwhelm business-men and business offices," a new figure emerges—the files-disposal expert. "He is a man, essentially, who knows how to throw typewriting away." This "essential man" is a figure of the Atomic Age. The author writes (with striking glibness for 1954): "The files disposal business boomed in about 1947 when the atom bomb threatened to clean out everybody's files with one whoosh, and businessmen thought that, if they didn't have such an awfully bulky lot of stuff to keep, they might save a few of the more important things in caves or underground vaults."[13] Here, in miniature, is the cold war experience of abundance and expansion subverted by a continual sense of physical vulnerability and paranoia. Protecting the files would at least close the potential information gap in a postapocalyptic international business setting.

The *Différance* Engine

In *Discourse Networks, 1800–1900,* Friedrich Kittler applied the language strategies of poststructuralism to the technologies of discourse. For Kittler, the introduction of the typewriter to the field of textual production has profound and lasting effects, which are described in terms that bring us to the edge of cyberspace. What first characterizes typing as an act of writing is an effect of disembodiment: the first typewriters did not permit the user to see the printed characters until several lines later. Not until Underwood's refinement did "visible writing" become a possibility. Angelo Beyerlin, Germany's foremost typewriter manufacturer, wrote: "In writing by hand, the eye must constantly watch the written line and only that. It must attend to the creation of each written line, must measure, direct, and, in short, guide the hand through each movement. For this, the written line, particularly the line being written, must be visible. By contrast, after one presses down briefly on a key, the typewriter creates in the proper position on the paper a complete letter, which not only is untouched by the writer's hand but is also located in a place entirely apart from where the hands work."[14] Even a visible typewriter hides the empty space that lies before the writing (the field of potentiality). Thus, "Underwood's innovation unlinks hand, eye, and letter" in a historically unique moment of disjuncture.[15] The hands appear *here*, while writing appears *there*. Typing thus produces an information space divorced from the body: a protocyberspace.

This disembodiment results from the emphatic standardization already described as a consequence of the keyboard array. If the act of handwriting had been a "continuous transition from nature to culture," that is, from prelinguistic thought to sign, then the act of typing was "selection from a countable, spatialized supply."[16] Following the precepts set forth by Derrida in *Speech and Phenomena,* Kittler makes a valuable distinction between a handwriting that *appears as* a direct emanation from the body, from nature, and a typewriting that is clearly mediated by cultural systems.

The described effect of a disembodied textual mechanics separates Kittler from the more utopian version of typing history provided by Marshall McLuhan. Like Richard Current before him and Kittler after, McLuhan emphasizes the structural impact of the typewriter and related technologies (although his main source seems to have been *The Wonderful Writing Machine*: "A modern battleship needs dozens of typewriters for ordinary operations"). As one might expect, however, McLuhan's emphasis on technology as "the extensions of man" leads him to stress, not the displacements of disembodiment but the integration of functions that occurs through typing: "At the typewriter, the poet commands the resources of the printing press. The machine is like a public-address system . . . as expediter, the typewriter brought writing and speech and publication into close association. Although a merely mechanical form, it acted in some respects as an implosion, rather than an explosion."[17] All these disparate functions are brought together and introjected within an increasingly empowered body. Cyberspace becomes the ultimate terrain for this implosive integration of functions, as human and data are made equivalent. McLuhan's utopian technoneurology serves a function similar to Gibson's cyberspace, as a metaphor that "naturalizes" technology to compensate for the human's alienation from the speed, power, and pervasiveness of contemporary technological configurations. (Gibson's formations seem by far the more richly complex of the two.)

Typecasting

The keyboard standardized the appearance and spacing of letters, and some worried that the typewriter spelled an end to the ability to write. The typewriter would thus yield a loss of bodily control, or perhaps even a loss of the body itself. The result, however, was a handwriting that aspired to the perfection of the typewritten standard. The typewriter thus makes potential cyborgs of us all, in our attempt to match its machine-tooled perfection. Ironically, the computer age has also introduced personalized fonts, developed from the handwriting of the user. The computer now simulates the human's fallible and uniquely shaky scrawl, albeit in a new standardized and storable form. Is it live, or Personal Font™?

(For the nostalgic, however, the computer can recall and reproduce the hyperbolic regularity of Machine Age typewriting. What exactly is the Courier font, in all its clunky glory, doing on my Mac?)

Speed Typing

In 1839, Michel Chevalier wrote about the American in motion that "he is always in the mood to move on, always ready to start in the first steamer that comes along from the place where he has just now landed. He is devoured with a passion for movement; he must go and come, he must stretch his limbs and keep his muscles in play. When his feet are not in motion, his fingers must be in action; he must be whittling a piece of wood, cutting the back of his chair, or notching the edge of the table, or his jaws must be at work grinding tobacco." "We are born in haste," says an American writer. "Our body is a locomotive going at the rate of twenty-five miles an hour; our soul, a high-pressure engine."[18]

Ever the technophile, Mark Twain was one of the first to purchase a typewriting machine (the story of his purchase appears, with suspiciously minimal variation, in every typewriter history). He praised it with reckless enthusiasm. But Twain's attitudes toward technology are truly ambivalent; as his *Connecticut Yankee* demonstrates, machination can produce unparalleled devastation. Nevertheless, one biographer argues that "The Yankee and the Machine were twinned in his mind. Both were tests of a perfectible world in which, contrary to all his insights and experience, friction and mechanical difficulties were equivalents of ignorance and superstition. Both expressed a secular religion which had as an unexamined article of faith a belief not in eternal life but in *perpetual motion*."[19] Perpetual, agitated kinesis marks the American spirit. The body is a machine, perfectible and progress oriented, while—at the same time—the machine becomes a body.[20]

The symbiosis of typewriter (machine) and typewriter (user) probably reached an apotheosis around the speed-typing exhibitions that swept the country for about thirty-five years beginning in the late 1800s. "Typewriter speed queens and kings were celebrities of a minor luminosity."[21] Before the battles, typewriter manufacturers had been content to boast that typing was twice as fast as the hand, but now these typewriter cyborgs, these carbon paper cowboys, left the natural hand far behind on the evolutionary ladder. One charming and slightly scary photo shows the 1926 amateur (!) champion, Stella Willins, posing in a motorcycle sidecar with her typewriter (of course) perched precariously before her. It's as though her typing must be measured in mph instead of wpm.

Unlike *Neuromancer's* renegade cowboys, these jocks were largely corporate owned—perhaps they belonged to the Underwood Speed Training Group or a similar organization. They did, however, have their own "decks": "Each typist had his own racing typewriter. . . . He carried it to matches, or on exhibition tours, in a big plush-lined case . . . and he worried about it the way a concert violinist worries about a Stradivarius. . . . The machines were stocked models but souped up, like a hot-rod racing automobile."[22] The "speed queens" (and kings) displayed intense concentration during a match, their fingers endlessly moving in conditioned-reflex perfection. "The slightest trace of self-consciousness was a fatal drawback."[23] (In *Neuromancer*, Case, too, yearns for the "bodiless exultation of cyberspace," the dissolution of self within the information vectors of the machine. For Gibson, though, this is both a dissolution of self and a self regained.) Kinesis alone produces the technologized subject.

Keep Jane's Fingers Dancing

Of course, there is another step in this cyborg dance. Despite the sporting aspects of these thoroughbred competitions, speed typing also represents the apotheosis of the Taylorist vision in which every gesture is designed to maximize productivity. *The Wonderful Writing Machine* reports that "motion studies" of the new electric typewriter revealed a 6 percent energy savings, "Which is pure bonus as long as the boss doesn't expect his patient stenographer to accomplish 20 per cent more, now that he's broken down and bought her an electric."[24] Throughout Bliven's book, secretaries are presented as a naive, patient, but secretly controlling group of girls (or ladies, to be more polite), coddled by bosses who can't afford to lose them. Yet the increase in the speed of office information processing calls forth a commensurate increase from the human user. The not so shocking truth is that the shift to electric typewriters was not grudgingly performed by gruff but lovable bosses giving their secretaries a bonus but by managers determined to maximize profits. The trend has obviously continued: Jeremy Rifkin reports that whereas a secretary once averaged about thirty thousand keystrokes every hour, a worker at a Video Display Terminal is expected to average eighty thousand.[25] Some bonus.

Surveillance of worker output is also so much easier in cyberspace, since every terminal can measure and report the number of keystrokes to a central managing position. *Processed World* magazine once featured a parodic ad for "Press®," a product designed to monitor employee pace: "If Jane's [keystroke] count drops below your chosen margin for more than three minutes, a subliminal warning flickers at the top of the screen. And if Jane still hasn't pulled herself together after two more minutes, a healthy 1-second jolt of 50 volts pulses out of her specially modulated keyboard and grounds harmlessly through her chair. It's guaranteed to get her moving again!"[26]

The Mysterious Interior of Machine #HH 5166247

The Wonderful Writing Machine features a chapter that concentrates on the labor of "final adjusting" as it is performed by Horace Stapenell ("a modest man"), as employee ("one of the best") of the Royal Typewriter company in Hartford, Connecticut. The author provides Horace's name, address, and biography before moving into a detailed explanation of his job. Just as Horace is a fairly ordinary guy, so the machines he works on are "standard-width carriage machine[s] with a standard keyboard." Those Johnny-come-latelies, the portables and the electrics, get their adjustments, mysteriously enough, "in other departments in other parts of the factory." Horace works in Department 10–C, and "10–C men hang around together." The chapter then becomes a tour through the inside of the typewriter, as we watch Horace make minute adjustments to bring the entire complex mechanism into alignment. The lines must be straight, the spacing even, the mechanism smooth and unresistant.

Horace is a real typewriter cowboy ("typewriters have been the focus of his whole working life"), fully jacked into his machine ("All his senses except taste are involved"). Once again, a symbiosis operates as man and machine are each explored simply in terms of the other. The figure of the human exists to present the space of the machine, and the machine is thereby humanized. Unlike the human typewriters and secretaries, Horace's work is measured by how *slowly* he proceeds: he "spends as much as three hours adjusting a single typewriter." And despite the monotony of his labor Horace has developed his own system, subtly different from those of the other workers around him ("They are the distinctions between working as at a craft and *working as a machine*").

The chapter details all the operations that Horace is likely to make, elaborately fetishizing each mechanism of the complex whole. The chapter frankly reads like ad copy: the more clarity the descriptions offer, the more the machine is mystified and mythified. An assembly line worker is inscribed within the rather different history of skilled handcraftsmanship, while the "standard" typewriter is itself invested with the precise workmanship of a town clock in Switzerland. It is as though the loss of *the hand* in the switch from handwriting to typewriting calls for its reappearance at some other part of the "discourse network," and so the writing machine is machined by a particularly careful, knowing, but very human hand.[27]

Dylan Goes Acoustic (or Clapton Unplugged)

Thus, the wonderful writing machine is invested with all the romance of a pretechnological mechanical marvel, like an elaborate automaton. In his volume on postmodernism, Jameson offers an interest reading of the modernist text: "Modern art . . . drew its power and its possibilities from being a backwater and an archaic holdover within a modernizing economy: it glorified, celebrated, and dramatized older forms of individual production which the new mode of production was elsewhere on the point of displacing and blotting out. Aesthetic production then offered the Utopian vision of a more human production generally; and in the world of the monopoly stage of capitalism it exercised a fascination by way of the image it offered of a Utopian transformation of human life."[28]

Despite the postmodern trappings of *Neuromancer*, Istvan Csicsery-Ronay Jr. located the significant modernist impulse at work in the subtextual celebration of art and creation that underlies much of Gibson's writing.[29] Its mode of production on a manual (hand-powered) typewriter links the work to Jameson's theory of modernism and uneven technological development. The typewritten manuscript belongs to a different historical moment than the postmodern cyberspaces of *Neuromancer;* in this sense, Twain was far more progressive than Gibson. When Twain, around 1883, produced the first typewritten manuscript, *Life on the Mississippi*, he was distancing himself from older modes of textual production, while with *Neuromancer*'s manuscript Gibson proclaims his fidelity. (It's tempting to regard *Neuromancer* as the *last* typewritten manuscript, even if it isn't true.)

The Mechanics of Fiction

Spatialization of information, disembodiment, exaggerated kinesis, information overload (cyberblitz), and the passage into the realm of the machine— these are the familiar tropes of Gibson's *Neuromancer*. But those figures are prefigured by a range of earlier discourses surrounding emergent information technologies, including those from the later nineteenth century (Twain, Sholes) as well as the middle of the twentieth (McLuhan, Bliven) and later (Jameson, Kittler).

Twain had invested fortunes in a typesetting machine developed by a James Paige (with fulsome praise, he compared it to all the most marvelous recent inventions, including the difference engine developed by Charles Babbage). The machine "became 'an inspired bugger,' 'a cunning devil,' and, after passing through a 'sick child' stage, a 'magnificent creature' ranking second only to man."[30] Justin Kaplan argues that through this anthropomorphism Twain expressed both his hopes and "his basic layman's ignorance, his credulity in the face of what seemed to him a divine mystery only because he knew hardly anything about mechanics."[31] Twain thus relies on nature for the conceptual metaphors that will render the mechanical susceptible to thought; he reaches with eagerness for the inconceivable, but can only do so in terms of the already conceived.

Gibson might be understood to do the same, but instead of nature he draws on the paradigm of industrial technology. Thus, cyberspace is as mathematically precise as a blueprint ("the cool geometric intricacy of Zurich commercial banking"), and, despite "the horizonless fields," its data systems comprise "an endless neon cityscape" and even "the old RCA Building" makes an appearance. ("The Kuang program dived past the gleaming spires of a dozen identical towers of data, each one a blue neon replica of the Manhattan skyscraper.")[32] Case, the cyberspace cowboy, loses his body but becomes a vehicle.

> Case had the strange impression of being in the pilot's seat in a small plane.
> A flat dark surface in front of him suddenly glowed with a perfect reproduction of the keyboard of his deck.
> "Two an' kick ass—"
> Headlong motion through walls of emerald green, milky jade, the sensation of speed beyond anything he'd known before in cyberspace. . . .
> The Tessier-Ashpool ice shattered, peeling away from the Chinese program's thrust, a worrying impression of solid fluidity, as though the shards of a broken mirror bent and elongated as they fell—
> "Christ," Case said, awestruck as Kuang twisted and banked.[33]

Relentless kinesis is one aspect of *Neuromancer's* postmodern amphetamine rush, but it also evokes the locomotives, automobiles, and aeroplanes of the Machine Age when, as industrial designer Norman Bel Geddes proclaimed, *"Speed is the cry of our era, and greater speed one of the goals of tomorrow."*[34] If cyberspace is a "consensual hallucination" that enables computer users to make sense of both their actions and the circulation of information, then that hallucination works by continually referencing the kinetic urban landscapes of Machine Age modernity.

Gibson shared Twain's "basic layman's ignorance" of the new machine's real operations. He relates in an interview: "When I started writing this stuff, I'd never touched a computer. And I think it gave me a certain strange edge in terms of imagination, in that I wasn't really hindered by what was possible." After he got a computer, he began to understand their real world mechanics: "I somehow thought that they were these silent, crystalline engines. I never really thought about how they worked. [Elsewhere, Gibson writes that he 'assumed the data was just sort of, well, *held* in a *glittering mesh* of silicon.'] And then I realized it was this piece of clumsy Victorian technology. . . . And at that point I sort of lost something, you know?"[35]

Rust Never Sleeps

While Gibson may have written *Neuromancer* on a manual typewriter, the Voyager Company let me read it on my Powerbook. A single floppy contained the entire trilogy: *Neuromancer*, *Count Zero*, and *Mona Lisa Overdrive*.[36] Using the search engine, I pretend to determine the prevalence of machine culture references in Gibson's writing. Did you know that there are twelve references to "rust" in the first book, nineteen in the second, and a whopping twenty-six in the last? Accelerated decrepitude, as Pris says in *Blade Runner*.

The Adding Machine

William Burroughs is an acknowledged and obvious influence on Gibson's writing. Together, Burroughs and Brion Gysin developed the cut-up and fold-in methods of rearranging typewritten text, releasing the words from the mechanically determined linearity. "You cannot *will* spontaneity," wrote Burroughs, whose family was responsible, incidentally, for the Burroughs adding machine, "But you can introduce the unpredictable spontaneous factor with a pair of scissors."[37] The typewriter is liberated from the mechanics of instrumental reason through these dadaist interventions. In "Technology of Writing," Burroughs had this advice for new writers: "One more thing: Sinclair Lewis said: 'If you want to be a writer, learn to type.' This advice is scarcely necessary now. So then sit down at your typewriter and write."[38] David Cronenberg's adaptation of *Naked Lunch* featured a typewriter that talked out of its ass.

The virus is one of Burroughs's most pervasive metaphors: the cut-up is a virus that destroys syntax and the rational domination of meaning. He once advocated the use of a Silence Virus to escape from the controllers of language, who are also then the controllers of the self (David Porush observed that the "noise" generated by the cut-up is a form of silence).[39] In 1992, Gibson released *Agrippa:* a software text with a built-in computer virus that would erase the text as it was read, and a book of illustrations that would fade more slowly over time.[40] The permanence of data is undermined by Gibson's own viral play. The author becomes an exterminator, a files-removal expert.

Afterword: Gibson's Afterword

Nothing kills a good critical analysis like an author who beats you to it. The Voyager Company's electronic edition of the cyberspace novels featured an afterword written by Gibson in the summer of 1992. He discusses his Hermes 2000 in loving terms, his subsequent forced experiment with a nightmarish Royal, and his latest acquaintance with an Apple computer. He recognizes the perceived irony of his writing *Neuromancer* on a manual machine but rejects it ("Some readers, evidently, find this odd. I don't.") The books may "pretend, at times, and often rather badly, to be about computers, but really they're about technology in some broader sense." At the heart of *Neuromancer* lies the continuity of machines and history. "I suspect they're actually about Industrial Culture," he wrote, "about what we do with machines, what machines do with us, and how wholly unconscious . . . this process has been, is, and will be."[41]

3

X-Bodies: The Torment
of the Mutant Superhero (1994)

1. Origin Stories

I don't read superhero comics anymore. I'm probably not as worried about my dick as I used to be. Well, *that* isn't exactly true—but I no longer deal with it by reading about mutant musclemen and the big-titted women who love them. I still read comics: several alternative titles (*Hate, Eightball, Dirty Plotte*) continue to engage, and there's been *Sandman* and *Swamp Thing* to look forward to, but it's those costumed characters, always fighting (whether for truth and justice or because it's what they do—and *they're the best at what they do*—or because it beats working), who have lost their charm, their appeal, and their relevance to my life. When I was contacted by the *Uncontrollable Bodies* editors to write an essay on "the body" that would incorporate autobiographical elements and a writing style less beholden to academic language, I wasn't sure whether they were responding to my work on terminal identity or an earlier study of Jerry Lewis.[1] My work was more invested in bodily control, its lack and loss, and the fragmentation of identity than I'd suspected. Meanwhile, here were these hyperbolic, dual-identitied bodies that I would ignore each week in my search for more "adult" comics. Those superbodies, it must be said, made me nervous. Clearly it was time to jack back into superhero culture to see what was happening, and to whom.

Elsewhere I have argued that narratives constitute adaptive technologies: the metaphorical cyberspaces of William Gibson's *Neuromancer* allowed a wholly legitimate envisioning of the invisible spaces of information circulation.[2] In its turn, that envisioning permitted a reconception of human possibility within electronic culture. More than just a mythological reconciliation, an illusion, fiction yields what Jameson has called a "cognitive mapping" of a (possibly reconfigured) subject into an intolerable space.[3] When it's working, narrative can become a testing ground for the conditions of being. Peter Brooks has written that "modern narratives appear to produce a semioticization of the body which is matched by a somatization of story: a claim that the body must be a source and a locus of meanings, and that stories cannot be told without making the body a prime vehicle of narrative significations."[4] Admittedly, Brooks is writing of Proust and Lawrence, not of Plastic Man or The Thing; still, I would maintain that superhero narratives do present a significant somatization of modernist and postmodernist social concerns. Superhero comics embody social anxiety, especially regarding the adolescent body and its status within adult culture. Superhero bodies are mysterious, invested with magical abilities and a metamorphic pliability; if they are marginal bodies in the body of literature, this still should not blind us to their importance. "So far from using bodily magic as an escape," the anthropologist Mary Douglas argues, "cultures which frankly develop bodily symbolism may be seen to use it to confront experience with its inevitable pains and losses. By such themes they face the great paradoxes of existence."[5]

Superhero comics present body narratives, bodily fantasies, that incorporate (incarnate) aggrandizement and anxiety, mastery, and trauma. Comics narrate the body in stories and envision the body in drawings. The body is obsessively centered upon. It is contained and delineated; it becomes irresistible force and unmovable object. The body is enlarged and diminished, turned invisible or made of stone, blown to atoms or reshaped at will. The body defies gravity, space, and time; it divides and conquers, turns to fire, lives in water, is lighter than air. The body takes on animal attributes, merges with plantlife, is melded with metal. The body is asexual and homosexual, heterosexual, and hermaphroditic. Even the mind becomes a body: it is telepathic, telekinetic, transplantable, and controllable. Brainiac's brain sticks out of the top of his head, on display as part of a visible, external body. The body is an accident of birth, a freak of nature, or a consequence of technology run wild. The superhero body is everything—a *corporeal*, rather than a *cognitive*, mapping of the subject into a cultural system.

Anyone who thinks that the superhero heyday has passed has only to step into a comics store to see rack upon rack of zingy new titles. The X-Men are movie, TV, and arcade game stars, Batman is in the movies and on TV, and new publishing ventures are burgeoning.[6] Television and cinema want to appropriate the mass-market merchandising megaclout of the superhero genre. Even Superman made it back into the papers (though the reports of his death were greatly exaggerated). The superhero, a popular icon since the 1930s, has become newly, and increasingly, ubiquitous.

At the center of the revival are the X-Men, once relatively minor characters in the Marvel Comics pantheon. The original stories from the middle 1960s lacked the cosmic grandeur of Stan Lee and Jack Kirby's *Fantastic Four* or *Thor* comics or the nerdy charm of Spiderman by Lee and Steve Ditko, but there was something of interest in the title's exploration of adolescent alienation. Recruited by the telepathic Professor Xavier, the X-Men are teenaged mutants, powerful but undisciplined. Under the cover of his exclusive School for Gifted Youngsters, Professor X teaches his X-Men to control their powers in order to face the threat posed by "evil mutants" bent (of course) on the domination of humanity. When a revamped mutant team was launched in the 1970s, however, the title caught on with adolescent readers. Replacing the all-white antics of the Beast, Iceman, Angel, Marvel Girl, and Cyclops was a more ethnically and visually diverse bunch. The Beast became more bestial, Cyclops more tormented; Marvel Girl was reborn as Phoenix, and an African woman known as Storm took over the leadership of the team. The mysterious, violent, nearly indestructible Wolverine became one of the most popular characters in comics. Scripts by Chris Claremont emphasized domestic interaction and introspection. *The Uncanny X-Men* spawned numerous offshoots, including *X-Men, X-Force, X-Factor, X-Men 2099,* and limited series with individual characters (especially Wolverine). The mutants provided enough torment and combat to propel the superhero revival that continues today, a revival fueled by inexhaustible reserves of adolescent angst.

The revival continued, and in the 1990s revisionism took a dark turn. Superman died (none too poetically—he was just *beat up*) and came back with Daniel Day Lewis's hair. Batman broke his back and returned in a semicyborged state. Marvel unleashed darker versions of its own classic heroes. Most of this was in response to the rise of Image Comics, the fastest-growing company in the history of the medium. Image was formed by some renegade writers and artists from the mainstream houses (mostly Marvel), and its roster includes some of the hotter names in the business. Their titles clog the shelves just as in-house advertisements clog their pages. The Image titles specialize in even more intensely exaggerated visualizations of the (barely) human body; there is a powerful hysteria working beneath the surface of muscles, cleavage, masks, and laser beams.

Superhero comics remain a largely subcultural phenomenon produced largely by young males for somewhat younger males. The recent boom in comics sales in the United States dates from the early 1980s when specialty stores arose to cater to an obsessively knowledgeable audience.[7] Titles began to be produced for the "direct sales" market—these were readers who knew what they wanted, and the industry was only too happy to oblige. As in *Trek* fandom, the lines between creators and consumers have been very permeable, and today's fanboy reader may be tomorrow's writer, artist, editor, or publisher (copyright control has somewhat shifted from companies to creators). Most recently, there has been an explosion of so-called collectibles: T-shirts, caps, action figures, trading cards, stamps, pins, watches, and "special" editions with embossed foil (or even holographic) covers have provided ever more opportunities for unrestrained consumption.

The following does not pretend to be an ethnography of superhero comics culture—I haven't done the research. I have relied on a conjunction of theoretical and ethnographic writings: Klaus Theweleit on the soldier-male and Wolfgang Schivelbusch on industrial shock, Alan Klein on the "comic book masculinity" of bodybuilding subculture, and Mary Douglas on bodily rituals as social symbolism.[8] I want to demonstrate that what superheroes embody are ambivalent and shifting attitudes toward flesh, self, and society. Where once superhero comics whimsically presented bodies armored against the shocks of industrial society, too many current characters now seem to simply incarnate problematic and painfully reductive definitions of masculine power and presence. In the 1970s and 1980s, mutant superheroes gained in popularity, and these X-bodies encourage an alternative understanding of the superbody hieroglyph (one that coexists with hypermasculine fantasy). The mutant body is explicitly traumatic, armored against the world outside yet racked and torn apart by complex forces within. The mutant body is oxymoronic: rigidly protected but dangerously unstable. In its infinite malleability and overdetermined adolescent iconography, the mutant superhero is a locus of bodily ritual.

There is also an autobiography entrenched in "X-Bodies," and I'm forced to realize that the autobiographical subject isn't me, the adolescent dreaming of bodily strength and cosmic consciousness, but me, the adult academic who feels compelled to write about superhero comic books. At 7 A.M. one Sunday, in bed with someone I'm no longer in bed with, I opened my eyes and had a magic thought: *mutant superheroes*. This could be a fertile field, encapsulating a striking number of body issues. But the topic was perfect in another way—

it was true to my reputation, and when people asked what I was working on I could wear an expression of embarrassed pride and say *mutant superheroes*! People could cluck knowingly, laugh appreciatively, or leave quickly. *Oh, that Scott!* they would say. I tried it out at a couple of parties.

Beyond the not so shocking shock value of comics, though, I do like the things. In early drafts of this essay I "sutured" the complex pleasures I derive from comics to the reductive discourses of the academy, the very approach I abhor the most. Academia presented me with an imperfect double of my self—*Bizarro Bukatman*. I knew that it was clobberin' time. I had to rediscover my fondness for the medium, and for the genre of superhero fantasy, without surrendering my intellectualism. I needed to recapture my own fragmented experience—my trauma, my anxiety, my hurt, my humor, my play, my intelligence, my body, my grace, my clumsiness, my fantasy, and my creativity.[9] My greatest battle.

The writing process has taken its toll. To walk up to the hip chick working the register at St. Marks Comics, a woman who clearly doesn't care whether Wolverine is stronger than Lobo, requires nerves of steel. I had established myself as something of a groovemeister, buying the latest alternatives and Vertigo grunge-horror books, but now I was clutching back issues of *Spawn* and *Cyber Force*. I would ask for separate receipts in a pathetic attempt to separate myself from my "research" purchases, but it was useless. I had clearly lost all hipster credibility.

2. Industrial Strength

I have a picture of myself at around age eight, dressed as Green Lantern. I think (I hope, I *pray*) that it was Halloween. Green Lantern was always my favorite of the "classic" superheroes; there was that streamlined costume (no cape!), the power ring, and the secret oath.[10] The ring worked by sheer force of will—thought made physical. In the pages of *Dr. Strange*, Steve Ditko would endow mystical rays and magical incantations with an eerie physicality all their own, but the world of Green Lantern was more familiar in its fancies. Even as a child I was charmed and slightly mystified by the literalness of GL's power ring emanations: huge green hands grabbed falling airplanes, and giant ears eavesdropped on crooks. The power ring also cranked out modern machines: an enormous emerald derrick would pick the criminals up and deposit them in jail or great green springs would cushion a descent (nor were these the only signs of an industrial consciousness—GL's streamlined look suited his secret identity as jet test pilot Hal Jordan). With the ring, the self was no longer bounded by a body but only by its own self-conception. I doubt that I realized it then, but here was Freud's omnipotence of thoughts gelled into an ornament that could compensate for (my) physical weakness.

There are deep uncertainties operating in superhero narratives that mark a symbolic return to a presymbolic space of primal drives and primal fears as well as later anxieties that are at once psychoanalytical, social, and historical. Wolfgang Schivelbusch reminds us of the disorienting experience of industrialization and its concomitant trauma, the industrial accident. "It must be remembered," he writes, "that railway accidents have this peculiarity, that they come upon the sufferers instantaneously without warning, or with but a few seconds for preparation, and that *the utter helplessness of a human being* in the midst of the great masses in motion renders these accidents peculiarly terrible." [11]

The human body is not designed for the stresses of mechanical operation. As Gustave Claudin observed in 1858 of his rapidly changing world, "These discoveries . . . bend our senses and our organs in a way that causes us to believe that our physical and moral constitution is no longer in rapport with them. Science, as it were, proposes that we should enter a new world that has not been made for us. We would like to venture into it; but it does not take us long to recognize that it requires a constitution we lack and organs we do not have." [12] The superhero, who appears on the American industrial landscape in the 1930s, possesses a new kind of body—only the Man of Steel has the constitution, organs, and abilities equal to the rigors of the Machine Age.

Superman makes his initial appearance following the sustained shock of World War I. Schivelbusch notes the newly unleashed terror of sudden death. Where once a soldier could prepare himself for combat, "from the eighteenth century on, such a state of readiness no longer existed. The wound caused by mass fire occurred suddenly, invisibly; it came 'out of nowhere.'" [13] By contrast, the superhero body is a body in a permanent state of readiness (*this is a job for* . . .). What's more, if random death now appears from nowhere, the superbody is more than merely resistant; it bears its own mysterious power. Such powers are often technological (well, pseudotechnological) in origin: Superman is "a strange visitor from another planet," Green Lantern was entrusted with his power ring by the Guardians of the Galaxy, Captain America was injected with an experimental supersoldier serum, and on and on. As embodied by the superhero of the 1930s and 1940s, the "utter helplessness of the human being" in the face of industrial stress has been overcome—technological trauma has produced its own antidote. [14]

The first sign that all was not perfect in superhero land turned up in the postwar era. In the 1960s, American superheroes were saddled with mysterious and wholly arbitrary "weaknesses." Superman had Kryptonite as his *bête verte,* and, okay, I could accept that. At least Kryptonite was some *thing.* But Green Lantern's ring failed to work against anything yellow. Why? So, like, was his ring only partly effective against orange? Where on the spectrum does yellow end, officially? When encountering a new hero, you had to know two things—what was his power, and what was his "Achilles' heel"? They were concomitant, each the inevitable consequence of the other. Thus, a writer's convenience took on the force of an ontology.[15]

It was against this background that the Marvel superheroes of the 1960s appeared "realistic." There were arbitrary weaknesses for these heroes, but self-doubts aplenty, yeah. These more psychologized figures quarreled, got depressed, and questioned themselves. The Marvel heroes were rarely gifted by birth or by choice; they were instead transformed in young adulthood by (sort of) varied forces: radioactive spider bites; cosmic ray bombardment in near Earth orbit; gamma ray bombardment at a military testing ground; a collision with a truck bearing radioactive waste; and a (nonradioactive) stick that, when banged on the ground, made you into Thor, the Norse god of thunder. These comics presented as obvious an allegory of pubescent metamorphosis as one could imagine—The Hulk, for example, got big and hairy and his voice changed. Go figure.

Identity is the obsessional center of superhero comics, as revealed by endless processes of self-transformation and the problematic perceptions of others—Batman hunted by police, Lois hunting for Superman's secret identity. The secret identity is a major issue for the superhero, but if Hal Jordan is the "secret" identity why does Green Lantern wear the mask? Writing about narratives from the Odyssey to the Prisoner of Zenda and beyond, Peter Brooks has written that "It is on the body itself that we look for the mark of identity, as writers of popular literature have so well understood. . . . The bodily marking not only serves to recognize and identify, it also indicates the body's passage into the realm of the letter, into literature: the bodily mark is in some manner a "character," a hieroglyph, a sign that can eventually, at the right moment of the narrative, be read."[16]

The superhero body is marked in at least two senses: the secret identity constitutes the body *secretly* marked—this weenie is recognized (by the reader) as the conquering hero—but costume and logo constitute the superhero body as *publicly* marked. Mask, costume, and logo are marks that guarantee the superhero body passage into the field of the symbolic (the logos).

Like the golem of Jewish mysticism, we might say that the superhero is con-structed in the field of writing (the creation of a golem depends upon a mys-tical word inserted into the clay creature's mouth or ear, but in the 1920 Ger-man film the inscription is placed in the center of its chest—logo position).[17] Thus, the acquisition of costume, mask, and logo might constitute a "*sym-bolic* birth," or *rebirth* into the symbolic, which, as Marie-Hélène Huet argues of the golem and other "ex-utero procreations," transfers issues of birth and identity from the field of maternal power to the realm of the patriarchy.[18]

Alan Klein observes of bodybuilding that "the hypermuscular body" in bodybuilding "is supposed to communicate without an act; its presence is its text."[19] The superhero body is similarly written, but when read it will yield a secret. Hence the fascination with *origin stories* in the comics: the secret is a secret history, a story embodied by the mark on the surface of the body. In these postmodern times of emphatic surfaces and lost historicities, origin tales are no longer so stressed: the hyperbolically muscular heroes of Image Comics are nothing more or less than what they look like; and the marked body has become an underdetermined sign as issues of identity recede to the background.[20] Most of these heroes seem not to have secret identities at all, which is just as well—some have purple skin and are the size of small neigh-borhoods. But then why are they wearing masks?

Clearly the mask serves to protect the self by placing a barrier between sub-ject and world (Klein: "bodybuilders wind up using their bodies as a mask, a male persona with which to ward off insecurities").[21] The mask, no matter how minuscule, is a sign of the rebirth as what Klaus Theweleit has referred to as the *armored body*.[22] The disturbingly repetitive and consistent memoirs of German *Freikorps* figures reveal a careful deployment of disciplinary and mili-tary apparatuses that turn the body into a part of a machine, delibidinalized through the imposition of boundaries drawn from outside the subject. The ego is further severed from the weakness and frailty of the flesh through pain: aggressiveness against "outsiders," killing what is not "them," externalizes the fear of ego dissolution. Hence the masculinist aversion to the liquidity as-sociated with the monstrous feminine—*Freikorps* males exhibited a desire to annihilate the female and reduce her to a "bloody mass." The woman bears libidinal energies that are not beholden to reason; they exemplify the *flow* that threatens to wash away all that is rational (all that is *the subject*) in a cata-clysmic flood.[23] *Antiwoman* becomes a code for *antilife*.[24] Body and psyche are united as the subject becomes a weapon, an armored figure hiding both the erotic and the mortal truths of its being.

Superhero bodies, despite their plasticity, are armored bodies, rigid against the chaos of surrounding disorder. While permitted the narcissistic luxury of self-doubt, their power and their ultimate triumph are guaranteed; their stories are already written.[25] We are deep within what Theweleit called "the conservative utopia of the mechanized body."[26] Writing about the investment that surrealism and dadaism also had in the armored body, Hal Foster noted the "tension between binding and shattering tendencies, the play between sadistic and masochistic impulses." Surrealism was defined by the struggle "between the erotic and the destructive, the one never pure of the other."[27] In cruder form superhero comics replay this struggle unabated, as the display and experience of power become especially hysterical. Erotic energies are sublimated into (other) bodily traumas, emissions, and flows: battles or the task of controlling the power are acts of self-protection that channel energy flow into focused blasts of multicolored destruction. Self-protection, though, is a blind for self-annihilation. Theweleit writes that in battle, "The man longs for the moment when his body armor will explode, strengthening his rigid body-ego; but a body such as his cannot atomize, as does the mass, by allowing itself to be penetrated, fragmented, and thus destroyed. His body atomizes only if he himself erupts outward. He desires to move beyond himself, bulletlike, towards an object that he penetrates."[28]

The longing for orgasmic battle begins to account for the appeal of the superhero team (Fantastic Four, Justice League of America, Avengers, etc.). Schivelbusch, whose notion of a "stimulus-shield" echoes Theweleit's armored body, notes that after World War I "warriors no longer did battle individually but as parts of the new combat machine. . . . The new military organization concretized the entirely specific sense of the word [*shock*]: the clash of two bodies of troops, each of which represented a new unified concentration of energy by means of the consolidation of a number of warriors into one deindividualized and mechanized unit. What was new in this military clash was its unheard-of violence (due to the concentration of energy) as well as the degree of attrition of its elements; the latter occurred in direct proportion to the degree of energy concentration."[29] Teamups became popular during World War II as a kind of superhero Popular Front movement against the Axis powers. Thus, they were originally a battle formation, an *Überkorps* of reciprocally reinforcing body armors. But their popularity survived the war, and in the 1960s such teamups were rampant. One is tempted to turn to Will Wright's study of narrative structures in the cinematic western: he found that such 1960s and 1970s releases as *The Magnificent Seven, The Profes-*

sionals, and *Butch Cassidy and the Sundance Kid* were marked by the "organization man" mentality of a newly powerful corporate capitalism.[30] Indeed, the superhero groups not only included frequently fractious members,[31] as did their western counterparts; they also featured jet planes, uniforms, and secret headquarters replete with boardrooms and global communications setups. The Fantastic Four even had their own skyscraper—the Skidmore, Owings and Merrill–style Baxter Building (all of these headquarters were revealed in panoptic cutaway views detailing the locations of hangers, living quarters, training areas, and missile launchers). It's difficult to imagine corporatist fantasies resonating loudly among ten-year-old readers (*Hey, you got to be the Trilateral Commission last time!*); still, the corporation, the fraternity, the secret clubhouse, and the playground all provide alternative concepts of home and family.[32]

Within the comics' massive pitched battles, obsessively hyperbolized in any number of recent titles from Image Comics such as *Brigade* or *WILDC.A.T.S.,* the action is an incoherent jumble of power beams and body parts, and superheroes and supervillains can't be easily distinguished. Although the supervillain may be considered the raison d'être for the superhero, the hero's creation is always precedent, and so the hero summons forth his own nemesis. But these are not battles between individuals, this is *war:* an unprecedented concentration of energy released in an explosion of nearly orgiastic pleasure and hysterical excess. The Image superhero tends toward battlefield (and action film) rhetoric.

> [Wed. 7:02 P.M., Cyberdata Technologies Building, lower Manhattan]
> —(We've still got to find Velocity, grab Timmie and get out alive. I always knew my S.E.A.L.S training would come in handy some day.)
> —*Heatwave to all units top to bottom. Rock and roll.*
> —*EEEYAA-HEY!*
> —(You'd think I'd be used to it by now, but Ripclaw's war cry still sends chills up my spine.)

The ensuing battle in *Cyber Force* #3 covers eight densely illustrated pages.[33] Ripclaw leaps into the fray, his clawed hands lunging forward toward the hapless reader. Where once the heroes respected the classical, clean, six panels per page layout common to American comics, now their pent-up fury overpowers the containing/constraining boundaries of the panel or even the page itself. Theweleit's analysis of the soldier-male is rhetorically tailored to that fantasied soldier-male, the superhero: "War is a function of the body of these men. . . . In war, the man appears not only naked, but stripped of skin; he seems to lose his body armor, so that everything enters directly into the interior of his body, or flows directly from it. He is out of control and seems permitted to be so. But at the same time, he is all armor, speeding bullet, steel enclosure. He wears a coat of steel that seems to take the place of his missing skin."[34]

In *one* panel, Heatwave stands in the foreground, firing his translucent pink energy beam out the bottom of the frame (*BZZZAK!*) while some armored guy with glasses fires his automatic weapon to the left (*BRAKAKAK!*) An enormous character in the upper-left midground is being shot at (*KRAKA BOOM! BOOM! BOOM!*) by about four guys with mobile armor spread out along the right background. The big one is saying: "I got ya covered, Heatwave, but that dude with the cannon's gettin' to be a real pain in the *butt*." The background is a purplish field, pierced by energy beams, explosions, smoke, and debris. The bodies become both armored and flowing in combat, as the seething energies repressed by the elaborate body armors of the superhero spurt from all directions and every orifice.

3. Androids on Steroids

It seems that every Image Comics character (Maul, Heatwave, Void, Ripclaw, Impact, Velocity, Grifter, Spartan, and the others) has been, is, or will be part of at least one superhero team (Team Youngblood, Brigade, WILDC.A.T.S., Cyber Force, Freak Force, StrykeForce, Bloodstrike, StormWatch, and so it goes). The editor's page in *Doom Force*, a parody scripted by Grant Morrison, perfectly described this kind of title (although the real targets were Marvel's *X-Factor* and *New Mutants*).

> Grant breathlessly painted a vivid word-picture of a colorful band of super-outcasts who bravely battle the world's most powerful menaces on behalf of the very same human race that rejected them. Ironically, these youthful warriors have much more in common with their enemies than with those they fight to protect, but their basic decency leads them to struggle for the cause of justice in a world they barely understand. Their grim, wisecracking demeanor and their good-natured bickering may fool you, but when the chips are down, they're prepared to sacrifice their very lives to protect the innocent—and each other.[35]

(Morrison also copyrighted names for future superhero use, so watch for Gridlock, Campfire, Eight-Track, Rim Shot, Mimosa, and Spatula.)

The Image books are a fanboy wet dream.[36] The art is replete with extensive crosshatching—the tiny lines that have dominated superhero comics since Rob Liefeld introduced the style. In his indispensible formal analysis, *Understanding Comics*, writer-artist Scott McCloud notes that "in the mid-1960s when the average Marvel reader was pre-adolescent, popular inkers used dynamic but friendly lines. . . . But when Marvel's reader base grew into the anxieties of adolescence, the hostile jagged lines of a Rob Liefeld struck a more responsive chord."[37] Liefeld, once featured in a Spike Lee Levi's commercial, was a founder of Image Comics, where those "hostile, jagged lines" are deployed in the service of a still-increasingly exaggerated bodily presence.[38]

The Image body is massively muscled, locked into a "dynamic," heroic pose. Despite accoutrements such as logos, masks, gauntlets, epaulets, and other superhero accessories, the bodies are essentially presented as nudes (costumes are more coloration than cover-up). The team books feature an assortment of freakish figures either frozen in a group pose or locked in prodigious battle with other characters on the other side of the embossed wraparound cover. Where comics art once emphasized a vigorous flow of line that would lead the eye from panel to panel, recent comics turn each page into a stiffly posed pinup of flexed muscles and dramatic shading. The narrative, not very important to begin with, is further devalued against this fetishism of the superhero's overstated iconographic status; always spectacular in superhero comics, the body is now hyperbolized into pure, hypermasculine spectacle. The superhero body becomes autoreferential; it can only be compared to those of other superheroes and not to the common world of flesh, blood, muscle, and sinew.

This spectacle of the body resembles other such spectacles in contemporary culture. The hypermuscled body has moved closer to mainstream culture, whether in the buff figures of music video, the bodily obsessions of academic cultural studies, the movie stardom of Arnold Schwarzenegger, American Gladiators, the underwear ads of Marky Mark, the increased coverage of bodybuilding events on cable TV—*stop the insanity!* The exaggerated musculature of the Image books suggests the parallel phenomenon of bodybuilding. As Klein and Sam Fussell have both noted, "One doesn't so much admire bodybuilders for what they can do as far as what they *look* like they can do. The look of power, virility, prowess, counts for more than function, and has more in common with the world of modeling, beauty contests, or cinema idols than that of sports heroes."[39] The *look* is the thing—to emphasize their supersolidity, bodybuilders adopt the Walk: "They burrowed their heads slightly into their shoulders to make their necks appear larger. They looked bowlegged, absurdly stiff, and infinitely menacing."[40] Bodybuilding contests present the body frozen into a set of poses that make the body *appear* powerful, and the final confrontation between contestants is the simultaneous "pose-down," in which each presents his body in as visually compelling a manner as possible. Superheroes present an image of active power, but being imaginary characters their power is also only an illusion.[41] The Image heroes are locked in a permanent pose-down of aggressive appearances and fetishistic display.[42]

It isn't surprising that the bodybuilder's body should emerge most consistently in the arena of superhero comics—comics and bodybuilding have been closely aligned for decades. Arnold came to stardom playing Conan the Barbarian, and Lou Ferrigno was The Hulk for a few years. Bodybuilding articles *sound* like superhero names: "Destroyer Delts," "Nuke Legs."[43] Bodybuilders *like* comics: "Comic-book depictions of masculinity are so obviously exaggerated that they represent fiction twice over, as genre and as gender representation. But for bodybuilders these characters serve as role models."[44] And let's not forget "The Insult That Made a Man Out of Mac," the one-page adventure of a skinny guy with sand in his face who takes a course from Charles Atlas and exacts his revenge. *Oh Mac,* his frighteningly fickle gal coos, *You ARE a real man after all*! Fans will be glad to know that Mac was reborn in Grant Morrison's technosurreal *Doom Patrol* as Flex Mentallo, the most famous superhero of all time, and, truly, who could argue the point? "I learned how to refine and manipulate the secret vibrational wavelengths of each muscle, each tendon." A battle against a government conspiracy spelled Mac/Mentallo's doom: "I thought if I flexed hard enough, I could make it happen. I thought I could turn the Pentagon into a circle. . . . I just flexed. In all the apartments of my building, people began to experience unusual phenomena: spontaneous, uncontrollable orgasms; visions of worlds folded into empty envelopes; astounding new ideas for leisure footware. There were reports of bizarre dreams, all containing the word 'obviously.' . . . And I kept flexing." By pitting the spiritual powers of "muscle mystery" against the articulate hierarchies of the military, Morrison exposes the emptiness at the core of bodybuilding fantasies—the lack of power that belies its emphatic appearance.[45]

Klein describes something called *roid rage:* aggressive behavioral outbursts that follow sustained steroid use.[46] I think of Maul from Image's *WILDC.A.T.S.,* my favorite goofy new character: "Maul can increase his body-mass exponentially," the *WILDC.A.T.S. Source Book* reports on the purple and green behemoth, "becoming bigger and stronger when necessary. He suffers a corresponding loss in intellect and self-restraint, though, which causes him problems." Maul is a close relative of Bruce Banner, a scientist who, when angered, transforms into a green-skinned, uncontrolled monster from the id known as The Hulk (*Is he man or monster . . . or BOTH?*). We are confronted with an aggressive hypermasculinity, a compensation for psychosexual anxiety that depends upon a ruthless suppression or (in the case of the *Freikorps*) an obliteration of the feminine. Thus, "the formidable bodies are responses to a shaky psyche . . . physique and psyche were different words for overdevelopment and underdevelopment. What bound them was compensation; the bodily fortress protected the vulnerability inside."[47] Superman is the hypermasculine version of Clark Kent (Jules Feiffer pointed out that his fake identity is our real one).[48] The hypermasculinity of bodybuilder or superhero-fantasy represents an attempt to *recenter the self* in the body, a reductive conflation of body with subjectivity.

While outsiders see a blatant narcissism in the mirrored gymnasiums and unrestrained body worship of the bodybuilder, Klein finds something else: "Narcissus fell completely in love with his reflection. The bodybuilder would like to, but can't. Inside that body is a mind that harbors a past in which there is some scrawny adolescent or stuttering child that forever says, 'I knew you when . . .' The metamorphosis is doomed to remain incomplete."[49] That scrawny adolescent is surely a close relative of the one with his arms filled with five copies of the latest Image slugfest. The act of bodybuilding only represents a more activist dedication to the same compensatory, hypermasculine, anxious, armored forms that superhero comics present to their similarly insecure readers.

In recent comics, muscular obsession reaches a new pitch. I'm continually struck by the attention to *neck muscles.* In his experience of male gym culture, Samuel Fussell noted that straights and gays preferred to work on different body parts—specifically, hets wanted megadeveloped lats (gays preferred a leaner, more classical, neck and shoulder line). This is interesting, if true, because the Image heroes have the biggest lats on the *planet.* Indeed, with their thick necks, bulging veins, and protruding tendons tightly swathed in colored skintight hoods, these heroes really become enormous *dicks* sheathed in an array of distinctly baroque (and somewhat painful looking) condoms— an effect both menacing and comical.

The women I know express the same revulsion toward images of body-

Figure 5. WILDC.A.T.S. in battle pose mode, art by Travis Charest.
(Courtesy of Image Comics.)

builders' bodies (*thank goodness*), and in fact men find these male bodies to be more "acceptable" than do women.[50] Superhero readers are also a very male and heterosexist group (with some exceptions for X-Men fans), unwilling to directly confront more nuanced definitions of masculine identity. The self-pity that underlies so many superhero titles since the 1960s (the *sensitive new age mutant* syndrome) indicates an awareness of emotional need but only within a hypermasculine context. A continuing character in *Eightball*, an alternative comic by Daniel Clowes, is the popular superhero artist (and total geek) Dan Pussey. In "The Origin of Dan Pussey," we visit him in high school as he withdraws ever further into fantasies of muscles and mutants: "See, at this point, now that the Ultimate Wars are over, Metallox is starting to feel like the other members of the Vengeance Battalion don't respect him as much because he's a Synthezoid. Okay, so here he is holding his arm with all the wires coming out of it and he says: 'You have fought long and hard in your galaxy to see that no man is judged by the color of his skin. . . . Is this any different? I, too, have wounds! I, too, feel the stinging loss of our courageous compatriot Heatgirl. My tears may be artificial, but my pain is no less real!" "Wow," his friend says, "I guess you're right! I never knew comics could be so . . . you know, like a real book!" Pussey complacently replies, "It really isn't all just BANG POW ZOOM stuff."[51]

This tension between hypermasculinity and (a disavowed) emotional complexity finds its most complete figuration in what I like to call "the really, really big guy" in contemporary superhero teams.[52] This phenomenon began with the Thing in the Fantastic Four ("This Man . . . This Monster" was one story), continued through the Hulk in the Avengers and the Beast (later, Colossus) in the X-Men, and has reached a peak in recent titles.[53] Maul, Beast, Coldsnap, Impact, Strong Guy, and Brick are the really big really, really big guys at the moment. These are the most explicitly monstrous bodies in the superhero canon and are often objects of self-pity—they are the strongest team members, but do they not bleed? Physical strength only hides the emotionally complex inner subject. Power is not self-aggrandizing; it is rather a cross to be silently borne (fortunately, thought balloons grant expression to this private torment). *Doom Force* even managed to parody the big guy phenomenon, as Shasta the Living Mountain (*I'm useless . . . everyone hates me because all I can do is turn into a mountain*) sacrifices her life for the team—superhero deaths being another terrific occasion for easy emotionalizing (it turns out that the team really didn't like Shasta, so they just go and get something to eat).

Hypermasculine fantasy is also revealed, with unabashed obviousness, in the approach to female superheroes. The spectacle of the female body in these titles is so insistent, and the fetishism of breasts, thighs, and hair is so complete, that the comics seem to dare you to say anything about them that isn't just redundant. *Of course*, the female form has absurdly exaggerated sexual characteristics; *of course*, the costumes are skimpier than one could (or should) imagine; *of course*, there's no visible way that these costumes could stay in place; *of course*, these women represent simple adolescent masturbatory fantasies (with a healthy taste of the dominatrix).[54] One might note that women participate more fully in battle than they once did. It's worth observing that they're now as powerful as their male counterparts. Women no longer have to suffer such wimpy powers as invisibility or telekinesis (*great*—they couldn't be seen, but they could move stuff around like Samantha on *Bewitched*). They no longer need protection; they are no longer victims or hostages or prizes.

Which is not to say that all problems have been solved. *WILDC.A.T.S.* featured two female team members. Zealot, with her swords and razors, "is superhumanly strong and skilled in the arts of killing with her hands and with any and all weapons." The notable lack of castration anxiety here lasts until one reads her origin story: she "was one of the three original founding members of the Coda, an ancient Sisterhood of assassins based in Greece." After centuries of service, "when she grew weary of killing for no reason other than money, she left the Coda and devoted her life to battling its values." Score one for our side—the demon woman is possessed and contained, killing for *its* (our) values. Then there's Void (with the Invisible Girl, the female superhero as *absence*), with a predictable array of telekinetic and teleportational skills, plus "a certain degree of clairvoyance." She has the liquid metal sheen of the Silver Surfer and *Terminator 2*'s T-1000, but they never looked quite so *naked*.

The rise of women's bodybuilding provides a limited parallel to the new prominence of female superheroes, since the practice has been read by a number of writers in cultural studies as a sign of resistance to traditional images of the female. Alan Klein, though, adds a valuable corrective to this uncritical embrace, arguing that women's bodybuilding is still bodybuilding.[55] The overdeveloped body remains a compensation for an underdeveloped ego, a way of hiding inadequacy behind an armored body. Klein may be underestimating the political significance of this gender shift, but his point is nevertheless well taken. Of course, female superheroes are not real women, nor are they created by women. At the time this essay was first published there wasn't a single Image title starring a female superhero, and their recent forays into this territory, such as Joseph Michael Linser's *Dawn*, remain firmly committed to maximum T&A and minimal costuming.[56] Female desire is absent — when male creators design women characters, they continue to indulge male fantasies. The new power of the female hero is cosmetic surgery, and the halo of power just adds a further level of exoticism to the spectacle of the female form.

Overall, the trend has been toward masculinized, even phallic, women — armed to the teeth and just one of the boys. Meanwhile (as they say in the comics), Grant Morrison has pointed to the disappearance of "the feminized superhero." The DC Comics of the 1950s and 1960s often subjected Superman to a dose of *Red* Kryptonite, an unpredictable substance that never worked the same way twice. Inevitably, the effect would be a temporary metamorphosis — Superman would gain the head of a giant ant or he might be unable to control his powers. The armored body became fluid, shifting in irrational and uncontrollable ways. Comics no longer "feminize" their heroes in this whimsical manner, a further sign of the repression that marks the hypermasculine construction.[57]

Hypermasculine trauma reveals itself through the incoherence and hysteria of endless combat: explosions, exposed flesh, and extraterrestrial invasions speak to the terror of the armored body.[58] Klein's evocation of bodybuilding is as applicable to superheroics. "We see men trying too hard to come across as invulnerable and in command," he writes, "because to be less than that is not living up to our advance billing as leaders, dominators, controllers — in short, masters of the universe."[59]

4. The Torment of the Mutant Superhero

When the body engages in the violence of battle, the armor slips. Energies are no longer so thoroughly contained. Similarly, the *mutant* superhero presents itself as a problematic figure. Mutants are genetic accidents; their powers are neither products of radioactive ingestion nor interplanetary travels. They are the aliens among us — to avoid prejudice, mutant superheroes hide their abilities. Mutant powers are stigmata that must be kept hidden from the unreasoning mob of mere normals. Mutant superheroes are not invulnerable; not only are they distinguished by (a frequently maudlin) emotionalism, but their first and most dangerous enemies are their own bodies. Optic blasts shoot from the eyes of the X-Men's Cyclops; he must shield them at all times.

Figure 6. Zealot of the WILDC.A.T.S., art by Jae Lee.
(Courtesy of Image Comics.)

Cyclops was the first star of the X-Men; with his ellipsoid yellow and ruby visor covering his deadly eyes he was at once statuesque and sleekly streamlined. But the fashionable mask of Cyclops is more than a mark of his superheroic status: this mask cannot be removed, for to do so would be to unleash death and destruction upon the world. The visor's deadly secret evokes such figures of the monstrous feminine as Medusa and Pandora's Box. But the struggle of Cyclops involves holding back this energy, containing it within himself; to release it would be to destroy his own sense of being (the woman he loves can never see his eyes, he realizes).

These are traumatized, eruptive bodies; the energies that are normally unleashed only in battle now continually threaten to overspill their fragile vessels. The mutant superhero is both armored and flowing. The armored body enforces categories of being by buttressing self against nonself, but mutant heroes are explicitly presented as "categorical mistakes." Theweleit's dissection of the structures that reinforce the subject against the disorder of a chaotic reality echoes Mary Douglas's arguments regarding ritual and somatic meaning. Douglas defines ritual as a metaphorical system for maintaining and communicating ideas of social order: "the magic of primitive ritual creates harmonious worlds with ranked and ordered populations playing their appointed parts. So far from being meaningless, it is primitive magic which gives meaning to existence. This applies as much to the negative as to the positive rites. The prohibitions trace the cosmic outlines and the ideal social order." [60] Rituals establish and preserve categories and hierarchies; they perform rules of social interaction. Those organized around the familiar space of the body constitute a narrow field of meaning: "the range of situations which use the human body for expression . . . derive essentially from the quality of social relations." [61] Following Mauss, and rejecting more psychoanalytically based readings, Douglas maintains that the body is always an acculturated body, an always metaphorical body. Where it figures prominently within cultural rituals, "the human body is always treated as an image of society . . . there can be no natural way of considering the body that does not involve at the same time a social dimension." [62]

More specifically, Douglas argues that the body and its boundaries mark a concern with social boundaries and hierarchical order.

Interest in its apertures depends on the preoccupation with social exits and entrances, escape routes and invasions. . . . The relation of head to feet, of brain and sexual organs, of mouth and anus are commonly treated so that they express the relevant patterns of hierarchy. Consequently I now advance the hypothesis that bodily control is an expression of social control—abandonment of bodily control in ritual responds to the requirements of a social experience which is being expressed. Furthermore, there is little prospect of successfully imposing bodily control without the corresponding social forms. And lastly, the same drive that seeks harmoniously to relate the experience of physical and social, must affect ideology.[63]

Thus, the body can serve as a sign of disorder, a categorical mistake: "when a monstrous birth occurs, the defining lines between humans and animals may be threatened. If a monstrous birth can be labelled an event of a peculiar kind the categories can be restored."[64] Mutants, while they want to fit in, know their birthright is to exist "outside" the normative. They are categorical mistakes of a specific type; they are, in short, adolescents. The first mutant superheroes were the X-Men: "The Most Unusual Teen-Agers of All Time!" Such "marginal beings" pose a question and a threat to the social body, which must somehow reincorporate this "ambiguous species"[65] or brand it (with an *X*?) as taboo.

The audience for mutant superhero comics is clearly targeted: an issue of *X-Factor* featured a comics-style ad for Stridex, an acne medication—it seems Cyclops doesn't suffer the trauma of red facial eruptions alone (Stridex even sounds like a mutant superhero). Where once Cyclops lamented his impossible desire for normalcy in one brief panel per issue (*I've no right to try to date Jean [Marvel Girl]—not while my eyes make me a potential danger to anyone near me!),* later Claremont issues might feature a five-page conversation between young ex-lovers, culminating in one crying herself to sleep (*Shut up, Peter, please! Don't say any more! It hurts too much!*). It must be said that this infusion of romance comics discourse did, in fact, extend the appeal of the X-Men beyond the confines of superhero subculture.

The appeal to adolescents immediately connects to Douglas's hypotheses regarding power hierarchies and structures of authority within cultures. In her studies of religious ritual, Douglas has located a correlation between the control of spiritual powers and the position within the social hierarchy. She distinguishes between internal powers that reside within the subject and external forces subject to mastery. "This distinction between internal and external sources of power is often correlated with another distinction, between uncontrolled and controlled power. According to widespread beliefs, the internal psychic powers are not necessarily triggered off by the intention of the agent."[66] Like the eruptive body of the mutant superhero (Havok, Storm,

Random), internal powers are uncontrolled; where once superheroes guaranteed social stability, they now threaten to disrupt it. Douglas further correlates controlled power and social authority, noting that

> where the social system explicitly recognises positions of authority, those holding such positions are endowed with explicit spiritual power, controlled, conscious, external and approved—powers to bless and curse. Where the social system requires people to hold dangerously ambiguous roles, these persons are credited with uncontrolled, unconscious, dangerous, disapproved powers—such as witchcraft and evil eye. In other words, where the social system is well-articulated, I look for articulate powers vested in the points of authority; where the social system is ill-articulated, I look for inarticulate powers vested in those who are a source of disorder.[67]

At issue is not whether our social system is well or ill articulated; at issue is the mapping of the adolescent subject onto a social order that is perceived by that subject as arbitrary, exclusionary, and incomprehensible. "What supreme irony!" Professor X muses in a couple of thought balloons. "The Sentinels had been created to destroy the X-Men—and yet, it was necessary for *us* to smash *them* in order to save humanity—the humanity that *hated* us!"[68]

Douglas suggests "that the contrast between form and surrounding nonform accounts for the distribution of symbolic and psychic powers: external symbolism upholds the explicit power structure and internal, unformed psychic powers threaten it from the non-structure."[69] The mutant superhero, like the adolescent, is inarticulate within the social system—a categorical mistake that upsets notions of order and hierarchy through an investment with dangerous, disapproved, and uncontrollable powers. The body of the mutant superhero is in fact a ritualized body, "a symbolic system, based on the image of the body, whose primary concern is the ordering of a social hierarchy."[70] Under the tutelage of Professor X, the mutants are sited both inside and outside society; their powers move from uncontrolled and eruptive to controlled and articulate. By constructing such an alternative social order, the categorical mistake is resituated as a fundamental force of social cohesion. "The rituals," Douglas notes, "work upon the body politic through the symbolic medium of the physical body."[71]

A recent series called *Marvels* retells the history of the Marvel universe by shifting attention to the citizens of New York, who can only catch brief glimpses of Thor as he rockets by a D train stalled on the Manhattan Bridge.

Superheroes are the stuff of legend, and Captain America is sublime: "Just to catch a glimpse of him—always in motion. Always moving forward—like a force of nature in chain mail. Never a hesitation or a backward glance. We were in awe of him. Of *all* of them."[72] The narrator is a middle-aged, grey-mustached photojournalist named Phil who lives out in the 'burbs with his wife and two daughters. Kurt Busiek's careful script and Alex Ross's painted artwork are perfect complements. The colors are real world muted, but the heroes' costumes are rendered in impossibly vivid tones. The faces are not the generic cyphers worn by most comics characters but instead have a kind of lumpy individuality. Fashions and hairstyles are appropriate to the New Frontier period—even the cars are accurate. Such details evoke a vague nostalgia for a comfortably quotidian past sometimes glimpsed in aging issues of *Life* magazine. Into this reality of bad haircuts and littered streets, the "Marvels" gain an understandable power to astonish.

The second issue of *Marvels* concentrates on the mutant problem. The unveiling of the mutant-exterminating Sentinels is retold from Phil's point of view as he watches events unfold on a black and white TV in a bar. Phil, the normal guy, gives voice to the articulate structures of authority. "They were the dark side of the marvels," Phil reflects. "Where Captain America and Mister Fantastic spoke to us about the greatness within us all, the mutants were death." A mob scene is lit only by the infernal red glow emanating from the visor of Cyclops. Phil learns to whistle a different tune when he finds that his daughters have been harboring a small mutant girl in their basement (doesn't everybody?).[73] The li'l mutant is nearly hairless, with enormous wet eyes brimming with tears ("A-are you going to send me *away*?")—her victimized vulnerability combines Walter and Margaret Keane's waif drawings, E.T., starving Ethiopian children, and Cindy-Lou Who. In these sequences, sad to say, the story loses its edge. Nevertheless, Busiek effectively mythologizes the relationship between the freakish "muties" and the glorified (if rather white-bready) "Marvels."

The bodily torment of the mutant superhero expresses a desire, a need, to transcend the confines of the body, to exist as pure spirit. As usual, however, such desires are fraught with ambivalence; hence the heightened transgression of its corporeal boundaries is accompanied by the hardening of the body. Still, the eyebeams of Cyclops, the telekinetic powers of Marvel Girl, the elemental forces controlled by Storm, even Wolverine's extensible adamantium claws—all of these pull the body past its margins. Douglas emphasizes that "the orifices of the body . . . symbolize its specially vulnerable points. Matter issuing from them is marginal stuff of the most obvious kind. Spittle, blood, milk, urine, faeces or tears by simply issuing forth have traversed the boundary of the body."[74] Mutant superheroes bear overdetermined inscriptions of marginality revealed in every bodily trauma and transgression. The saga comprises a massive passing narrative, as these stigmatized bodies attempt to hide behind a veil of "normalcy."

Douglas's model of social hierarchy contains clear gender correlations, although she doesn't address the issue.[75] Theweleit's terminology is useful: controlled and external power corresponds to the masculine armored body, while uncontrolled, internal power is analogous to the fluidity of the feminine. Articulate power is therefore the province of the masculine with the feminine relegated, by definition, to the inarticulate power operating outside systems of social authority. The mutant is thus a feminized figure, and the construction of an alternative social order acquires an ideological relevance that begins to transcend adolescent narcissism. The emphasis on uncontrolled powers that exist beyond the articulate structures of social authority points to a preference for the spiritual rather than the material aspects of reality, and in ritual and myth, Douglas argues, "to insist on the superiority of spiritual over material elements is to *insist on the liberties of the individual* and to imply a political programme to free him from unwelcome constraints."[76]

It's worth considering the resurgent popularity of the X-Men in the context of Generation X, the group of 1990s twenty-somethings that comprised a significant part of the mutant superhero audience. Generation X walked a fine line, ferociously absorbing (and regurgitating) popular culture while performing a self-conscious marginality that mixed historical eras. The modern primitive fascination with such body arts (or rituals) as tattooing and piercing fetishized the body as a spectacle of marginality, not to mention the body in pain—mutant stigmata.[77] Marvel and Image advertised upcoming mutant titles called *Generation X*. The alternative community represented by the mutant band, combined with the pop nihilism and colorful violence of the superhero comic, made these titles perfect light reading for homesick slackers who envisioned themselves as unstuck in space and time, lost in an America in which all the good stuff had already happened.

In *Natural Symbols*, published in 1970, Douglas continually returns to the issue of student rebellion and the assault on cherished hierarchies: "His teachers live in one universe, they cherish boundaries and smell conspiracy against sacred forms; he lives in another universe in which no particular form is sacred; form as such is distinct from content and inferior to it; he opposes classification as the expression of empty form, the very emblem of evil."[78] Thus, the archenemy of the X-Men is Magneto (which, in my opinion, is not pronounced "mag-neat-o"), the self-proclaimed leader of the Brotherhood of Evil Mutants, who believes that mutants, Homo Superior, must subjugate Homo Sapiens once and for all.[79] Magneto has become something of a dark (and not unsympathetic) deity in recent years, but his obsessions are precisely with power, definition, and hierarchy. On the other side are the government representatives who want to exterminate mutants or at least institute a Mutant Registration Act. Again, social structure is advanced as an empty emblem of evil.

Mutant bodies are explictly analogized to Jewish bodies, gay bodies, adolescent bodies, Japanese or Native or African American bodies—they are, first and foremost, subjected and subjugated and colonized figures. If they are victims, however, they are also valuable sources of disruption and challenge—transgressive, uncontrollable, and alternative bodies. As on *Star Trek: The Next Generation* (ST:TNG), issues of gender, ethnicity, and sexual preference have received remarkable attention (and is the resemblance between patriarchal, bald Professor X and patriarchal, bald Captain Picard only coincidental?).[80] *Star Trek* and *X-Men* present ethnically, sexually, generationally, and genetically diverse companies of humans, mutants, and aliens taking their places within flexible structures of cooperation and tolerance. The group is something more than a battle unit and clearly takes the form of an idealized, alternative society—one in which all members, and therefore no members, are outcasts.[81] In the rejection of traditional political thought that marked American student rebellion in the late 1960s, Douglas observed that "the young radicals of today express contempt for the physical body, read the mystics and cultivate non-rationality."[82] Mutants just wanna have fun.

The seething, mutated, cyborged, and ceaselessly flowing bodies of these superheroes "express contempt" for the physical body but in a deeply ambivalent form. If the flowing body is also an armored body, if its physical presence is protected and exaggerated, then that physicality has itself become a symbol for the (teen) spirit lodged within. As I argued in my study of postmodern science fiction, the body may be "simulated, morphed, modified, retooled, genetically engineered, and even dissolved," but it is never entirely eliminated: the subject always retains a meat component.[83] As in cyberpunk, a profound ambivalence, and even hysteria, regarding the status of the body in contemporary technoculture is revealed. And so: *X-Bodies* as in taboo; *X* as in impure and polluted and under erasure; but also X as in X rays, with their power to reveal; X as in extreme; X as in *ex*—the *ex-men*.

5. Now Our Weird Heroes Each Remain Eccentric

Doom Patrol, scripted by Grant Morrison for nearly four years, recrafted comic book trauma, moving well beyond the defensive postures of the hypermasculine. In the first Morrison issue, Cliff Steele (Robotman: human brain in a metal body) immediately demolishes armored body fantasies: "Can you imagine how crude robot senses are, compared to human ones, huh? All I have are memories of the way things used to feel or taste. You know, they say that amputees feel phantom pains where their limbs used to be. Well, I'm a total amputee. I'm haunted by the ghost of an entire *body*! I get headaches, you know, and I want to crap until I realize I don't have any bowels." A friend tries to help: "I can't stand by and watch you destroy yourself." Steele replies, "Me? How *can* I destroy myself?" He pounds his head through a wall to emphasize the point, but still cannot feel *anything*. We are past the neurotic self-involvement of teen mutants here and are nearing complete psychotic breakdown: these folks were *never* normal.[84]

Aside from Robotman, The Doom Patrol included Negative Man, who was possessed by a radioactive spirit that flew from his body to perform superdeeds, and Elasti-Girl, who could make isolated parts of her body grow or shrink. Morrison rebuilt the group by ditching Elasti-Girl, remaking Negative Man as Rebis (a hermaphroditic blend of two human bodies and that spirit), and adding the fabulous Crazy Jane, who suffers from sixty-four multiple personalities, each of which has its own "meta-human ability." Morrison never imposed normative values on his team: Jane is not "cured" by developing a unitary sense of self, by "controlling" her multiple personalities; instead she learns to permit each of her personalities to dominate when appropriate.[85] The struggle in *Doom Patrol* is not to be accepted but to accept oneself.

The psychic and physical traumas of the group are matched by the slippages of reality to which they are continually subjected. An early enemy was the Brotherhood of Evil, now reformed as the Brotherhood of Dada, whose first act is to trap Paris within a recursively structured painting. One enemy, The Quiz, has "every superpower you haven't thought of"—to fight her involves thinking of lots of superpowers *really quickly* (unfortunately, nobody thinks of "the power to create escape-proof spirit jars"). In later episodes they befriend Flex Mentallo and the sentient Danny the Street ("Sometimes it's an alley in Peking, sometimes a back street in Toronto") and battle the Men from N.O.W.H.E.R.E., whose every utterance is based on the same acronym: *Naked old widows hover earlier round Easter. Never open William's head evil reptiles emerge.*[86]

Perhaps *all* of this is occurring inside Jane's head; perhaps the entire concept of superheroes is only a psychic formation in the first place (*gasp*). Protesting the trend toward more "realistic" approaches to superhero comics, Morrison argued that "The idea that you could bring something as ridiculous as superheroes into the real world seemed to me completely insane. . . . I was more interested in comics as what they were, as ridiculous garish combination[s] of words and pictures about people with ludicrous talents."[87] Nothing could illustrate Morrison's point better than the Fantastic Four stories of the 1960s. The FF were typical of Marvel's characters in that they were both weirder and more human than their forebears. The rubbery Reed Richards (Mr. Fantastic); Sue Storm (the Invisible Girl), his bride; her brother Johnny, the Human Torch; and gruff, lovable, but deeply traumatized Ben Grimm, transformed into an odd pile of orange rocks known as The Thing, comprised one of the most affectionate of superhero teams—and why not? They were family.

Their adventures took them to hidden lands, other dimensions, and the edges of the universe; Jack Kirby's baroquely cosmic creations never again seemed either as perfect or as true. The comic reveled in juxtapositions of galactic scale with human banality. Kirby's humans were always stylized, simple, and dynamic, and the visual flatness of the characters was enhanced by Joe Sinnott's clean, clear inking. But Kirby's cityscapes were so many abstract geometric shapes piled atop one another, and the vast machinery and elaborate costumes that were hallmarks of his art were detailed, obsessive, and faintly psychotic. In his best work, machinery seemed to merge with the human (or alien) figures; the biological was stylistically severed from the world. The FF pages fairly vibrated with color, drama, and dynamic movement, and even the word balloons and sound effects added to the overall effect. Readers of my generation can hardly forget the thrill of turning the page and finding Kirby's classic six-panel pages supplanted by a grand one- or two-page spread, replete with exploding suns, surging nebulae, a massive alien figure, or perhaps a "psychedelic" photo montage. Meanwhile, Stan Lee's dialogue ranged in style from Ben's Brooklynese ("Can'tcha see I'm tryin' ta dislike ya?!!") to the faux Shakespearian flights of the Silver Surfer, herald of Galactus, eater of planets ("Incredible? Nay, it is *supremely* cred-

Figure 7. The cosmic extravagance of the Fantastic Four, art by Jack Kirby
and Joe Sinnott. (Courtesy of Image Comics.)

ible! Earth is but a twinkling dot . . . a paltry pebble . . . in the vastness of
space!"). Hyperbole? "The World's Greatest Comic Magazine!" the covers
proclaimed ("The Brutal Betrayal of Ben Grimm" was "Possibly the most dar-
ingly dramatic development in the field of contemporary literature!"). Cultural studies academics please note: nobody took this stuff too seriously. It
was playtime, and it *was* fun, and it was sometimes moving, and it provided
the dizzying shifts of spatiotemporal scale and perspective that make science fiction a genre to consider. The Lee/Kirby *Fantastic Fours* are perfect

examples of the "garish" and "ludicrous" entertainments to which Morrison referred; one issue of *Doom Patrol* featured an affectionate parody (*And Men Shall Call Him—HERO!*).[88] Foregoing angst for absurdism, *Doom Patrol* stories elevate and enhance the conventions of the genre to construct darkly liberating cutups that infect the readers' reality and open doors of illogical possibility. The traumatic body of the superhero now signifies a traumatized *reality* rather than an inadequate psyche. In a world where our government feeds radioactive cereal to unsuspecting test subjects, the Doom Patrol makes nicer comrades than the solipsistically suffering X-Men—and why not? They're family.

6. The Never-Ending Battle

Writing "X-Bodies," I dream: I'm in a comics shop and discover lots of new *Green Lantern* titles. I'm obligated to buy them all, secretly glad of the excuse. GL . . . my old alter ego has returned. I am, at once, the academic reader, the adolescent comics fan, and the high-flying superhero. Clearly, some early anxieties are not completely behind me.

Confronting the autobiography that underlies "X-Bodies," I see that my battle against the evil forces of academia is neatly designed to keep me on the margins. With no permanent appointment, I stand peering over the fence and wonder *what do academics want?* but the real question I keep ducking is *why won't I give it to them?* For one thing, the academy keeps refusing to tell me about *my* self. My reclamation of my own experience is part of a very appropriate struggle to legitimate the personal, the physical, and the aesthetic within a field that has privileged the authoritative, the cognitive, and the textual.[89]

Very heroic—but then there's my irrational fear of losing my self by joining a community (*any* community). My writings validate my own past, and thus my own self. Superheroes, science fiction, and Jerry Lewis—I'm the emperor of the nerds, the god of geeks. I rescue the terminally trivial, make it respectable and perhaps, on occasion, sexy. Yet have I arranged to be taken unseriously? Am I engaged in a continuing activity of careerist self-sabotage, a cartoon anarchist being blown apart by his own bomb, Professor Kelp blowing up his lab? Is the real rescue I'm trying to make the rescue of my terminally trivial, maybe respectable, and, on occasion, sexy self? Well past adolescence, I lead a double life—inside and outside academia, inside and outside superhero subculture. I'm loving and duplicitous, a wreck and in control, armored and flowing, I'm Professor Kelp and Buddy Love. I'm a mutant superhero, asserting my phallic invincibility, fighting old battles. Maybe it's time to hang up the cape.

And maybe not. Really, this self-mythologizing is getting out of hand. The fantasy to surrender is the one with the monolithic entity of academia tearing away at my own unified, noncontradictory (and still wacky) self. I'll stand by the work I've done. I am a proud academic—still committed to rigorous intellectual inquiry and supportive pedagogy despite the narrowness of so many of the "approved" academic discourses. The uncontrol that marks marginalized mutants and Professor Kelp is only mine to a point—I am also, after all, Professor X, the mutant in control. If, then, life as a mutant superhero is mine, I'll wear the cape proudly. Keep the cape and scrap the armor (my own official superhero oath). Then I can decide which way to fly (my shrink said that, not me).

(And the Silver Surfer said this—) *I was born to soar . . . to ride the currents of space . . . not to be confined within a barren structure!*[90]

TWO

1 Nature dwarfs technology until the mothership dwarfs
nature in *Close Encounters of the Third Kind,* effects supervised
by Douglas Trumbull. (Courtesy of Columbia Tristar.)

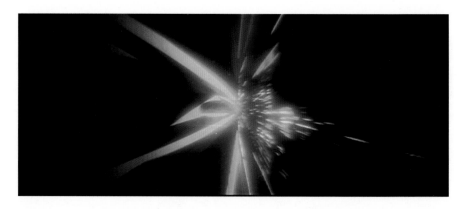

2 The Stargate sequence in *2001*, effects by Douglas Trumbull.
(Courtesy of Metro-Goldwyn-Mayer.)

3 *Blade Runner*'s infernal city, special effects by Douglas Trumbull.
(Courtesy of Fox-Lorber Productions.)

4 *The Right Stuff*, on the edge of transcendence,
special effects by Jordan Belson.
(Courtesy of the Ladd Company.)

5 Fitz Hugh Lane, *Castine Harbor and Town*, 1851
(Courtesy of the Putnam Foundation, Timken Museum
of Art, San Diego.)

6 Frederic Edwin Church, *Twilight in the Wilderness*, 1860.
(Courtesy of the Cleveland Museum of Art.)

7 Frederic Edwin Church, *Cotopaxi*, 1862.
(Courtesy of the Detroit Institute of Arts.)

8 Chorines as skyscrapers in a poster for *42nd Street*.
(Courtesy of Photofest.)

9 The noirish opening of "The Girl Hunt Ballet" in *The Band Wagon,*
set design by Oliver Smith. (Courtesy of Metro-Goldwyn-Mayer.)

10 Times Square in the film version of *Guys and Dolls,* set design

11 The city boldly abstracted in *The Band Wagon,*
set design by Oliver Smith.
(Courtesy of Metro-Goldwyn-Mayer.)

12 *Astro City* #1, cover art by Alex Ross. (Courtesy of Image Comics.)

13 Panels with crayon effect in *A Superman for All Seasons,*
art by Tim Sale. (Courtesy of DC Comics.)

14 In the superhero city, the fantastic supplants the utilitarian. Art by Tim Sale, from *A Superman for All Seasons*. (Courtesy of DC Comics.)

15 Gotham's urban canyons: Batman under a blood red sky in
Legends of the Dark Knight, cover art by John Cassaday.
(Courtesy of DC Comics.)

16 *Transmetropolitan* #22, cover art by Geoff Darrow.
(Courtesy of Grant Morrison and Darick Robertson.)

17 Superhero as dandy: Martin Nodell's version
of the Green Lantern, 1940, sculpted by
William Paquet based on designs by Steve Rude.
(Courtesy of DC Comics.)

The Artificial Infinite:
On Special Effects and the Sublime

All my modes of conveyance have been pictorial.
Mr. Booley (from Charles Dickens's "Some Account
of an Ordinary Traveller")

In the eighteenth and nineteenth centuries, as new technologies and social formations displaced the haptic in favor of the visual as a source of knowledge about an increasingly complicated set of lived realities, popular culture offered a surfeit of spectacular forms that compensated for the lack of touch with what might be termed a hyperbole of the visible. An apparently direct address to the spectator depended on techniques of perspectival composition, trompe l'oeil, a hiding or deemphasis of the frame, an often overwhelming scale, and a mimesis of the natural. Historians tend to agree that underlying the fascination with these displays were anxieties regarding urban growth, technological development, and social change. The spectacle was a simulacrum of reality, but spectators were not duped by these illusions— by paying admission the customer indicated at least some understanding of the rules of the game. Some pleasure, however, clearly derived from responding to these entertainments as if they were real. Visual spectacle provided a reassurance in the form of a panoptic power (minus the inscribed and very real power relations described by Foucault)—the human subject was, after all, capable of perceiving and comprehending these new conditions through the projection of an almost omnipotent gaze out into the represented world.

The cosmic displays of science fiction cinema, produced by technologically advanced optical effects, surely derive from a similar drive for scopic mastery. The overwhelming perceptual power granted by these panoramic displays addressed the perceived loss of cognitive power experienced by the subject in an increasingly technologized world. In acknowledging anxiety while ultimately producing a sense of cognitive mastery, these entertainments frequently evoked the rhetorical figures of the sublime. The nature of popular, commercial entertainment suggests that this was actually a tamed sublime rather than truly awe-inspiring, transcendent visions; nevertheless, the sublime became an important mode for these mareoramas, landscape paintings, stereoscopic views, and science fiction films.

The stock scripts and relatively wooden performances of science fiction cinema shouldn't distract one from the articulations of meaning located in the mise-en-scène as well as the state of the art technological spectacle on display.[1] While there are relatively few director-auteurs in SF film, cinematic style (as well as authorial consistency) can be located in the fields of art and effects direction. The special effects work of Douglas Trumbull is particularly distinctive and sustained in its evocation of the sublime, and this essay will concentrate on sequences from his films. Trumbull supervised the Stargate sequence of 2001 and produced the luminous alien spacecraft of Close Encounters of the Third Kind (see color figs. 1, 2). He worked in conjunction with "visual futurist" Syd Mead on Star Trek: The Motion Picture and Blade Runner (see color fig. 3). Beyond his work as an effects designer, Trumbull directed two features, Silent Running and Brainstorm — both interesting in themselves — while developing his 65mm, 60 fps Showscan exhibition system. Finally turning away from Hollywood and a system that was, as he put it, "multiplexing itself to death," Trumbull turned to "special venue" productions, developing multimedia technologies for theme parks or World's Fair exhibitions. The popularity of simulation rides in a surprising range of settings has provided new opportunities for Trumbull to experiment with the kind of experiential cinema that has been his forte since the 1960s. The attention to spectacle and the conditions of exhibition reconnects Trumbull's work to the early history of the cinema as well as to the history of precinematic phantasmagoria.

In Trumbull's effects sequences, the sublime is elicited around a massive technological object (or environment): the Stargate (2001), the mothership (CE3K), V'ger (Star Trek), and the city (Blade Runner). It is technology that inspires the sensations characteristic of sublimity; therefore, it is technology that alludes to the limits of human definition and comprehension.[2] The special effect unfolds before the human gaze and becomes susceptible to an encompassing control that inheres in the very act of seeing. Trumbull's sequences, however, are different from other effects work in their ambivalence:

they are neither unabashedly celebratory (*Star Wars*) nor darkly condemning (*Alien*). As with the panoramas and other displays of the last two hundred years, then, Trumbull's effects are rooted in an ambivalent relation to new technologies, and like those other forms, they depend on new technologies for their very effect(s).

Concerning Visuality

The ability to cognize is very often dependent on the concurrent ability to envision and thereby conceive, and this can be equally true for both quantitative information and abstract conception. Therefore, debates over the place and meaning of observation and visual representation within culture take on a crucial importance. This is generally, although not unanimously, regarded to be a period of information proliferation, by which it's understood that less information comes to the subject via direct sensory, bodily experience and more, far more, arrives in mediated, representational forms. If, as some theorists of culture would have it, mediation is im-mediately tantamount to manipulation, then the proliferation of mediated experiential modes will indeed produce a vapid, inertial society of spectacles and simulations. But, on the other hand, if visuality comprises a more complex and open phenomenon, then the range of observer positions will be less circumscribed and possibly less debased. The relationship between visual experience and cognition, then, always an active topic for philosophical debate, becomes increasingly crucial as a means of understanding the place(s) available to the subject in this heavily technologized and electronically mediated culture.

Jonathan Crary's extended essay, *Techniques of the Observer,* has already proven its value in the fields of art history, cinema studies, and cultural studies. Crary's analysis of paradigmatic shifts in the construction of "observation" is set against the context of electronic culture—his opening question ("How is the body, including the observing body, becoming a component of new machines, economies, apparatuses, whether social, libidinal or technological?") straddles historical and contemporary moments.[3] The model Crary constructs is grounded in the process of modernization, under the conditions of which the observer "is made adequate to a constellation of new events, forces, and institutions that together are loosely and perhaps tautologically definable as 'modernity.'"[4] Classical models of vision collapse, along with "their stable space of representations. Instead, observation is increasingly a question of equivalent sensations and stimuli that have *no reference to a spatial location.*"[5] The idea that increasing industrialization and rising urban concentration should challenge older paradigms of spatiovisual experience is not new—for example, Henri Lefebvre wrote:

> The fact is that around 1910 a certain space was shattered. It was the space of common sense, of knowledge, of social practice, of political power, a space thitherto enshrined in everyday discourse, just as in abstract thought, as the environment of and channel for communications; the space, too, of classical perspective and geometry, developed from the Renaissance onwards on the basis of the Greek tradition (Euclid, logic) and bodied forth in Western art and philosophy, as in the form of the city and town. Such were the shocks and onslaughts suffered by this space that today it retains but a feeble pedagogical reality, and then only with great difficulty, within a conservative educational system.[6]

Their periodization may be at odds, but I think Crary and Lefebvre are concerned with the same epistemological rupture. Lefebvre even shares with Crary the sense that this is not simply a shift within the field of "representation" but the disappearance of a particular lived, *bodied* conception of spatiality. Crary's emphasis is less on changing spatial conceptions than on the implications of a culture founded on a new relationship between visuality and experience, a relationship that now "depends on the denial of the body, its pulsings and phantasms, as the ground of vision."[7]

Representation begins to have less to do with the world "out there" than with the physiological conditions of vision, conditions that can now be simulated. Thus, the experience of a three-dimensional image is no longer any guarantor of "reality" but is more on the order of a physiological sleight of hand. Crary brilliantly argues that a range of aesthetic techniques generally lumped under the heading of *realism* "are in fact bound up in non-veridical theories of vision that effectively annihilate a real world."[8] The absence of spatial verifiability uproots signs from an ostensibly stable field of meaning, whereupon meanings and values can be exchanged more freely.

The separation of the visual and the haptic thus resulted in an overemphasis on the former. The "empirical isolation of vision" permitted its "quantification and homogenization" while at the same time, the objects of visual contemplation were "sundered from any relation to the spectator's position within a cognitively unified field."[9] A veritable explosion of visually based toys, displays, and environments appeared, as if to compensate for the diminished role played by the remaining senses. These objects and environments, however, were irreducibly situated within the increasingly centralized and disciplinary conditions of industrial capitalism. Where some might see the construction of a "transcendent subject" no longer limited to a single set of spatiotemporal coordinates, Crary, following Foucault, sees a model grounded in systems of surveillance and control, in which the observer becomes, almost literally, "a component."[10]

Crary emphasizes the kineticism that emerged in the nineteenth century. Visual experience was "given an unprecedented mobility" that was "abstracted from any founding site or referent." Crary tracks this mobility into the field of representation, noting that "the traveling artist's kinesthesia demanded and elicited a new and complexly fluid state of mind. Locomotion was consonant with the experience of mobile and mutable aspects or shifting effects."[11] This analysis is consonant with some others, which also link the emergent kinesis of the Machine Age to a set of epistemological reconfigurations and adaptations on the part of the mobile observer. The nineteenth century saw the expansion of travel and the rise of tourism for the middle classes. Vision was put in motion around the rise of railway travel, with its new emphasis on what Wolfgang Schivelbusch has dubbed "panoramic perception." The replacement of the slow, horsedrawn coach by the speeding train shifted the rider's attention from foreground to the middle and backgrounds. The windowed and enclosed train put the world behind glass and effectively filtered out auditory, olfactory, and haptic sensations of the world beyond the window, forcing a reliance on sight as the sole source of information.[12]

Crary's sociology differs significantly from that of Schivelbusch, however. While for Crary "panoramic perception" would demonstrate the severing of visuality from the body, Schivelbusch describes a reconfiguration of the body in relation to the shifting nature of spatial apprehension. Despite their common suspicion of industrial capitalist culture, Schivelbusch remains committed to a phenomenological perspective that is less concerned with judging than with mapping alterations in lived experience. Whatever it is that Schivelbush is describing, it is not a removal of the bodily experience from the field of industrial development—the velocity that produces a panoramic view is also the velocity that cripples and pulverizes bodies, whether in crashing railway carriages or across the fields of wartime carnage. Panoramic perception (even in its simulacral, cinematic variation) remains a most definitely embodied phenomenon.

It is the absence of a phenomenology that weakens Crary's generally excellent work, and that absence tends to schematize some of his most provocative arguments. The body, as an experiential field, simply disappears from his consideration, repressed as surely as he claims it was in the historical past.

It is worth noting that while vision may be detached from the body of the observer it is constantly reattached to an at least partially illusory body. There is a being at the center of the panorama, enjoying the view. The body isn't at the center of Paris; it's at the center of an exhibition, a display—still, it's at the center of something. As at Disneyland, where real and simulated motion are intricately combined, the actual position of the observer's body becomes a means of support for an illusionistic position.

Why is the body constantly being recalled into being by amusement park rides or panoramic addresses? Undoubtedly, Crary could argue that the loss of the body is the precondition for creating that equivalence of signs and values that obtain when vision is decorporealized, "liberated" from direct physical verification, and so the support that I'm describing would serve as an ersatz reembodiment to further ground the ideological operations of industrial capitalism. Indeed, every moment of potential liberation that Crary describes is immediately recontained by the disciplinary society: "But almost simultaneous with this final dissolution of a transcendent foundation for vision emerges a plurality of means to recode the activity of the eye, to regiment it, to heighten its productivity and to prevent its distraction. Thus the imperatives of classical modernization, while demolishing the field of classical vision, generated techniques for imposing visual attentiveness, rationalizing sensation, and managing perception."[13]

I think that I'm allowed to be unsatisfied with this. It isn't wrong; it's brilliant—but it's not the whole story. Indeed, Crary provides some clues of a world beyond his monolithic historical read. He acknowledges the existence of oppositional modes but argues that "it only becomes legible against the more hegemonic set of discourses and practices in which vision took shape."[14] That's a start, but I would still resist the reading of this "set of discourses" as all determining. Crary is altogether too eager to reduce a vast array of cultural phenomena to a single hegemonic model of hegemonic practice.

So Crary winds up aligned with the very tradition he critiques. When he discusses "techniques for imposing visual attentiveness, rationalizing sensation, and managing perception," he isn't simply describing a historical position; he's inadvertently presenting us with an astute analysis of the academy in a nutshell—the academy that can't abide discourses of the body (only discourses about it), the academy that can't accommodate a plurality of interpretive positions (only the faux plurality of identity politics). Can we liberate the study of visuality from the academy's own predilection for rationalized sensation and managed perception?

Barbara Stafford offers a very different set of terms with which to understand visual culture. While her theoretical models are less elaborated than those of Crary, she describes a pervasive shift from a culture grounded in visuality and physical experience to one dominated by textuality and instrumental reason.

Stafford's histories reveal the diversity of visual culture in the eighteenth century. If research into the physiology of perception "objectified" the viewer, this objectification was often a prelude to further revelations concerning, or discoveries of, natural law. Such "rational re-creations" as automata, kaleidoscopes, miniatures, illustrated texts for children, and even the phantasmagoria of magic lantern presentations served as forms of "phenomenalized instruction," according to Stafford, erasing "the dualism between mind and body, art and craft, science and technology."[15] Stafford emphasizes the construction of "an informed and performative gaze" operating within a field of "sensationalized knowledge."[16] As for the illusionism attendant upon most of these phenomena, Stafford notes that these were "licit effects" (a lovely phrase); their principles were to be revealed and explained to the audience or observer.[17] Yes, the world and the observer were inscribed within a field of knowledge and therefore within the disciplinary apparatus that Foucault correctly describes, but this is not the sole aspect of visuality that needs to be acknowledged (and I have no doubt that Crary would concur).

So the constant address to the body that marks the panorama and, later, the amusement park attraction, is not simply a writing of the body into an expanding field of signification; it is also a means of inscribing new, potentially traumatic phenomena and perspectives onto the familiar experiential field of the body. They are holdovers from a time when, Stafford writes, "spatial and kinesthetic intelligence were not yet radically divorced from rational-linguistic competence and logical-mathematical aptitude."[18] Empirical positivism may have suffered at the hands of the perceptual skepticism exercised by eighteenth-century British philosophy, but enough faith in "direct" and "unmediated" experience survived to be flattered at the fairground.

If I'm arguing for the validity of an "embodied knowledge," I do so not from a belief in the existence of some empirically verifiable truth, but from my conviction that knowledge grounded in the conditions of physical experience permits a necessary accommodation—perhaps we should call it an adaptation—to a new set of lived conditions. Crary is correct to emphasize the separation of observation from spatial referent, but if he wants to follow the macroscopic, strategic model upon which Foucault's historiography depends then I'll counter with de Certeau's emphasis on the range of interventionist tactics available to the subject within these broader structures, tactics that are the very stuff of individual adaptation to the strategies of centralized power structures. While the incorporation of the body into a range of primarily visual entertainments constitutes for Crary a colonization of that body, I think it represents a compensation for the declining centrality of sensory experience, a valid (i.e., useful) means of recentering one's experience of a decentered world. If this was, in some ways, complicit with dominant ideological agendas, it is also, irreducibly, a necessary means of being in the world.

Corporeal Mappings

Now the sense of displacement or disorientation produced by the environment of the industrial city gave rise to new entertainments that produced a cognitive and corporeal mapping of the subject into a previously overwhelming and intolerable space. Panoramic perception became a fundament of the Machine Age, a function of new architectures of steel and glass; it defined the arcades and department stores of consumerist abundance as well as a set of spectacular forms that reinforced the new dominance of an epistemology of vision. Telescopes, microscopes, maps of continents, geologic periods, and human anatomy further extended the reach of human perception, as Stafford notes: "The extension of vision permitted a new form of travel. Opaque depths were opened up, becoming transparent without the infliction of violence. The veil of the invisible was gently and noninvasively lifted. The eye could easily voyage through and beyond the densities of a plane, or silently journey beneath the stratified level."[19]

Travel provided the metaphor for a broad evocation of a spatiotemporal continuity wedded to a utopian dedication to "progress"; Susan Buck-Morss writes that "Railroads were the referent, and progress the sign, as spatial movement became so wedded to the concept of historical movement that these could no longer be distinguished."[20] Journeys to new heights, new perspectives, and new worlds became the substance of such recreations as the packaged tour, the panorama, the scenic garden, and the world's fair. In popular literature, Jules Verne took his readers aloft in a hot air balloon to go *Around the World in Eighty Days* and fired them from a cannon to bring them

From the Earth to the Moon. As Buck-Morss notes, new modes of conveyance became linked to new fields of knowledge and new possibilities for human advancement.

Here, then, is the start of at least one thread of what we have come to refer to as the Information Age, as an abundance of physical data was fitted to the epistemological desires and requirements of the public consciousness. Spectacular displays depended on a new mode of spectatorial address—essentially, *you are there* (even though you're not)—linked to new technologies of visual representation. Of course, these presentations can, in their turn, be traced to the geometric specificities of perspectival composition, which situated the observer in an illusory relation to the scene observed: now the spectator was granted vivid revelations of the insides of the human body, astronomical phenomena, and newsworthy events. Panoramas of exotic ports evoked an immersion in faraway places.

> The panorama struck a responsive chord in the nineteenth century. It satisfied, or at least helped to satisfy, an increasing appetite for visual information. A revolution in travel had made the world seem smaller. The growth of a literate middle class and the burgeoning newspaper industry meant that many more people were aware of a greater number of happenings over a larger area of the globe. It is not surprising that people should desire visual images of a world of which they were becoming increasingly aware through the printed word. The panorama supplied a substitute for travel and a supplement to the newspaper.[21]

Bodily experience and cognitive understanding were thus both supplemented —and largely replaced—by a reliance on vision within a simulacrum of the real.

Most popular were panoramas of one's own city, which became perceptible in a manner previously impossible. If the visual was now largely removed from the confirmation of haptic experience (a fundament of the Information Age), then, first, the visual would become a hyperbolically self-sufficient source of knowledge and information for the general public as well as the scientist and, second, a significant set of entertainments would recall the body into a pleasurable ersatz existence. The panorama and its successor, the diorama, would eventually incorporate simulated motion, lighting, and sound effects, platforms to rock or even move the audience, photography, and even, in the case of Hale's Tours, cinema. Such attractions have made an important return: Trumbull developed the "Ridefilm Theater," a simulator-theater system that featured a fifteen-passenger motion base encompassed by a 180 degree spherically curved screen. High-resolution images, projected with synchronized movement, produce a striking sense of kinesthetic immersion in a complex technological space.

Special Effects

A too easy historicism has tended to divide cinematic representations into naturalist and antinaturalist categories. Within this schema, special effects hark back to the imagistic manipulations of Méliès, but it should be clear that even the supposedly naturalistic Lumière brothers were purveyors of spectacle and novelty. Cinema is, of course, a special effect, and that is how it was regarded by its initial audiences. The illusion of motion, with its consequent sensations of temporal flow and spatial volume, provided enough innovation for spectators already familiar with a range of spectacular visual novelties. If cinema's unique blend of spatiotemporal solidity and metamorphic fluidity was largely assigned to the representation of narrative, the effect(s) of the medium nevertheless remained central to the spectatorial experience.

Writings on early cinema by both Tom Gunning and Miriam Hansen describe a "cinema of attractions," an "unabashed eclecticism" that was figured in a direct address to the viewer. According to Gunning, "this is an exhibitionistic cinema," while Hansen, following Jean Mitry, writes that "The frontality and uniformity of viewpoint is clearly the mark of a *presentational*—as opposed to *representational*—conception of space and address."[22] The presentational mode ultimately yielded to a more univocal narrational system that stabilized space and introduced "the segregation of the fictional space-time on the screen from the actual one of the theater or, rather, the subordination of the latter under the spell of the former."[23]

Nevertheless, Gunning argues that the fascination of the attraction "does not disappear with the dominance of narrative, but rather goes underground, both into certain avant-garde practices and as a component of narrative films, more evident in some genres (e.g. the musical) than in others."[24] The genre of science fiction often exhibits its spectatorial excess in the form of the special effect, which is especially effective at bringing the narrative to a spectacular halt. Science fiction participates in the presentational mode through the prevalence of optical effects that in fact *re*-integrate the virtual space of the spectacle with the physical space of the theater.

Special effects redirect the spectator to the visual (and auditory and even kinesthetic) conditions of the cinema and thus bring the principles of perception to the foreground of consciousness. This idea is at the center of Annette Michelson's superb analysis of *2001: A Space Odyssey*. The expansion of the visible field to cineramic proportions, the removal of perceptual clues to verticality and other conditions of physical orientation, and the sustained evocation of bodily weightlessness, the imposition of the rhythms of respiration and circulation on the soundtrack all contributed to the profound redefinition of haptic experience undergone by the voyagers in the audience.[25] If *2001* is more radical in its affect than other works of narrative cinema, visual effects remain central to science fiction for closely related reasons. "If we think of what it is that science fiction 'does,'" writes Brooks Landon, "surely we must acknowledge that its frequently mentioned 'sense of wonder' derives from 'a new way of seeing.'"[26]

The special effects of contemporary cinema are thus only a more recent manifestation of optical, spectacular technologies that created immersive, overwhelming, and apparently immediate sensory experiences such as "Renaissance" and elevated perspectives, panoramas, landscape paintings, kaleidoscopes, dioramas, and cinema — a cinema, to borrow from Gunning and Eisenstein, of attractions.

The Sublime in Science Fiction

The presentational mode described by Gunning or Hansen exceeds the logics of narrative and exaggerates the poetics of spectacle and thus bears a relation to certain conceptions, in poetry and painting, of the sublime — especially the sublime as figured in American art of the nineteenth century.[27] The classical conception of the sublime, as described by Longinus in relation to spoken rhetoric, emphasizes its power to enthrall and elevate the mind of man; in a famous passage, Longinus celebrated its unambiguous glory through his own little special effects sequence, writing that "our soul is uplifted by the true sublime; it takes a proud flight, and is filled with joy and vaunting, as though it had itself produced what it has heard."[28]

Joseph Addison and Edmund Burke were largely responsible for transforming the sublime from Kantian doctrine to aesthetic strategy. The field of the sublime was comprised of the majestic, the awe inspiring, and the literally overpowering: it spoke the languages of excess and hyperbole to suggest realms beyond human articulation and comprehension. The sublime was constituted through the combined sensations of astonishment, terror, and awe that occur through the revelation of a power greater, by far, than the human. Those commingled sensations result from the rhetorical construction of grandeur (either grandly large or small) and the infinite. The object of sublime rhetoric is often not entirely available to vision or description: uniformity (the similarity of all parts) and succession (a sense that the object extends on and on) characterize this "obscurity." The sublime initiates a crisis in the subject by disrupting the customary cognized relationship between subject and external reality. It threatens human thought, habitual signifying systems and, finally, human prowess: "the mind is hurried out of itself, by a crowd of great and confused images; which affect because they are crowded and confused."[29] The final effect is not a negative experience of anxious confusion, however, because it is almost immediately accompanied by a process of appropriation of, and identification with, the infinite powers on display. The phenomenal world is transcended as the mind moves to encompass what cannot be contained. And so the sublime is grounded in a pervastive ambivalence—the tension between diminution and exaltation is evident in the oxymoron of Burke's "delightful horror" and in Kant's description of "a quickly alternating attraction toward, and repulsion from, the same object."[30]

As telescopes provided tantalizing glimpses of worlds beyond our own, astronomy provided a new and exalted ground for the rhetoric of the sublime. In 1712, Joseph Addison wrote of the infinitude of the heavens in language typical of the mode.

> When we survey the whole earth at once, and the several planets that lie within its neighbourhood we are filled with a pleasing astonishment, to see so many worlds, hanging one above another, and sliding round their axles in such an amazing pomp and solemnity. If, after this, we contemplate those wild fields of ether, that reach in height as far as from Saturn to the fixed stars, and run abroad almost to an infinitude, our imagination finds its capacity filled with so immense a prospect, and puts itself upon the stretch to comprehend it. But if we rise yet higher, and consider the fixed stars as so many vast oceans of flame, that are each of them attended with a different set of planets, and still discover new firmaments and new lights that are sunk further into those unfathomable depths of ether, so as not to be seen by the strongest of our telescopes, we are lost in such a labyrinth of suns and worlds, and confounded with the immensity and magnificence of nature.[31]

Here, in a sense, the cosmic trajectories of 2001 are prefigured not only in the evocation of astronomical scale but in the description of successive levels of macrocosmic order that ultimately yield to a chaos that signals the very limits of our ability to comprehend the vastness of the universe. The universe is without end, it confounds us, but the rhetoric of the sublime paradoxically permits an understanding of these sensory and conceptual limits. The rhetorical threat posed by the sublime is finally, then, not really that much of a threat.

The precise function of science fiction, in many ways, is to *create* the boundless and infinite stuff of sublime experience and thus to produce a sense of transcendence beyond human finitudes (true to the form of the sublime, most works produce transcendence of, and acknowledgment of, human limits). Indeed, the objects of science fiction are characterized by a spatio-temporal grandeur revealed by the titles alone: *A Space Odyssey, Last and First Men, When Worlds Collide, The Star Maker* (and consider the titles of early science fiction magazines: *Astounding, Amazing, Thrilling Wonder Stories, Weird Tales*). The conclusion of Richard Matheson's *The Shrinking Man* (1956) links the micro- and macrocosmic in an infinite continuum of religious transcendence. Science-fictional objects are sublimely obscure: the city of Trantor in Isaac Asimov's Foundation series, covers an entire planet—one of the boundless cities of SF—and there is the spaceship that begins *Star Wars* (1977): too large for the screen—or our consciousness—to hold. Science fiction is immediately and deeply bound to the tropologies of the sublime. Burke's "artificial infinite" is echoed in *2001*'s "Jupiter and beyond the Infinite": rhetorical allusions to the unrepresentable forms of infinity.[32]

As in the parable of Prometheus, however, humanity's o'erreaching is frequently followed by the punishment of the gods. Arthur C. Clarke's "The Nine Billion Names of God" (1952) posits a religious order that has enlisted the aid of a computer to determine all the names of the story's title. The lamas believe that this task of enumeration is humanity's purpose and that upon its completion our history, too, will end. The rationalist technicians, hurrying to escape the wrath of the order once the computer has executed its run, are finally confronted with the limits of being: "'Look,' whispered Chuck, and George lifted his eyes to heaven. (There is always a last time for everything.) Overhead, without any fuss, the stars were going out."[33]

Clearly, SF participates in the "delightful horrors" of sublime experience. Humans are often dwarfed by the presence of a greater power, and the only appropriate response seems to be the awe and shaking terror of the astronaut in the penultimate sequences of *2001*.

Landscape Painting and Special Effects

The figures of sublime rhetoric were developed and understood primarily with reference to poetic language and were first related to the register of the visual arts only with suspicion. With the unintentional influence of Burke in the nineteenth century, however, painting became a new site for the instantiation of the sublime. While the concrete and exteriorized representations common to painting had long been regarded as deficient when compared to poetry's grand abstractions, Burke's categorization of sublime effects ("obscurity, privation, vastness, succession, uniformity, magnificence, loudness, suddenness and so on") proved easily applicable to the painter's depiction of the natural order.[34] Andrew Wilton has studied Turner's painting within the context of eighteenth-century notions of the sublime and argues that painting's concreteness, once regarded as its very limitation, now became its great strength: "The vast, the remote, the obscure, qualities that give rein to the imagination, can be enumerated in respect to landscape more easily and precisely than in connection with religious, mental or abstract ideas."[35] The representation of natural phenomena—mountains, sky, flora—became the means of meditating on the magnificence of their Creator (and the magnificent powers of reason that could ruminate upon that magnificence).

The landscape sublime is rooted in an activity of contemplation, in the attempt to grasp what fundamentally cannot be grasped. The breadth of nature proves ideal in stimulating the dynamic cognitive processes that exalt the mind that engages with it. The artworks most closely associated with the sublime are therefore often detailed and scrupulous revelations of nature's grandeur—but less from an impulse toward mimesis than from the encouragement of specific spectatorial behaviors.[36] For landscape painting to inspire dynamic contemplation, however, it is not enough to duplicate external form. Many artists, Turner and Church among them, provide a kind of viewing instruction in the depiction of a frequently tiny figure fixed in contemplation of the very wonders that the painter has chosen to embellish.[37]

Spectacular and monumental elements, all encompassed by a dynamic spectatorial gaze, are easily found among the plethora of special effects sequences in the history of the cinema. If the poetics of the sublime anticipated the thematics of science fiction, then the visual sublime elaborated through painting just as surely prefigures the visible excesses of SF film, and they are particularly pronounced in the filmwork of Douglas Trumbull.

An examination of Trumbull's work reveals a surprisingly coherent aesthetics. A Trumbull sequence is less the description of an object than the construction of an environment. He has expressed a dissatisfaction with the flatness of most special effects sequences, which require rapid cutaways to distract the audience: "I like the idea of creating some crazy illusion that looks so great that you can really hang on it like a big master shot of an epic landscape."[38] ("Epic landscape" suggests the affinity between Trumbull's effects and the majestic paintings of Turner, Church, Bierstadt, and so on.) The work privileges a sense of environmental grandeur: the widescreen effect becomes an enveloping thing, such as the roiling cloudscapes that presage the appearance of the mothership in *CE3K*, the gorgeous and monstrous Los Angeles of *Blade Runner*, or the amorphous, infinite interiority of V'ger in *Star Trek*. The Stargate sequence in *2001* features scarcely any objects; it emphasizes instead a continuum of spatiotemporal transmutations.

Wilton isolates some relevant techniques in Turner's style. Citing the moments of turbulence in Turner's painting, his language evokes a powerful spectatorial kinesis: "Views through arcades, avenues of trees, tunnels of rock, even vortices of dust or storm, create an arrow-like retreat through the picture-space that is often at odds with the calmer perspective of the principal view. These distortions . . . impose a *dramatic mode of vision* upon the viewer, who is compelled to enact with the eye leaps and plunges, ascents, *penetrations* and progressions that plot for him the three-dimensional presence of the perceived landscape."[39] Such turbulent moments are usually grounded within the calmer description of a larger landscape, just as Trumbull's kinetic effects are rooted in the narrative progression of a feature film. In American landscape painting, the work of Martin Johnson Heade also puts the spectator in motion, this time in an act of spatial penetration of the picture plane: "The lines of the juncture between the higher ground on the perimeter of the marsh and the edge of the marsh itself also expand to exaggerate and reinforce the visual experience of rushing into deep space. In no other American landscapes does spatial recession play such an important role or is it developed with such careful geometric precision" (Powell, 83). Trumbull's effects are also grounded in a phenomenologically powerful spatial probing.[40]

Trumbull emphasizes the spectatorial relation to the effect/environment. To some degree, all special effects are so inscribed: the effect is designed to be seen, and frequently the narrative will pause to permit the audience to appreciate (or groove on) the technologies on display (what, in a somewhat different context, Laura Mulvey once referred to as "erotic contemplation"). However, Trumbull's sequences are different. Where John Dykstra's work in *Star Wars* or *Firefox* (1982) is all hyperkinesis and participatory action, Trumbull's work is especially contemplative. If he desires to create effects "good enough to look at for a long period of time," then his sequences have encouraged precisely this kind of activity.

Further, and regardless of the director involved, these scenes frequently include an explicit and pronounced spectatorial position within the diegesis: witness the cutaways to an astronaut's frozen features, Spielberg's typically slack-jawed observers, the crew of the starship *Enterprise*, or the disembodied eye that holds the infernal city reflected in its gaze. Much of this is typical of cinematic science fiction, a genre that is almost defined by its incorporation of new technologies of vision.[41] But, again, Dykstra's work on *Star Wars* is not so inscribed: the passage of the first, impossibly enormous spaceship is witnessed by the audience, but there is no spectator *within* the diegesis (the same holds for the climactic explosion of the Death Star). The presence of the diegetic spectator stages an extended encounter with the sublime, rehearsing (and hyperbolizing) the filmic spectator's own response.

In *Star Trek: The Motion Picture*, to take the most obvious example, the spectatorial function is taken by the crew of the U.S.S. *Enterprise*, which has been brought out of mothballs to confront an immensely powerful techno-organic entity that is heading (as usual) for Earth. The visual centerpiece of the film (aside from the hilariously fetishized *Enterprise* itself) was the mysterious V'ger entity; essentially an old Voyager spacecraft with some loose screws. The V'ger model, as designed by Syd Mead (who would also work with Trumbull on *Blade Runner*) was sixty-eight feet in length and peppered with lamps, fiber optics, neon tubing, and laser lights, all augmented with additional animation effects and Dykstra's computerized camera. V'ger is perhaps exemplary of the sublime object in its boundlessness (although one should note a blurred distinction here between sublimity and monotony). Trumbull's unit developed a computerized multiplane system (Compsy) that provided complex movements through the ethereal, multi-layered space within V'ger as well as some beautiful streaked footage of the *Enterprise* flying through a "wormhole" in space.[42] Although the film is poorly paced and plays like a high school version of *2001*,[43] the effects work is not without interest. The extended penetration of V'ger places the human within and against the alien landscape. In these shots of a touchingly diminutive *Enterprise*, the human is nearly lost, barely visible against V'ger's dark monumentalism. There is, perhaps, a similarity here to the tiny figures that occupy the lower foreground of Church's South American paintings—"insertions of culture into nature," Barbara Novak calls them.[44] Of course, V'ger is not natural but is possessed of the brutal force that one associates with nature: this is a distinction to which I shall return.

Through the prevalence of such temporally distended special effects sequences, science fiction clearly participates in a *presentational* mode of cinematic discourse. Audiences may use a diegetic human figure as a provisional guide through the immensities of alien space, but this character does not serve to defuse or anchor the spectator's own phenomenological experience.[45] The passage into the kinetic lights and amorphous shapes of the Stargate sequence in *2001*, to take another example, is explicitly directed *right at* the viewer. Close-ups of David Poole, the astronaut, do not reintegrate us into a fictional (*re*-presentational) space; neither do they situate Dave as a psychologized subject meant to focus audience identification. Cutaways to human observers in Trumbull's sequences reestablish scale and reemphasize the "otherness" of the sublime environment, but they do not mediate the experience through the psychology of characters who are, uniformly, stunned into a profound passivity. In their increasing magnification they suggest something of the "extraordinary intensity" of the close-up as celebrated by Jean Epstein. Fictive and theatrical spaces are collapsed, as diegetic and cinematic spectators are, in a metaphorical sense, united. (Michelson argues that *2001* is predicated on just such a confusion between astronaut and spectator.[46] In other SF films, these tropes are often present but in less overt form.) The presence of diegetic spectators, then, here actually enhances the presentational aspect of the cinema while also evoking the sublime.

America (and beyond the infinite)

In the nineteenth century, America revealed its obsession with the relationship between nature and human power and human destiny in prose, paint, and politics. A rhetoric of progress mingled with the sense of a people chosen by God and history, privileged to engage with, and tame, a New World that still seemed to bear the fresh touch of its Creator. The vast reaches of the American West seemed to test the will of the nation's new citizens, and the emerging technologies of industrial capitalism were extraordinarily suited to the colonization and economic exploitation of these territories. Alan Trachtenberg has written that "the American railroad seemed to create new spaces, new regions of comprehension and economic value, and finally to incorporate a prehistoric geological terrain into historical time" (this powerful spatiotemporal collapse echoes Buck-Morss's contention that spatial movement analogized historical progress).[47]

In an oft-quoted section of "Nature" (1836), Emerson—who also could be somewhat delirious about train travel—narrates a state of mind characteristic of the transcendental sublime: "Standing on the bare ground,—my head bathed by the blithe air and uplifted into infinite space—all mean egotism vanishes. I become a transparent eyeball; I am nothing; I see all; the currents of the Universal Being circulate through me; I am part or parcel of God. . . . In the wilderness, I find something more dear and connate than in streets or villages. In the tranquil landscape, and especially in the distant line of the horizon, man beholds somewhat as beautiful as his own nature." Emerson's debt to Kant is evident in his version of the sublime as exaltation and in his description of the ego's dissolution, which is ultimately recuperated in the beauty of human nature.[48] His "transparent eyeball" anticipates the infradiegetic but impossibly positioned spectators that populate Trumbull's effects sequences, and it provides a strikingly direct gloss on Trumbull's evident transcendentalist bias.

The landscape took on a centrality in American painting, which became "immersed in nature."[49] In the union of sublime aesthetics and transcendental philosophy, one critic has written that "the sublime experience was transformed into a new mode of landscape expression; the traditional sublime setting was augmented by the transcendental sublime sensibility, a sensibility that found its roots in man's internal perception of time and space."[50] This sensibility found its clearest expression in the genre of luminist painting. Barbara Novak has defined *luminism* in relation to transcendentalist philosophy as an aesethetic that emphasized impersonal expression, horizontality, minute tonal gradations, intimate size, immobility, and silence (see color fig. 5). The luminist work is marked by a "calculated control": an order is imposed on visible reality.[51] Stroke is deemphasized because stroke implies the artist, paint as a medium rather than a transparent representation, and an ongoing temporality. And of course the luminist work is defined by its representation of light: a cool, hard, palpable light (not diffuse) spread across a glassy surface. "The linear edges of reality are pulled taut," Novak writes, "strained almost to the point of breaking."[52]

Luminism was not the only means of evoking the sublimity of the American landscape. The monumental paintings of such nineteenth-century figures as Copley, Cole, Church, Bierstadt, and others constructed a visual rhetoric of the sublime far removed from the solitude and silence of the luminists, although there were numerous shared concerns.[53] "The landscape painter must astonish his audience by the immediacy of his *effects*," Wilton writes.[54] While much of this immediacy was achieved through the hyperbolized detail of the rendering, the scale of the works also meant to overwhelm the sensibility of the spectator. These representations of exotic landscapes in the American West or South America were too large and too detailed to be "taken in" with a single glance; the spectator's gaze had to be put in motion to assimilate the work. Furthermore, this especially exhibitionistic mode of representation was often exhibited like a fairground attraction. In its construction of a dynamic, kinetic gaze, as well as its mode of exhibition, the monumental landscape painting takes its place alongside such contemporaneous "phantasmagoria of progress" (Buck-Morss) as the diorama and magic lantern show.

The paintings of Frederick Church are particularly appropriate to consider alongside Trumbull's effects. The astonishing, bold color experiments (special effects) that Church unleashed in depicting his twilight skies and volcanic eruptions were the result of new technologies in cadmium-based pigment production (see color figs. 6, 7). These effects were put in the service of atmospheric and cosmological phenomena: not just the sky but the sun and moon, a meteor, and the aurora borealis. One critic has pointed to the promise of revelation that underlies the dramatic scenography and monumental scale of Church's later paintings.[55] Another writes of "Twilight in the Wilderness" (1860) that "The painting defies simple categorization as a 'luminist' work of art, but there can be no doubt that the subject of the picture is, literally, American light, symbolic of the new world Apocalypse. It is a compelling work of art which combines two aspects of the sublime, the traditional interest in nature as object and the transcendental concern for nature as experience, through color, space, and silence."[56]

The dual contexts of luminism and "great pictures" provide a further context for the Stargate sequence. The passage through the Stargate is a voyage "beyond the infinite," a movement beyond anthropocentric experience and understanding. Using slitscan technologies, Trumbull created a set of images that were little more than organized patterns of light—the very stuff of cinema. Light, with its implications of revelation and blinding power, is also the very stuff of the sublime.

> Light is . . . the alchemistic medium by which the landscape artist turns
> matter into spirit. . . . In American art especially, light has often been
> used in conjunction with water to assist spiritual transformation, either
> dissolving form, as in some of Church's large South American pieces, or
> rendering it crystalline, as in the works of Lane. In the former, light is
> more closely attached to what we generally call atmosphere, and has a
> diffusive, vaporous quality. In the latter, light itself partakes of the hard
> shiny substance of glass. In all instances, the spirituality of light signals

the newly Christianized sublime. In the large paintings by Church and Bierstadt light moves, consumes, agitates and drowns. Its ecstasy approaches transcendence, but its activity is an impediment to consummating a complete unity with Godhead.[57]

In *2001*, light's transformative power illustrates, embodies, and enacts precisely the supercession of the human (and the human's rebirth as a superhuman, a Star Child).

The Sturm und Drang of the Stargate sequence is clearly different from the luminism of Fitz Hugh Lane, but I would argue that the sequence participates in both of these tropologies of light, moving from the diffusion and mutability of the first section to the color-tinted, crystalline silence of the landscapes at the end. Light "moves, consumes, agitates and drowns," but there is nevertheless a stillness that subtends the sequence's last minutes. Here the landscape becomes more concrete but commensurately more barren, and sky and sea blend as the horizon disappears. The penetrating camera movements persist but are now overwhelmed by the quietude of these enormous and empty worlds.[58]

John Wilmerding has written about Church in terms that seem just as applicable to the Stargate sequence: "while Church's handling of composition and paint only peripherally borders on luminism," he nevertheless notes "the sense of vast stillness verging on an imminent crescendo of light and sound."[59] The "imminent crescendo" directs us to the function of sound here and in other sequences. While most are accompanied by tumultuously loud sound effects or scoring, language is, in every instance, absent. Again there is a conflation of two tropes found in the American landscape sublime: the evocation of Apocalypse ("sublimity overwhelms with a deafening roar") and the quietude of luminism ("the spectator is brought into a wordless dialogue with nature").[60]

Technological Encounters

Mark Seltzer has astutely proposed that "Nothing typifies the American sense of identity more than the love of nature (nature's nation) except perhaps the love of technology (made in America)."[61] To the American paradigm that opposed nature's might and human will, American painters, poets, essayists, and novelists added the newly unleashed forces of technology to produce what Leo Marx has labeled "the rhetoric of the technological sublime."[62] The anxiety surrounding the new prominence of technology has received much attention since the Industrial Revolution, and its representation has hardly been limited to science fiction.

In nineteenth-century America, technological anxiety was transformed by a sense of destiny. "Above all, the rhetoric conveys that sense of unlimited possibility which seizes the American imagination at this remarkable juncture."[63] This rhetoric of unlimited possibility does not, however, mask some residual anxieties, as a surfeit of landscapes featuring decimated woodlands and smoke-obscured vistas demonstrates: "The new significance of nature and the development of landscape painting coincided paradoxically with the relentless destruction of the wilderness in the early nineteenth century."[64] As Rosalind Williams notes in her study of subterranean environments in the nineteenth century, "Technological blight promotes technological fantasy."[65] The presence of the sublime in science fiction, a deeply American genre, implies that our fantasies of superiority emerge from our ambivalence regarding technological power rather than nature's might (as Kant originally had it). The might of technology, supposedly our own creation, is mastered through a powerful display that acknowledges anxiety but recontains it within the field of spectatorial power.

What Buck-Morss refers to as the "phantasmagoria of progress" (panoramas, world's fairs, and the like) are visual displays that concretized metaphors of progress to provide some means of contending with the complexity of what Walter Benjamin called a "new nature." By this, she contends that Benjamin meant

> not just industrial technology but the entire world of matter (including human beings) as it has been transformed by that technology. There have been, then, two epochs of nature. The first evolved slowly over millions of years; the second, our own, began with the industrial revolution, *and changes its face daily.* This new nature, its powers still unknown, can appear ominous and terrifying to the first generations confronting it, given "the very primitive form of the ideas of these generations" who have yet to learn to master, not this nature itself, but humanity's relationship to it.[66]

The sublime is thus figured in these spectacles as an idealist response to significant and continuing alterations in lived experience. Hence the sustained reappearance of the sublime in popular, technologically based entertainments. Then and now, the language of consumption and the display of spectacle grounds the spectator/visitor and hides the awful truth that an en-

Figure 8. Gardens in the machine from *Silent Running*, directed by
Douglas Trumbull. (Courtesy of MCA/Universal.)

vironment that we made has moved beyond our ability to control and cognize it: hence the experience of technology as both alien and enveloping in Trumbull's effects sequences. The simultaneous fascination with and fear of technology's beauty, majesty, and power reveal a necessary ambivalence, and through this ambivalence the sublime becomes a crucial tool of cognitive mapping.

Technology has come to comprise an environment, a second nature "with its own attendant pleasures and hazards."[67] Nature is displaced by technology in *2001, CE3K,* and *Silent Running,* and this displacement is complete in *Star Trek* and *Blade Runner.* Buck-Morss notes that the new space of the Crystal Palace, a space permitted by new technologies of glass and steel architecture, "blended together old nature and new nature—palms as well as pumps and pistons."[68] Technology permits a containment of nature in the Crystal Palace and the crystalline domes of *Silent Running* (the garden in the machine perhaps). But the appearance of nature has become little more than nostalgia for a pastoral ideal. If the rhetoric of the technological sublime in nineteenth-century letters was characterized by the appearance of "the machine in the garden," then, at the end of the twentieth century, we would have to note that the machine *is* the garden.[69]

The significance of this shift was discussed by Thomas Weiskel, who noted that the sublime "must now be abridged, reduced, and parodied as the grotesque, somehow hedged with irony to assure us we are not imaginative adolescents." He adds that, the infinite spaces of nature or the cosmos "are no longer astonishing; still less do they terrify."[70] In the absence of nature's grandeur, then, perhaps technology constitutes a new ground for human definition and for our obsession with infinite power and possibility.

Theorists of postmodernism emphasized the moment's technocultural underpinnings and the rise of invisible networks and decentered fields of power that were seen to characterize electronic and nuclear technologies. The aesthetics of John Pfahl's series of photographs (from the early 1980s) of power plants in their "natural" settings are troublingly, shockingly ambivalent: nuclear (and other) technology becomes truly awe-ful, somehow simultaneously coexisting with nature, dominated by nature, and dominating over all.[71] The startling rise of mediating electronic technologies has precipitated a crisis of visibility and control. If cultural power now seems to have passed beyond the scales of human activity and perception, then culture has responded by producing a set of visualizations—or allegorizations—of the new "spaces" of technological activity. Most SF remains unflaggingly conservative in its language and iconography, but it still remains the genre most committed to narrating the ambiguities that mark the technological contours of contemporary culture.

The ambivalent relationship between technology and human definition is evident in the mothership sequence in *Close Encounters of the Third Kind*. First, one must note the sky in the film's night scenes—abundant stars allude to the infinite reaches of space: as we know, "theorists of the sublime attached much importance to the associational significance of the sky, and usually placed the night sky full of stars at the head of their list of its sublimities."[72] For landscape painters, clouds also afford the opportunity to depict "the storm cloud, with its obvious propensities for sublimity,"[73] and *CE3K* provides strikingly exaggerated clouds, substantial yet strangely liquid and far more animated than the dumbfounded characters themselves (see color fig. 1).

The star-filled skies presage the appearance of the mothership. The ship's design was inspired, according to Spielberg, by the sight of an oil refinery—the sublime is thus constituted around an anxious technological object (compare this to Pfahl's contemporaneous reactor shots). We might additionally note how nature, in the form of Devil's Tower, dwarfs the humans who nestle against it until the mothership, in its turn, dwarfs nature (see color fig. 1). The complex relationship between nature and technology is also manifested in the first appearance of the mothership, which emerges from behind the mountain, that is, from the earth, instead of the improbably starry sky. The scale of the ship further indicates the subjugation of nature by the power of technology—Spielberg wanted it to be "so big it would blot out the stars." Finally, while the ship is defined by brilliant and beautiful light, it is also distinguished by the black shadows that swallow the observers: for all its beauty, the mothership is something of a dark, visually negative force. Burke noted the same dialectic between light and its absence in Milton's descriptions of God: "Dark with excessive light thy skirts appear." The subsequent communication between human and alien happens via music and color, continuing the avoidance of linguistic rationalism and so remaining firmly within the experience of the sublime. In Trumbull's films, as a rule the effects sequences unfold, if not in a reflective silence, then at least in the absence of language. ("The eye is not the only organ of sensation by which a sublime passion may be produced," Burke wrote. "Sounds have a great power in these as in most other passions. I do not mean words.")[74] The tension that obtains between visibility and obscurity, the explosions of vivid chromatics and sound, the evacuation of language and narrative—all this speaks to the powers of the human sensorium even as it also seems to diminish and displace the human.

Artificial Infinities

Artificial infinities abound in SF: generation ships, outer space, cyberspace, boundless cities, cosmic time, galactic empires, *2001*'s mysterious monolith, the endless underground cities of the Krel in *Forbidden Planet*. Rosalind Williams has written about the craze for artificial environments that punctuated the fancies of the nineteenth century and notes that these industrial fantasies have continued unabated into the present era "in the form of retreats into personal or collective environments of consumption—the artificial paradises of the shopping mall or of the media room, for example. This is a journey further inward, a retreat from technology into technology."[75]

Trumbull's accomplishment is the articulation of the tension between anxiety and identification as we strain to assimilate the imagined infinities of technological power. Such tension is exemplified in the opening sequences of *Silent Running*, as a lush, natural forest is slowly revealed to exist within the hypertechnologized spaces of a vast spacecraft—nature is now enclosed and redefined by the experience of the technological, as "man's traces" become increasingly more evident until they finally overwhelm.[76] The ending is even more complex: the drones are left to care forever for the forests as they drift through deep space. The spaceship explodes in a, well, *sublime* pyrotechnical display (a new sun). The drones tend to the forest in a series of interior shots.

Then the drifting domed biosphere is seen in its entirety, slowly receding in the visual field. Culture (the ship) is superseded by nature (the pure light of the explosion); then the natural (forest) is contained by the technological (dome), which in its turn is contained by the cosmological (space).

The archetype of the artificial environment is, of course, the industrial city, revisited and hyperbolized in *Blade Runner*. The oil refinery motif of *CE3K* has become more pronounced, as the entire city is now explicitly figured as an anxious technological object. There is no more nature, only its simulacra in the form of synthetic animals and humans, and no escape from the encompassing technological landscape. Williams argues that "in the late twentieth century, our technologies less and less resemble tools—discrete objects that can be considered separately from their surroundings—and more and more resemble systems that are intertwined with global systems, sometimes on a global scale."[77] In *Blade Runner,* as the hovercar glides above and through the city, we indeed "take a proud flight" and attain a position of conceptual mastery over the complex and superbly synchronized urban scene. The film provides two fields of vision: there is the physical reality beyond the windshield and a graphic display of what must be an electronic traffic corridor along which the car glides. Each view explains the other as urban space and information space map each other to produce an intertwined global system.

The phantasmagoria of progress involves a sustained immersion within an artificial, technological environment that suggests technology's own ability to incorporate what it has generally excluded. If the disappearance of nature is seen as a consequence of a burgeoning technosphere, then utopian technologies will incorporate Arcadia (Crystal Palace, Futurama, *Silent Running*). If technology is seen as a dehumanizing force that leads to an impoverishment of spirit, then utopian technologies will permit a new emergence of spirituality and cosmic connectedness (V'ger, virtual reality). It might even be argued that cinema is the very paradigm of an artificial, technological environment that has incorporated utopian fantasies of nature, kinetic power, spiritual truth, and human connection.

Conclusion

Trumbull's effects are not the sole staging ground for sublime experience in electronic technoculture—it is evident that the rhetoric of the sublime has made a somewhat massive return. Baudrillard's kinetic cyberblitz, the technomysticism of *Mondo 2000*, the transcendent possibilities envisioned in Gibson's cyberspace trilogy, a new attention to its rhetoric within philosophy and the academy, and millennial fantasies of various stripes all point to the renewed relevance of the sublime.

The reasons for its return are not difficult to fathom. The sublime came to prominence in response to the increasing secular rationalization of modern life and was later co-opted as a mode of accommodation to the power of industrial technology. The late twentieth century presented a historically analogous time of technological development and expansion, and so it was hardly surprising that this rhetoric should recur to ground an understanding of an ostensibly new phenomenon. Just as Gibson's cyberspace recast the new "terrain" of digital information processing in the familiar terms of a sprawling yet concentrated American urbanism, the sublime becomes a means of looking backward in order to recognize what's up ahead.

But there's something else going on. The sublime not only points back toward a historical past; it also holds out the promise for self-fulfillment and technological transcendence in an imaginable near future. Under the terms of the sublime, technology is divorced from its sociological, rationalist underpinnings to become a technology without technocracy, a technology beyond the scope of human control. There is thus an inevitability to the fact of technological progress, and thus accommodation becomes the one valid response. The sublime presents an accommodation that is both surrender and transcendence, a loss of self that only leads—*back? forward?*—to a renewed and newly strengthened experience of self.

Thomas Weiskel's revisionist approach to the Romantic sublime understands this characteristic ambivalence as a repressed content, namely, the playing through of an oedipal scenario. On some level, then, the return of the sublime represents a throwback to fantasies of masculinist dominance, and to this interpretation Trumbull's endless penetrations into vast unknown regions would seem to lend themselves. "I think we may infer," Weiskel writes, "that the 'imminent danger' [Burke] to which we are exposed and from which we are then released in the sublime moment is an unconscious fantasy of parricide."[79] There are elements of this scenario in each of Trumbull's sequences as the human—character and cinematic spectator—is first overwhelmed before being granted some measure of cognitive control. The destabilizing function is then subverted and recontained by the narratives of some of these films: Spielberg's parricidal anxiety becomes especially evident when *Close Encounter*'s omnipotent aliens emerge from the "mothership" resembling the doe-eyed third world waifs of a Margaret Keane painting. Human superiority is (re)assured in relation to these diminutive *and neutered* figures. *Star Trek's* new captain literally mates with the female manifestation of V'ger in a transcendent, transspecies union that nevertheless somehow remains comfortably heterosexual.

The sublime's rhetoric of confrontation and mastery smacks of phallocentrist bias, while the landscape sublime's predilection for the "virgin landscapes" of South America and the North American West aligns it all too neatly with the colonialist usurpation that called itself manifest destiny. Its mystical overtones no longer jibe with a secularist culture that remains deeply suspicious of spiritual value. Despite these condemnations, however, any number of theorists and artists have attempted to "rescue" the sublime, finding in its confrontational power an ethos of exploration and self-discovery that meshes with my sense of Trumbull's effects work.

Patricia Yaeger has specifically challenged the masculinist modalities of sublime rhetoric. Despite its status as "old-fashioned, outmoded [and] concerned with self-centered imperialism," she contends that because "it is a literary genre or moment concerned with empowerment, transport, and the self's strong sense of authority, the sublime is a genre the woman writer needs." The sublime preserves a sense of the other, or "alienness," even in the face of cognitive assimilation, and it can encompass the intimate as well as the grandiose. The other need not be "obliterated or repressed" but can be preserved in a newly dialectical self-other relation. Citing Weiskel and Neil Hertz, Yaeger argues that one can locate a desire to merge with the other in the sublime moment, and thus the oedipal struggle for control may be a feint that masks more primordial (and less gendered) desires. "Subject and object have entered into an intersubjective dialectic of grandeur in which the poet refuses to annex what is alien, but revels, for a brief poetic moment, in a pre-oedipal longing for otherness and ecstasy."[80] What she terms the "feminine sublime" thus addresses the crucial problem of how to produce "a model of the self that permits both a saving maintenance of ego-boundaries and an exploration of the pleasures of intersubjectivity."[81]

In *Agon*, Harold Bloom connects sublimity to the questioning traditions of gnostic thought. Like the sublime, "Gnosis is more than or other than rational," Bloom writes. "And yet this need not be considered either a mystical or a visionary experience, since in Gnosis the knowledge is neither of eternity nor of this world seen with more spiritual intensity. The knowledge is of *oneself*."[82] The confrontation leads back to a confrontation with a self that is neither fixed nor given, but comes into being through the act of interrogation. Bloom refers to gnosis as "performative knowledge," a knowledge that can only emerge via experience. Further, the experience of "the Sublime moment proper" opens a "gap of negation or disjunctive generation of meaning."[83] The sublime thus depends on a disruption followed by a performative adaptation that yields a dynamic knowledge of a dialectically constituted self. Yaeger and Bloom might be approaching the sublime from very different directions, but for both the trope offers something more than phallocentric reassurance.

Bloom has devoted some attention to the sublimity of science fiction and fantasy: "What promises to be the least anxious of literary modes becomes much the most anxious, and this anxiety specifically relates to anterior powers."[84] Again, ambivalence—the eddies between the polarities of bondage and freedom—structure the experience of the text. The sublime enacts an ambivalent relation to authority, while the technological sublime enacts a conflict between a humanity ever more tenuously linked to nature while ever more imbricated with the "anterior powers" of technocultural structures. If a positive value can be assigned to the return of the sublime in SF cinema, then it lies in a rhetoric of scopic destabilization that yields a new subject position with regard to the source of technological anxiety. Unlike *Star Trek*, *2001* does not "explain" its ultimate trip and so denies its viewers the firm ground provided by cognitive comprehensibility. I would argue that in *2001* Kubrick and Trumbull have emphasized and foregrounded the phenomenological instability that has always been more or less present in science fiction cinema. If SF too often seems anchored (or mired) in rationalist cant, then the "performative knowledge" provided by inventive special effects moves the spectator beyond the rational to a space beyond the infinite. Despite the recontainments and reassurances that are the function of these films' narratives, scopic instability and cognitive accommodation remain fundamental to, and implicit in, our experience of the works.

Barbara Novak describes another moment when advanced technology was employed to (re)present advanced technology: "The most exciting visual encounters with the railroad were those that took place through the mediation of yet another machine—the camera. The photographer, having already accommodated one machine within his artistic perspective, had much less difficulty than painters in accommodating still another."[85] As with the privileged views provided by panoramas, elevated views, photographs, and the cinematograph, special effects encourage engagement with a reality that seems to defy engagement. Through the "magic" of special effects, a contemporary rhetoric of technological sublimity is produced by technological means. Cinematic *affect* is rooted in cinematic technology, but *effects* emphasize those underpinnings; if cinema is rooted in illusions of light, for example, then optical effects endow light with an overwhelming physicality. Science fiction cinema uses state of the art effects to "accommodate still another" realm of machinery. The effects put machinery in motion, offering technology up to dynamic contemplation (and in the ridefilm theaters machinery in motion puts the spectator in motion as perception is now supplemented by bodily experience).

However, one must acknowledge (at least briefly) the recurrent fantasies of sexuality and power at work within many of these texts. The mythology of the frontier is clearly evoked in narrative, image, and technique, as a penetration of sublimely mysterious and fluid interior spaces becomes the precondition for masculinist mastery (one might refer to this as regeneration through cyberspace). But this overdetermined phallocentric *thrust* should not blind us to the overwhelming need to map ourselves into the anxious spaces of first industrial and now electronic culture. Cognition, one hopes, does not necessarily imply domination, and, while the science fiction narrative often speaks to militaristic male fantasies, the spectator's immersion in a technologized environment presented by the wide-screen special effects sequence retains phenomenological validity and importance. To invoke a transcendentalist, Thoreau's admiration of the Native American was grounded in their relation to nature: "Perception, rather than domination or calculation, is his forte."[86] Relations among perception, cognition, knowledge, and power are neither simple nor, I suspect, absolute, and the phenomenological status of these phantasmagorias of progress merits an attention that moves beyond simply classifying such spectacles as masculinist, colonialist, or consumerist.

But we should remember Tom Gunning's argument that "effects are *tamed* attractions."[87] The reflexivity of special effects (a technology of technology, a cinema of cinema) indeed encourages some sense of identification and mastery. The effect is possessed of its own hypnotic grandeur: it is designed to inspire awe, but always within a reassuring sense of play (here I'll simply note the number of fanboy magazines devoted to effects extravaganzas). Rapture replaces terror in most of these artificial infinities. There is, ultimately, a denial of human limitations—a denial of death, really—that connects to science fiction's overall denial of sexuality, mortality, and fleshly bodies (what Vivian Sobchack has described as "the virginity of astronauts").[88]

Special effects, in the cinema and in their extension to virtual reality systems, are but the latest in a series of popular cultural entertainments that emphasize what Stan Brakhage has referred to as the "adventure of perception." Despite their emphasis on perceptual mastery and the magisterial gaze, these recreations significantly balanced sensory pleasure and cognitive play.[89] The effects sequences of the science fiction cinema are significant for what they say, as well as for what they do not say, about our complicated relationship to complex technologies at this precarious historical moment. This ambivalence permeates the culture of visuality. As Miriam Hansen wrote with regard to the development of cinema's moving camera, "The mobilization of the gaze promises nothing less than the mobilization of the self, the transformation of seemingly fixed positions of social identity. This mobilization, however, is promise and delusion in one."[90]

5

The Ultimate Trip:
Special Effects and Kaleidoscopic Perception

*The screen was a second sky, where what you saw was nothing
compared to the anticipation of what you might at any moment
witness: a shooting star, a spaceship, an apocalypse.*

Geoffrey O'Brien

It must have been my early love of planetariums that made me want to become an astronomer. So imagine my surprise, disgust, and resentment on discovering that astronomy consisted of something more than sitting in the dark and gazing upward into the abyss. There were mathematical operations to perform, physical laws to consider, and endless, endless cataloguing. My career as a scientist did not survive this rude awakening, which I think occurred in the first week of my first year of college. But here I am, attending to the discourse of science fiction cinema, still embracing that experience of sitting in the darkness and peering into infinity.

My pleasure at the planetarium, then, may not have been, as I had thought, an awakening to the pleasures of rationalist thought but rather the reverse, a sustained and licensed engagement with the irrational. There, in the middle of the Museum of Natural History in the middle of the afternoon, the lights would go out, a simulated Central Park would surround me, and one by one the stars would come out. It was as romantic a vision of Manhattan at night as any by Walt Whitman, George Gershwin, or Woody Allen. But it wasn't science. There were facts, and plenty of them, but these facts mostly proclaimed an inconceivable vastness. They blinded me with science. These facts were mind-altering substances and when combined with the immersive visuals emitted by the Zeiss projector, well, let's say that hallucinogenic experience was masquerading as rationalist discourse.

There is a branch of spectacle that always ends up aligned with the project of education. The cosmic excesses of planetariums echo the cosmological dramas of so-called hard (science-based) science fiction. World's fairs have always been marketed as uplifting, informative experiences (never mind the midway). Since the eighteenth century, toys have often been valued as "rational recreations." The joys of large-screen cinematic entertainment have been brought back by IMAX films as well as such novelties as 3-D glasses but always in the Exxon-sponsored name of saving the planet. "Interactive" museums are trumpeted for their ability to engage the minds of their young visitors, but observers can't help but note that the main thing these children seem to be learning is how to push buttons.

Why, for at least the last three centuries, has this veneer of education clung to visual spectacle? Barbara Stafford attends to what she has termed "sensationalized knowledge" in the historical realms of entertainment and play. She describes the prevalent means by which spectacle became a means of "demonstrating truth" as "learning became the seductive coercion of perception."[1] The body was a part of the educational process—the mind had not yet been divorced from its perceptual and kinesthetic experience. So, for Stafford, such spectacles as interactive museums and IMAX entertainments are the last bastions of a sensationalized knowledge that explicitly incorporates mind with body. Stafford acknowledges that "all exhibitionism, whether functioning within art or science, possesses this double inclination toward irrationality and rationality," but her contention could stand even more emphasis.[2]

A utopian belief in the power of education is a legacy of the Age of Enlightenment, but in its privileging of rationality the Age of Reason seems to have produced, as an inevitable corollary, a suspicion of sensory pleasure, a distrust of bodily engagement. Such phenomena are not banished from the realm of experience, but they must be contained by, sublimated to, this faux educational project. Jackson Lears, in describing recent scholars of advertising and popular culture, shows that this legacy remains nearly intact. Such scholars could "sometimes fairly be said to harbor puritanical traits: a distrust of fantasy and sensuous display, a preference for production over consumption, a manipulative model of advertising as social control, and a masculine bias that led them to typecast the mass of consumers as passive and feminine."[3] They thereby implicitly "elevated the rational producer over the irrational consumer," and they embraced an ethic that devalued aesthetic experience.[4] But let's also note, as Stafford does, that the lowly conjuror and popular educators once "relied on the same battery of stunning newfangled devices to attract the consumer's gaze."[5] Perhaps educators, then and now, are the greatest of conjurors, producing illusions of education while actually feeding the public's phenomenal appetite for spectacle.

This is not meant to deny the very real educational effect of spectacular engagement. I could hardly agree more with Stafford's consideration of active perception and bodily intelligence—what she calls "good looking"— or with her skepticism regarding the discourse of a desensationalized knowlege. "[C]lassification and quantification were the Enlightenment's rational methods for controlling a mythic and carnal hypervisuality," she writes— the artificial infinity of the planetarium is thus contained by the cataloging of galactic types.[6] But Lears emphasizes that antimodernist tendencies co- existed in American culture with the rhetoric of rationalist progress. A barely disguised carnivalesque tradition showed itself in "scientific" demonstra- tions at world's fairs, which exemplified the "coming together of popular entertainments and popular edification in a corporate-sponsored pattern of progress. . . . The promise of magical transformation preserved the carniva- lesque tradition for a technological age."[7]

Industrial Light and Magic: what is evoked by special effects sequences is often a hallucinatory excess as narrative yields to kinetic spectatorial ex- perience. A consideration of special effects might help to restore a balance between the ideological critiques of representation (and narrative) that have long dominated cinema studies and a phenomenological approach that ac- knowledges that, as Steven Shaviro puts it, "Cinema is at once a form of per- ception and a material perceived, a new way of encountering reality and a part of the reality thereby discovered."[8] All too often film theory has sought "to ward off the cinema's dangerous allure, to refuse the suspect pleasures that it offers."[9] Despite the rhetorics of lack (in one discourse) and the empti- ness of spectacle (in another), he notes that what is really feared "is not the emptiness of the image, but its weird fullness."[10] Theory has performed its own acts of containment on unstable images, reducing fluidity to dichotomy and heterogeneous texts to univocal utterances.[11] Cinematic images are in- deed full and superbly weird: they are dreams that pull us toward the un- canny and the utopian. Something other than rationalist reduction is at work in these technological representations: some irrational aspect of technology keeps peeking out from behind the curtain.

Kaleidoscopic Perception

While special effects might seem like a mildly intriguing midway sideshow in the vast exposition of modernity, they exemplify some of the period's most pervasive rhetorics. The discourse of the modern overflows with evocations of delirium, immersion, and kinesis—apt metaphors for a civilization hurtling through a totalizing continuum called "progress." These were phenomena associated with the lived experience of urban concentration and industrial expansion. Technology becomes enveloping, inescapable, and incomprehensible, literally overwhelming. While the panorama may have provided one of the dominant metaphors for spectacular visual culture in the eighteenth and nineteenth centuries, it's worth remembering that the obscurity of the phantasmagoria was nearly as common a point of reference.

The dark distortions of the phantasmagoria are related to the brightly colored fragments seen tumbling in a kaleidoscope. The kaleidoscope itself was another important model of modernist perception, and its ephemeral collages possessed an immediate metaphorical value. Baudelaire, for example, was fascinated with them because, as Jonathan Crary reminds us, kaleidoscopes "coincided with modernity itself."[12] To "become a 'kaleidoscope gifted with consciousness' was the goal of 'the lover of universal life,'" that wanderer of urban landscapes known as the *flâneur*. The kaleidoscope became a machine that disintegrated any fixed perspective: "shifting and labile arrangements" became the new point of view.[13]

Kaleidoscopic perception—comprised of equal parts delirium, kinesis, and immersion—characterized the popular entertainments of the later nineteenth century, from expositions to magic lantern shows, panoramas, and travel tours. The descriptions surrounding immersive environments such as fairgrounds and amusement parks—distilled urban realms—were rife with delirious liberation, and while planners of vast world's fairs were inspired by rationalist visions of progress the midway nevertheless still beckoned and cacophony carried the day.[14] "The Fair is a succession of mental shocks," a contemporary journalist wrote, although he did add that these were, finally, "cumulative and educative."[15] According to one history, 1893 Chicago World's Columbian Exposition visitors could expect to encounter an array of strange buildings, peoples, and sounds ("the discord of . . . camel drivers and donkey-boys"): "Finally they would betake themselves to the Ferris Wheel, on which they were conveyed with smooth, gliding motion to a height of 260 feet, affording a transient and kaleidoscopic view of the park and all it contains."[16] The climactic and pleasurable circuit on the Ferris wheel does not restore order but underscores fragmentation and "kaleidoscopic" disunity. The loss of one's bearings is central to the experience.

Emphasizing delirium, kinesis, and immersion allowed mass culture to soothe some anxieties. But upon further consideration they also demonstrated a developing taste for delirium, kinesis, and immersion. At a time of increasing concentration of power and control, popular recreations offered oceans of irrational pleasures.[17] Technology was usually the vehicle for these effects, but this might be a technology unleashed against itself, against the rationalist control that usually adhered to technological culture. Special effects, usually nested within the rational discourse of science fiction narratives, possess a similar gesture toward an antirationalism, even an antimodernism. Terry Castle has analyzed "the invention of the uncanny" in Western Europe during the eighteenth century and locates a pervasive representation of the underside of rationalist, secular, Enlightenment values. She elaborates: "the aggressively rationalist imperatives of the epoch—also produced, like a kind of toxic side effect, a new human experience of strangeness, anxiety, bafflement, and intellectual impasse."[18]

Extending the boundaries of the known reminds us of all that remains unknowable. From the eighteenth to the twentieth centuries, science continually expanded the realm of the visible through measurement, representation, and revelation, using telescopes, microscopes, thermometers, X rays, photography, cinema, and digital modeling. Yet we live in the awareness that we are surrounded by the unseen, the immaterial, the phantasmatic. As Terry Castle writes, "The more we seek enlightenment, the more alienating our world becomes; the more we seek to free ourselves, Houdini-like, from the coils of superstition, mystery and magic, the more tightly, paradoxically, the uncanny holds us in its grip."[19] Castle argues that the symptoms of this repression were everywhere evident—for example, in the ghost stories and phantasmagoria of the eighteenth century. As Tom Gunning notes, they were equally present in the spiritualist photography of the nineteenth century, and—I would add—they find new expression in the hallucinatory special effects of twentieth-century SF and horror films.[20]

As noted in the previous chapter, cinema was regarded as something of a special effect by its initial audiences, even such skeptics as Maxim Gorky. The illusion of motion, and especially movement in depth (as Tom Gunning has noted) was sufficiently novel for audiences who brought to the cinema their own familiarity with panoramas, dioramas, phantasmagoria, amusement park rides, and other spectacular novelties.[21] Despite the seemingly inexorable movement toward a narrative structure that could ground these effects, this "aesthetic of astonishment" should neither be discounted nor relegated to the realm of "excess." Special effects emphasize real time, shared space, perceptual activity, kinesthetic sensation, haptic engagement, and an emphatic sense of wonder. The impact of these spectacles has only been redoubled in the era of IMAX, ridefilms, and a range of new, immersive, theme park attractions and other themed environments (such as the more recent hotels of Las Vegas, such as The Bellagio, The Venetian, and New York New York).

The Pleasures of the Spectacle

When the stolid spacemen of *Forbidden Planet* (Fred M. Wilcox, 1956) are given their tour of the wondrous technologies of the Krel, the camera performs a fascinating, slightly oblique roll from its omniscient vantage point high above the humans. Energies surge and mysterious objects shuttle through a space that is described as a cube of twenty miles per side. Until now, the camera had been notably static, and the film was reliant upon its striking wide-screen scenic design for its impact. Now, however, the power of the Krel seems to summon a corresponding cinematic power, as "we" crane and turn to encompass this immensity. The shot, of brief duration, still involves an array of effects—miniatures, mattes, animation, sound effects, and camera movement combine. Despite its Cinemascope proportions and Technicolor opulence, this shot is remarkably similar to one in the low-budget *The Incredible Shrinking Man* (Jack Arnold, 1957). Here, a diminutive Scott Carey escapes the family cat only to plummet down the basement stairs to land atop a pile of rags within a wooden crate. When he returns to consciousness, the camera takes on his perspective, looking upward at the newly formidable, clifflike walls of the crate. Again there is that small roll of the camera. Where the Krel laboratories are monumental and sublime, the basement is shrunken and domestic. Where *Forbidden Planet*'s camera is omniscient, *Shrinking Man*'s is subjective. And yet there is something strikingly similar about these shots. Both evoke a vertiginous sense of displacement and defamiliarization that is, when it works, the science fiction film's most significant accomplishment. But there is also something liberatory about these movements, especially in the contexts of the mundane camera work that precedes them both. If they destabilize us, then it should be acknowledged that we welcome the effect. We are moved away from the mundane, away from the ordinary—in some sense, we are moved away from the narrative and into the pleasures of the spectacle.

That slight twist of the camera suggests the visual play of the kaleidoscope. These are brief examples of something encountered in more extended form

Figure 9. The mighty machinery of the Krell in *Forbidden Planet*.
(Courtesy of Metro-Goldwyn-Mayer.)

in such films as *2001: A Space Odyssey* (Stanley Kubrick, 1968), *Close Encounters of the Third Kind* (Steven Spielberg, 1977), and *Altered States* (Ken Russell, 1980). The archetypal kaleidoscopic effects sequence, as found in these films as well as *Brainstorm* (Douglas Trumbull, 1983), *Johnny Mnemonic* (Robert Longo, 1995), *Contact* (Robert Zemeckis, 1997), and countless others, features a first-person camera engaged in a relentless movement of forward penetration, distortions of the visual field, and a distended sense of time.[22] The main characters take kaleidoscopic journeys, adventures of exploration in relation to monoliths, motherships, virtual realities, and the inner spaces of the human psyche. These are not so much journeys *to* other places or societies as flights *from* the strictures of instrumental reason.

Like kaleidoscopes, science fiction films are "toys" based in what Roger

Caillois categorized as *ilinx*—that is, something "creating vertigo by scrambling ordinary perceptions."[23] Science fiction cinema combines ilinx with mimicry (games of alternative realities) to create kaleidoscopic worlds comprised of inventive design and especially pervasive motion. Whether the movement belongs to the on-screen artifact or the camera that investigates it, optical effects sequences generate revelation through kinetic exploration. The panoramic space sequences in *2001* are the most sustained and astonishing. The drifting camera seems to be engaged in elegant and casual description, but at the same time it keeps moving in a single direction, leading to something—new objects, a different location. Each shot offers the film's odyssey in miniature.

Kaleidoscopic perception takes over with "the ultimate trip" of the Stargate sequence, a sublime and psychedelic display that propels Dave, the sole surviving astronaut, from Jupiter's orbital space to somewhere "beyond the infinite." The slitscan animation by Douglas Trumbull renounces traditional representation in favor of abstract forms that somehow evoke, at once, outer space, Oskar Fischinger, and the streaking, strobing neon of a nighttime car trip. Dave's face is frozen in contorted terror, his incomprehension evoking Arthur C. Clarke's axiom: "Any sufficiently advanced technology is indistinguishable from magic" (Clarke was, of course, *2001's* coauthor).[24] Arrayed lines of light emanate from the vanishing point along the screen's center horizon, and the effect is one of infinite expansion combined with relentless enclosure. Later in the eleven-minute sequence, tinted tracking shots above tundra, volcanic fields, and Monument Valley suggest our arrival at another world, unpopulated, caught between seismic upheaval and luminist repose.[25] Without a doubt, *2001* features the most vertiginous effects since *Ballet Mécanique*, the 1924 film by Fernand Léger and Dudley Murphy of which Jean Epstein growled, "Anyone enchanted by this abstract cinema should buy a kaleidoscope."[26]

The space station seen turning elegantly in Earth orbit near the start of *2001* recalls the Ferris wheel of 1893. Here, again, on this transplanetary ride, movement is relative, exhausting, and inexhaustible. In Stan Brakhage's *Anticipation of the Night* (1958) amusement park rides offer an unstable place of perceptual renewal, playful and disturbing, providing access to the "adventure of perception."[27] Cinema inherits the kaleidoscopic possibilities of amusement park rides—the moving image could initiate the same delirious renewals of visual and haptic perception.[28] *Anticipation of the Night*, with its hurtling drive into the forest and the night and out into morning, foreshadows (as does so much experimental cinema and animation) *2001's* journey through the Stargate—exaggeratedly subjective cameras journey into unknown territories. Both are lyrical and mesmerizing. *Dog Star Man* (Brakhage, 1964), far more complex than *Anticipation*, is nearly contemporary with *2001*, and there are important rhymes here, too: hypnotic and extended allegories structured around an upward, explicitly evolutionary, striving. Both juxtapose the spiritual with the carnal. Brakhage's more recent painted films, including *Night Music* (1986) and *Rage Net* (1988), are kaleidoscopic cinema at its most literal (i.e., at its most abstract), Stargate sequences without telos, their quality of attraction left intact, even accentuated, by the immersive scale of the 35mm screen.

Topsy-Turveydom

The escape from narrative logic (and logos) is hardly restricted to experimental cinema or science fiction. Perhaps the persistent expression of the uncanny is a form of resistance to authority and control—the very authority and control instantiated by the ruthless and ostensibly impersonal "logic" of a deeply instrumental reason. Certainly both *Anticipation of the Night* and *2001* explicitly depend on perceptual disorientation through a "pure cinema" that defies cognitive understanding.[29] Castle sees masquerade sequences as introducing "a curious instability into the would-be orderly cosmos of the eighteenth-century English novel." The masquerade is "the exemplary site of mutability, incongruity and mystery," "an unrecuperable textual event," and I see a relation to the later event horizon represented by special effects—"the sense of discontinuity and paradox may be intensified to a hallucinatory degree," and their colorful excess "adds an element of spectacle to the ordinarily quotidian landscape" of the work.[30]

What links these episodes, attractions, and genres is a phenomenological excess that alludes to a reality beyond the ordinary—"a world of endless, enchanting, metamorphosis."[31] This is very similar to Samuel Delany's conception of the paraspace in science fiction—a materially constituted other space, a field of heightened rhetorical performance where conflicts of the real world are played out, and in which the death of the subject (as we generally know and love it) is figured.[32] Paraspaces redefine and extend the realms of human experience and definition, obliterating any vision of fixed space, subjectivity, or language as new, radically mutating, ontologies emerge.[33]

So it is interesting that Castle describes the residue of the masquerade scene as "a world upside down" that represents a carnivalization of English narrative.[34] "The masquerade offered eighteenth-century culture an anti-image of itself: a kind of licensed topsy-turveydom . . . in which the very principles of order and distinction might be challenged." At the heart of the masquerade narrative there lies a utopian impulse characterized by an ontological movement. Castle argues that "In a rigidly taxonomic, conceptually polarized society, it opened up a temporary space of transformation, mutability, and fluidity. It embodied, one might say, a gratifying fantasy of change in a world that sanctioned few changes."[35]

What Castle and Delany observe in the historically variant literary genres of eighteenth-century masquerade narratives and twentieth-century science fiction can be extended to other cultural phenomena and media, including phantasmagoria, amusement parks, and cinema. Gunning's "cinema of attractions"—a prenarrative, performative mode marked by a direct address—is an exhibitionistic cinema whose "energy moves outward towards an acknowledged spectator rather than inward towards the character-based situations essential to classical narrative."[36] Gunning concentrates on an early cinema that predates the full emergence of sustained diegetic illusion, but he acknowledges that the attraction survives "as a component of narrative films, more evident in some genres (e.g. the musical) than in others."[37] In this case, the musical possesses a utopian mutability similar to that of the masquerade. Dance is a kinetic tactic of liberatory trespass.[38]

Masquerades and musicals demonstrate that spectacle possesses a utopian dimension that reveals itself through a resistance to narrative's authority. So where Gunning sees "tamed attractions" in the survival of such spectacular elements as musical numbers, montage sequences, stunts, or special effects, I see a more radical play.[39] Through their emplacement within an overall naturalism, it's possible to argue that attractions can take on a newly disruptive, interruptive function. The underlying assumption here is that narrative does not completely (or simply) contain (or tame) the energies characteristic of the attraction.[40] Spectacular elements that exceed the constraints of predictable and conservative narrative structures become expressions of utopian resistance through that licensed "topsy-turveydom."[41]

Castle and Gunning have both discussed the persistence of the uncanny in popular entertainment. While the supernatural was replaced with an emphasis on material explanation, Castle argues that this did not represent the dispelling of the uncanny but rather its diversion or displacement "into the realm of the everyday. Even as the old-time spirit world is demystified, the supposedly ordinary secular world is metaphorically suffused with a new spiritual aura."[42] She further notes what she calls the "technological embodiment" of this "spectralizing habit" in such image-producing machines as photography, cinema, holography, and virtual reality. Cinema has continued to reflect on its "spectral nature," as Castle puts it, in trick films and ghost stories.[43] Cinema always combines the material and the immaterial, the solid and the phantasmatic, the permanent and the ephemeral, the rational and the uncanny. Gunning and Castle agree that despite its scientistic underpinnings this is a "fundamentally uncanny" medium. Geoffrey O'Brien puts it eloquently: "Upon the motion picture—the most alluring mechanism of the age of mechanical reproduction—would devolve the task of reconstructing the imaginary worlds it had helped to dismantle."[44]

Movement and Utopia

That sense of the uncanny and nonrational is continually enacted, performed, by way of kinesis. Special effects sequences *move* (again, they exaggerate a fundamental property of the *movies*). Think of *Star Wars* (George Lucas, 1977) or even *Forbidden Planet*. The spectator is put *in motion* relative to the world onscreen. Recent developments in multimedia entertainment, including ridefilm systems, have supplemented this cinematic address with real bodily movement. I have suggested that such bodily engagement presages and encourages conceptual understanding. The interaction with phenomenal reality becomes haptic as well as visual, while the familiar terrain of the body grounds the experience of the novel and unfamiliar. Immersive media thus serve as both a physical and conceptual interface with new technologies.[45]

But there is more at work in this delirious kinesis. Movement becomes more than a tool of bodily knowledge; it performs an idea of utopia. Utopian discourse forms a sturdy subgenre in SF literature and is one of the genre's originary threads. Yet cinema has not been nearly as generous with its utopian visions. The disparity is partly historical; while much of the early literature was informed by philosophical discourse, SF films were aligned with the happier, cheaper thrills of horror, Saturday afternoon serials, and action adventures.[46] Furthermore, while the literature emerged from the widespread technological utopianism of the late nineteenth century, the films arrived after World War II and Hiroshima, coincident with the paranoid formations of the cold war.[47] Giant insect movies expressed a dystopian distrust of technologies that literally ran amok over the countryside.[48] In the United States, 1950s' xenophobia, the countercultural critiques of the 1960s and 1970s, and the anticorporatism of the 1980s all fueled dystopianism, while corresponding utopias were in short supply. But perhaps a site of utopian projection might be found outside the narrative in the embodied, kaleidoscopic perception presented through special effects.

Douglas Trumbull's tripartite multimedia installation for the Luxor in Las Vegas (*Secrets of the Luxor Pyramid*, 1994) illustrates the difference between utopian content and utopian form. The narrative is built around an ancient crystal, a solar eclipse, and warm, fuzzy thoughts. The first section ("In Search of the Obelisk") is seemingly set far below the Luxor pyramid in mysterious catacombs. A fifteen-person motion platform facing a wraparound screen pitches and yaws in synchrony with the filmed movement of a hovercraft that zooms through vast and beautiful crystalline chambers while dodging some very dull bad guys (both human and cosmic). There are no fixed verticals and few points of reference—the central pilot figure serves as sufficient visual anchor for those who need one, but the peripheral visions are vastly more compelling—producing a glorious experience of kinesthetic distraction. In the last section ("Theater of the Future") three versions of a future city are presented in giant screen splendor (one reminiscent of *Blade Runner*). The ultimate vision of organicist buildings nestled in a green environment is too common a utopian projection, however, and the glassy architecture is too reminiscent of the distinctly nonutopian Vegas Strip lying just beyond the doors. Nevertheless, *The Secrets of the Luxor Pyramid* remains effectively utopian. If the images of utopia are irreducibly banal, the experience of a kinetic, delirious, immersive, and yet still magisterial vision retains its affect. Ironically, the dystopian sequences, because they're envisioned through identical techniques, are therefore equally utopian. Cinematic utopia is thus not a function of what is described but of how.

There is some precedent for understanding kinesis in this way. Louis Marin argues that the "Utopic figure is simultaneously of the narrative and of the descriptive domain."[49] Movement is the fact of traversing terrain, crossing borders, and transgressing boundaries. Movement performs freedom, a resistance to strategic spaces of control. World's fairs and theme parks celebrate a tactics of movement—they aren't mapped in a linear fashion and they can't be taken in with a single, immobile glance. Of course, they also further the strategies of control by containing and predetermining the tactical decisions of their visitors (Fantasyland "or" Frontierland?). But strategies and tactics are always locked in a dialectical development; strategic control must always be threatened by tactical transgressions that must as surely be contained. And so it goes.

Narrative, no less than spectacle, is itself often defined by such kinetic transgression. Marin discusses the operating tension in narratives of utopia: these spaces must accommodate two incommensurable desires, for both infinite expansion and totalization and closure. The utopia is bounded; it maps and describes a totality: "The utopian representation always takes the figure, the form, of a map. In the complex unity of its ensemble . . . It gives a location to all journeys, all itineraries, all voyages and their paths: all are potentially present because they are all there, but implicitly it negates them all."[50] The utopia is always bounded; it describes, maps, contains, and inscribes a totality. But the absolute, atemporal, and inhuman spatiality of the map is transformed by the journey, the narrative of movement, that returns to absolute space a relative temporality, the duration that is proper to Bergsonian consciousness.[51] Boundaries are opened to a potential infinity of trajectories that can be called, after Michel de Certeau, space narratives. "The story does not . . . limit itself to telling about a movement. It *makes* it. . . . What the map cuts up, the story cuts across."[52] Hence *Blade Runner* (Ridley Scott, 1982), a film about the boundary definitions of the human, begins with the totalizing view, the map view from above, before moving to extract its narrative figure. An opposition arises between the reassuring boundary represented by the frontier (law) and the unreachable, and thus infinitely distant, line of the horizon (liberty): "The limitless horizon is one of the main characteristics of the romantic landscape, an indefinite extent related to the display of a transcendence at this extremity where it seems possible to have a glimpse of the other side of the sky, a 'beyond-space' encountered through the poetic and rhetorical figure of the twilight, in terms of which a bridge seems to be established between the visible and the invisible."[53] Marin's language is remarkably, perhaps deliberately, evocative of the "beyond spaces" of science fiction film, the "glimpse" that the genre provides of the invisible realms beyond the infinite. Cinema is both corporeal and ethereal, an equivocal bridge between realms of experience (*And when he had crossed the bridge*, the intertitle from *Nosferatu* reads, *the phantoms came to meet him*).

Trumbull's effects sequences center on massive technological objects or environments: his work extends the histories of both the romantic sublime and the technological sublime in American culture. Technology marks the limits of human definition and comprehension, but through the unfolding of the effect it becomes susceptible to the control inherent in the act of seeing.[54] When Marin writes of the doubled connotations of utopian spatiality in Thomas More and Edward Bellamy, his language also summons up Trumbull's fantastic topographies in *Blade Runner, 2001,* and *Close Encounters.*

> Utopia *as a city or landscape* develops and displays a virtual or potential spatial order. . . . It offers to the beholder-reader an ambiguous representation, the equivocal image of significations contrary to the concept of "limit": on the one hand the synthetic unity of the same and the other, of past and future, of this world and the beyond (and the frontier would be in this case the place where conflicting forces are reconciled), and on the other hand the active tracing of differences, the indefinite fight between opposite forces (in this case the frontier would open a gap, a space "in between" that could not exist except by the encountering of violent and resisting forces.[55]

In Trumbull's extensive, overwhelming tours of futurity—in *2001, Close Encounters, Blade Runner, Silent Running* (Douglas Trumbull, 1971), and his ride-films—the technological environment extends to and beyond the limits of the frame. The "limit" is immediately negated as the camera begins to move across the wide-screen expanse as well as into the deeper regions of the space. A tension is generated between a totalizing technological environment that can be taken in by a single, magisterial, omnipotent glance (as at a painting) and the trajectory of movement that explores, expands, and temporalizes that space.

Fredric Jameson has defined science fiction literature in terms of a similar spatial practice that permits an omniscient and totalizing gaze to take in the immensity of alternate futures or new worlds.[56] Marin, exploring the imperative of description in utopian discourse, writes of the contained space of utopia: "It would be a limited space where nothing would be beyond its frame. [Thomas] More says it this way: everything 'under the eyes of all.' No area is left hidden from the gaze which is not included anywhere, but which views the whole as a surface."[57] The omniscient and revelatory moving camera of SF film is a function of utopian discursive practice: a gaze from which nothing is hidden but that is not "included" within the fixed space itself. Geoffrey O'Brien describes filmgoing as "a more futuristic experience" than attending the circus or theater—the filmgoer becomes a "lone space traveler strapped down and watching the universe roll by outside his porthole."[58]

Utopian planning, whether fictional, proposed, or actually built, has often tried to contain the ambivalent energies that Marin describes. Consider European and American town planning in the nineteenth and early twentieth centuries: even preceding Bellamy's influential *Looking Backward,* utopia becomes an ode to radial symmetry and centralized planning.[59] Single-purpose zoning links otherwise divergent cities by James Silk Buckingham (Victoria), Ebenezer Howard (Garden City), and Le Corbusier (Radiant City). The "city" at the center of King Camp Gillette's proposed urban overhaul, described with zeal in *The Human Drift* (1894), doesn't even get a name: a hive of building types with precisely defined functions are arranged in repetitive hexagonal blocks to create potentially endless, repetitive neighborhoods, districts, and cities.[60] Obsessive and monotonous self-similarity pervades these spaces, producing a reductio ad absurdum of instrumental reason. Small wonder, then, that the dynamics of movement should become a counterutopian signifier against these locked-down signifieds. Boundaries and control yield before an act of movement that denies their very premises.

So utopia is less a place, a fixed site, than a trajectory. Actually, it's a field of possible, and multiple, trajectories. Robert Nozick has described the metautopia, "utopia" as a "framework for [multiple] utopias," and America, "the promised land," is perhaps *the* metautopian construct.[61] Following William James and D. H. Lawrence, Gilbert Seldes wrote of America that it was a land of "pluralities" and of the American that "He not only can make something of himself, he can make himself over."[62] America is a site of masquerade and self-transformation: citing Seldes, Ann Douglas writes that "the 'natural self' of the American was an actor, too. Citizenship in America was an almost infinitely multiple act of impersonation; the essence of the stable American identity was to have no stable identity at all."[63]

The Right Stuff

With the kinesis of spectacular visual effects, often accompanied by a sense of utopian possibility, movement becomes a passage across borders that promises resistance to external control. While this has reached an absurdly ahistorical apotheosis in recent American action films, some work has successfully explored the issues of freedom and American identity. In *The Right Stuff* (1985), Philip Kaufman's film based on—but very different from—Tom Wolfe's history of the Mercury space program, movement is linked explicitly to transcendence and implicitly to the spectacularity of cinema. The film begins with scratchy black and white footage, shot and projected in Academy ratio, until, with an airplane crash and red fireball, it explodes into color, multiple-channel sound, and 70mm Panavision. *Superman* (Richard Donner, 1978) begins with a similar shift from black and white footage explicitly figured as both historical and movie memory. The variable ratio of these films recalls John Belton's evocation of a 1926 screening of *Old Ironsides:* "Scenes of the launching of the USS *Constitution,* moving under full sail directly toward the camera, and the climactic sea battle were projected on [an] expanded screen with the wide-angle Magnascope lens."[64] Belton describes an address turned suddenly more direct: "The cumulative effect was that of an illusion of the image's movement into the space of the theater auditorium, breaking down the spectator's sense of the barriers of the proscenium."[65] (Old Ironsides seems to be a utopian inversion of the riverboat that plows through Huck Finn's raft, oblivious to the destruction it has wrought.)[66]

The special effects in *The Right Stuff* are diversely styled and similarly heterogeneous. The hyperrealistic earthscapes and miniatures seen in the orbital flights were produced, as were most effects in the years following *Star Wars,* through computerized motion-control cameras and blue-screen processes. Scenes of the X-1 rocketing to break the sound barrier go for a more historically accurate look, with the plane slipping in and out of the film frame to emphasize a devastating propulsion that always threatened to move out of control. One can almost see the invisible barrier in the air before the plane, and when that barrier finally crumbles the plane soars forth with determined and purposeful, yet also celebratory, grace. A dichotomy is established: two worlds on either side of the barrier, one subject to physical shock and embodied limitations, the other liberatory and effortless.

There is a third space, however, a liminal space that few of the film's characters are privileged to witness. As *über* test pilot Chuck Yeager pushes the X-1 to its limits, and as astronaut John Glenn moves toward earth orbit, *The Right Stuff* conveys the subjective transcendence of the transit outside the envelope—that domain lying on just the other side of the possible—the ephemeral passage into the world beyond. That passage is marked for the viewer through the imagery created by Jordan Belson. An abstract filmmaker since the late 1940s, Belson had been experimenting with music and color for decades. In 1957 he was the visual coordinator for the "Vortex Concerts" at San Francisco's Morrison Planetarium, filling the dome with hypnotically undulating patterns. (Among other things, he "filmed long scroll paintings through a kaleidoscope to produce dazzling flows of richly textured imagery.")[67] His later 16mm trance films, including *Re-entry* (1964), *Samadhi* (1967), and *Cosmos* (1969), encourage a meditative posture; shifting luminiscences remain a compelling point of mental and perceptual focus while quietly distorting the field of visual perception.[68] Science fiction filmmakers had been aware of Belson for some time: some of his existing footage had been used in the charmingly low-budget *Journey to the Far Side of the Sun* (Robert Parrish, 1969) as well as the *2001*-inflected *Demon Seed* (Donald Cammell, 1977). *The Right Stuff* was the first feature that he had worked on, as well as his first experience with 35mm production. He was an intriguing figure to invite onto a mainstream Hollywood production, because of both his relatively low-tech relation to cinema and his nonrepresentational approach.[69]

The gorgeous, streaky, intense blue that Yeager sees after surpassing the speed of sound fully conveys the transcendental mythologism of the test pilot sequences (see color fig. 4). At first Belson's footage (it's hard to call it imagery) is framed by the controls and cockpit windshield, but after a cut to Yeager's goggled face the blue is unbounded—unmediated—extending to the limits of the Panavision frame. The sequence not only represents (and presents) a transformed, distorted perception. It transforms the film into a more heterogeneous and self-aware text. Belson's work, lyric, abstract, and nonobjective, is reinvigorated by its narrative "setting" (setting as in the setting of a precious stone). If, in the narrative, it *represents* a utopian transcendence and the penetration of a new frontier, as narration it *presents* a utopian transgression of the realist representational codes that dominate narrative cinema.

The central problem confronted by *The Right Stuff* is how to resist corporatism within a fully technologized world. What becomes of the individual, and what "space" becomes proper to its (his?) survival? The film depends on an alternately ironic and beatific evocation of American frontier mythology to produce a sense of embattled masculinity in a world that has displaced power from people to systems (technocracy, mass media, politics). The horizon line of the desert across which Yeager's horse gallops and the horizontal line of the airplanes and the paths they trace across the sky are challenged by the vertical onslaught of the booster rockets that cannot be actively piloted, only passively ridden.

The rugged, individualist test pilot Chuck Yeager (played with leathery cowboy conviction by Sam Shepard) confronts his (or is it "the") future as his horse picks its way down a path. The telephoto lens magnifies some distortion in the image, and only then does the camera reveal the squat, orange rocket-plane being fueled, liquid oxygen spilling onto the natural landscape. The sequence was Kaufman's conscious attempt to confront the end of the Western genre.[70] The juxtaposition of past and future (implicitly passing over the present) is also reminiscent of the famous bone/spacecraft jumpcut in Kubrick's *2001*.[71]

Yeager nearly "pushes the envelope" to earth orbit, but his is no longer the way. The film really culminates the orbital flight of Glenn, whose squeaky-clean, "Dudley Do-Right," team-playing character is constantly mocked yet is nevertheless permitted to literally reach the heights that Yeager was denied. What the film describes is a massive technological, technocratic system that solely exists in order to launch one man beyond its reach, beyond itself. Thus, Glenn's transcendence is not a transcendence of self but a movement beyond the authority and rationality of systems. Unlike a Western, however, this frontier can only be crossed or occupied through the resources and control provided by that very system.

In the true spirit of American cinema, this drama is played out on the male body (indeed, many of the most appealing male stars of the 1980s are featured in the film). That body is alternately eroticized and dehumanized: as it becomes increasingly technologized, it also becomes less active, less powerful. *The Right Stuff* has been criticized for its inconsistent tone regarding these men, but it is actually more incoherent than inconsistent—due not to artistic failure but to the incoherence of its foundational, masculinist mythos and America's incomplete confrontation with its own violent history.[72]

The Right Stuff is hugely reflexive, incorporating much American film history. In his book on the film, Tom Charity notes that the movie references films or images by Orson Welles, John Ford, George Stevens, Anthony Mann, and Stanley Kubrick, not to mention the genres of the Western, the war film, screwball comedy, documentary, and the New American Cinema.[73] This last is crucial, but is the incorporation of abstract imagery in *The Right Stuff* or *2001* more than an appropriation, a "taming," of the radical energies of such avant-gardists as Fischinger, Brakhage, James Whitney, or Jordan Belson? With the handmade films of Brakhage and the Vortex performances of Belson, two figures who emerged from the romantic, masculine rhetoric of abstract expressionism, the hero is the artist himself, flying solo, smashing (or maybe overflying) the barriers of convention. Brakhage scratched his signature into the very substance of the emulsion. Mainstream cinema does somewhat tame these energies: the narrative explains and grounds the alterations in perception and assigns them to the characters onscreen, but it also makes them less authored, weakening the connection to an individual artist-hero. Yet at the same time the quotation of avant-garde form invokes the romanticism of a lost individuality, especially in *The Right Stuff*.

Through its provocative reflexivity, *The Right Stuff* is finally as much about the technological, technocratic system of Hollywood as it is about NASA's early years. Perhaps the last great epic of the Machine Age, *The Right Stuff* is an emotional evocation of a temporary transcendence that describes a sublime but ephemeral passage beyond its own boundaries.

Conclusion

Marin and de Certeau (and Trumbull and Kaufman, for that matter) are not being naively utopian in recognizing something potentially positive in these movements across boundaries, borders, and frontiers. Because utopia, in Marin's definition, cannot be at rest, cannot be "finished," it challenges totalizing systems of thought, which must be regarded as reifying, reductive, and false. Because it "is one of the regions of discourse centered on the imaginary," Marin continues, "utopia will never become a concept," and so it can serve as "an ideological critique of ideology."[74] Leo Marx noted the inability of nineteenth-century writers to reconcile the conflict between pastoral fantasies and the fact of technological progress, an inability that "can hardly be accounted artistic failure. By incorporating in their work the root conflict of our culture, they have clarified our situation, they have served us well. To change the situation we require new symbols of possibility."[75] As the technological contours of existence become more pervasive, Marx's appraisal remains at least as valid. Mere kinesis hardly constitutes a prescription for change, but it does speak the possibility of, and necessity for, movement in other senses of the word. Instrumentalism is undermined by an antiproductive, antiteleological, kaleidoscopic passage. *Under the pavement, the beach,* the situationists proclaimed, and challenged the gridworks of urban life with an unbounded landscape of pleasure. Similarly, vertiginous effects can gesture toward a transgression of the "similarity of organization" that marks Hollywood narrative structures. Causality and logic are deemphasized in favor of a spatiotemporal unfolding that *feels* different than more familiar, more transparent, cinematic styles, that *means differently.*

We are bombarded, stunned into submission, by special effects; technological space moves through our passive bodies. But we also move with it and sometimes even move against its overdeterminism. Our utopian impulses are incompletely contained by the encompassing forces of corporate culture. Jackson Lears argues that the market economy is something other than a system of financial control; it's also a mythology tapping an existent reservoir of antimodern feeling: "one can glimpse alternative visions of abundance surviving amid the emergent consumer culture, vestiges of the carnivalesque, glimmers of magical transformation . . . certain kinds of commodities could still carry a charge of animation, could still connect the self to the material world."[76]

The special effects sequences of science fiction cinema are not literally utopian—neither are they, in fact, nonnarrative, antirational, or transgressive. Instead, they articulate, as an embodied knowledge, a utopian discourse of possibility; they present the possibility of utopia, not its realization. They show us what utopia might feel like.[77] So on some level, effects aren't "about" technology at all, any more than my love of the hyperbolic sky of the planetarium was about my devotion to the scientific method. My experience might well be something more like Gaston Bachelard's experience of poetry, which "has an entity and a dynamism of its own; it is referable to a direct *ontology*."[78] At work in the poetic is not causality but its opposite, a reverberation (*retentir*) that, for the receptive person, "brings about a change of being."[79] The poetic image speaks to embodied subjectivity, and in doing so it serves as an antidote to the biases of mind. Bachelard's "poetry" is thus not so different from Marin's "utopia": "poetry appears as a phenomenon of freedom."[80]

Science fiction is a notoriously rationalist genre, but in the kinetic delirium of many effects sequences, the genre detaches from disembodied, de-sensationalized knowledges. As Bachelard noted, "At the level of the poetic image, the duality of subject and object is iridescent, shimmering, unceasingly active in its inversions."[81] His prose is unapologetically, insistently, liberatory: "To the function of reality, wise in experience of the past . . . should be added a function of *unreality*, which is equally positive."[82] Special effects exemplify the function of unreality in representations of technology, an escape from technocracy through the window of technological immersion. Technology provides the occasion, and the material base, for the antirational act/fact of kinetic utopian transgression but still within the context of technological experience. Under the guise of rationalism, technology becomes a new source for exaggerated sensual and sensory pleasures. High technology provides an antitechnocratic liberation: technocratic nightmares are simply sidestepped—or overflown—by the boundary-crossing, antiteleological dérive of special effects.

THE GRACE OF BEINGS

THREE

Taking Shape:
Morphing and the Performance of Self

Perhaps the immobility of the things that surround us is forced
upon them by our conviction that they are themselves and not anything else,
by the immobility of our conception of them.

Marcel Proust

If the nineteenth century dreamed of cinema, then the twentieth was dreaming of morphing.[1] As with the trope of virtual reality, morphing articulates
and condenses an array of philosophical positions and some specific desires
and anxieties. Its place within the public and critical imagination tells us
plenty about fantasies of disengagement and reengagement with historical
as well as technological realities. Like virtual reality, morphing enacts many
of the contradictory impulses of contemporary culture. It *embodies* them—
but it disembodies them even more. Virtual reality, through its construction
of computer-generated environments into which the (properly augmented)
subject could enter, promised a total spatial plasticity that exaggerated the
spatial reconstructions of earlier twentieth-century aesthetic forms, especially cinema. Morphing, a computer-generated transformation of a photographic base image, brought that level of imaginary mutability to the body
and self. Again, like VR, it had its precedents: its reshaping of perception and
bodily form recalls, say, surrealist collage or the atemporal unfolded perspectives of cubism.

Morphing is illusive but also deeply elusive; its amorphousness resists re-
cuperative attempts to nail it down. It aspires to the condition of the floating
signifier, but this is its fantasy, one that has to be critically and historically
examined. Around virtual reality and morphing, images of reality, identity,
and history are put up for grabs by a mutability so apparently radical that
these categories appear to be superseded, even obliterated. Like so many tan-

talizing digital dreams, morphing holds out the promise of endless transformation and the opportunity to freely make, unmake, and remake one's self.

I want to consider various coexisting aspects of time-based morphing sequences.[2] Morphing is, first, a way of seeing over time, an exaggeration of everyday perceptions of continuity and discontinuity. The act of perception implicates the perceiving self and is fundamental to its definition. Morphing's hyperbole thus makes it into an explicit, condensed *performance of vision*. The same enhanced temporality also enacts a *performance of memory*, yielding further self-(re)generation.

But it is important to contrast the phenomenology of morphing, its performative elasticity and continual remaking of the self, and the ideology of the cultural narratives that contain and situate it. Actually existing morphing, as used in science fiction, horror, comedy, and TV commercials, is more a means of reification than liberation. Morphing and the other "transgendered" and "transracial" possibilities of electronic culture (what I have elsewhere referred to as terminal identity) stand, ever more evidently, as feeble attempts to do an end run around history's place in the construction of identity. Michael Rogin correctly notes that "Current writing on gender, race, and popular culture celebrates the subversive character of cross-dressing for allegedly destabilizing fixed identities. Such accounts need to consider history if they are to carry conviction."[3] I want to examine morphing's slippery masquerade through its performance of racial repression in Michael Jackson's "Black or White" music video (1991) and the Jim Carrey film *The Mask* (1994). Rogin reminds us that "Postmodern performance"—and morphing is a postmodern performance if there ever was one—"has an unacknowledged genealogy in the mobile, protean, modernizing self." Yet such "self-effacement can serve self-promotion," he continues, and "American self-making brought with it a dark underside" of enslavement, exclusion, and appropriation.[4]

Morphing the Self: Time, Perception, Memory

Morphing, first of all, shares something with time-lapse photography. Images that recorded change over time precede the development of cinema—there are daguerreotypes that record the successive stages of a solar eclipse and later the serial exposures by Marey and Muybridge. But time lapse takes on a new power with cinema's introduction. Jean Epstein, along with Dziga Vertov and René Clair, the filmmaker most obsessed by the temporal reconfigurations of which the cinema proved uniquely capable, wrote that "a short documentary film which describes in a few minutes twelve months in the life of a plant from germination through its maturity and withering to the formation of the seed of a new generation" presents "the most extraordinary voyage." The passage of time is magnified (and revealed to be relative, local, as in Einstein's understanding), while natural processes are translated to the scale of human perception. "Thus, until the invention of accelerated and slow cinematic motion, it seemed impossible to see—and it was not dreamed of— a year in the life of a plant condensed into ten minutes or thirty seconds of an athlete's activity inflated and extended to ten minutes."[5] Time-lapse photography provided a revelatory look beneath the humanly perceptible surface of natural development.

At the same time it also allowed a comprehension of the thing seeing as well as the thing seen because temporal continuity implies the existence of a consciousness for whom duration occurs. Epstein comes very close to overturning Henri Bergson's premature consigning of cinema to the realm of discontinuity (based, for Bergson, on its division of movement into discrete still images), and he anticipates Gilles Deleuze by decades. For Epstein, "the cinematograph seems to be a mysterious mechanism intended to assess the false accuracy of Zeno's famous argument about the arrow."[6] Within the consciousness of the spectator, discontinuity is effaced. Movement becomes *effectively* continuous, indivisible, and is furthermore an act—a fundamental act—of consciousness. "Experience," Deleuze writes, "always gives us a composite of space and duration."[7]

Duration is founded on what must be called a persistence of memory; "there is no perception which is not full of memories," Bergson pointed out.[8] "Our successive perceptions are never the real moments of things, as we have hitherto supposed, but are moments of our consciousness."[9] Time-lapse insists upon the relationship between vision and temporality and is thus a most obvious illustration of duration and the way it can produce the continuity and history central to a sense of self. A single frame cannot illuminate or inform in this regard: the sequence alone can do this.

Much the same is true of morphing. Morphing also makes explicit the temporal nature of visual perception, and, with that, it implies the centrality of history to the existence of the self.[10] And because morphing is frequently linked to one's body, as the object that morphs, the self is still more closely linked to duration. Bergson's language even prefigures morphing, as he describes the true self as one "in which *succeeding each other* means *melting into one another* and forming an organic whole."[11] While I will demonstrate that morphing continually refuses history in the traditional sense, Bergsonian memory continues to function: "These two acts, perception and recollection, always interpenetrate each other."[12] Without recollection the universe could only be a set of disconnected spatial forms existing in a permanent now. Consciousness, which perceives space and experiences duration, makes the self and the universe at once. Bergson's language again pushes into the terrain of morphing: perception and recollection "are always exchanging something of their substance as by a process of endosmosis."[13] *Endosmosis*, according to the *Oxford English Dictionary*, is "The passage of a fluid 'inwards' . . . to mix with another fluid on the inside of it" and so is not dissimilar from morphing, wherein elements of one picture mix with those of another.

The complex significance of this interpenetration is most apparent when a crisis of memory occurs, when memory endosmotically pushes itself out to morph the physical world into alignment with its own "substance." The most extraordinary literary example occurs at the beginning of Proust's *A la recherche du temps perdu*, as Marcel awakens: "I lost all sense of the place in which I had gone to sleep, and when I awoke in the middle of the night, not knowing where I was, I could not even be sure at first who I was."[14] Marcel describes a separation of self from the objects of the world: "I would . . . open my eyes to stare at the shifting kaleidoscope of the darkness, to savour, in a momentary glimmer of consciousness, the sleep which lay heavy upon the furniture, the room, the whole of which I formed but an insignificant part and whose insensibility I should very soon return to share" (4). But a more lingering insomnia gives him "only the most rudimentary sense of existence," and "I was more destitute than the cave-dweller" (5).

Marcel is rescued by a powerful act of memory, but before allowing him the luxury of reorientation memory first unsettles him further: "the memory—not yet of the place in which I was, but of various other places where I had lived and might now very possibly be—would come like a rope let down from heaven to draw me up out of the abyss of not-being" (5–6). A great gathering of times and places occurs, drawn from memory, history, and even books recently read, as "everything revolved around me through the darkness: things, places, years." Temporal rhythms jumble: "*in a flash* I would traverse centuries of civilisation, and . . . would *gradually* piece together the original components of my ego" (6). Marcel's body, distracted by its own weariness, is initially an unreliable guide to memory's morphoses: "Its memory, the composite memory of its ribs, its knees, its shoulder-blades, offered it a whole series of rooms in which it had at one time or another slept, while the unseen walls, shifting and adapting themselves to the shape of each successive room that it remembered, whirled round it in the dark. . . . Then the memory of a new position would spring up, and the wall would slide away in another direction" (6). In this "waking dream" of "shifting and confused gusts of memory," the "various suppositions of which it was composed" have the indivisibility of lived experience (7).

The neurologist Oliver Sacks has written the case study of a Mr. Thompson who could summon nothing from his long-term memory; his loss of duration manifested itself in a frantic remaking of his life from moment to moment: "He would whirl, fluently, from one guess, one hypothesis, one belief, to the next, without any appearance of uncertainty at any point."[15] Sacks points to the obvious need for a life story to bind our moments of experience and cites Luis Buñuel on memory: 'Life without memory is no life at all. . . . Our memory is our coherence, our reason, our feeling, even our action. Without it, we are nothing."[16] Without memory, Mr. Thompson must keep morphing: "Abysses of amnesia continually opened beneath him, but he would bridge them, nimbly, by fluent confabulations and fictions of all kinds. . . . Mr. Thompson, with his ceaseless, unconscious, quick-fire inventions continually improvised a world around him—an Arabian Nights world, a phantasmagoria, a dream, of ever-changing people, figures, situations— continual, kaleidoscopic mutations and transformations."[17]

Proust and Sacks both describe vertiginous self-transformation as a function of memory's temporary or permanent loss. Unstable memory transforms the perception of physical reality. Contemporary science fiction, however, describes an opposite "endosmosis," a morphing that alters physical reality, which then affects memory and thus the self. In today's cyberworld of digitally produced and stored multiple realities, the mere fact of physical existence no longer guarantees the persistence of a fixed self. Increasingly, the sign of memory replaces actual memories. In *Blade Runner*, replicants are indistinguishable from humans because they have been programmed with memories and given photographs: visual and tangible totems of artificial remembrances. But it's of course worth "remembering" that, even for humans, memories are not merely objective intrusions of the past into our present: we make them—with Marcel, we select and distort; we misremember. To a certain extent our pasts are constructions; to a certain extent, so, too, are our selves. Sacks wonders what can be done for his patients with severe memory dysfunction: "Can we create a time-capsule, a fiction?"[18] This is just what *Blade Runner*'s Tyrell Corporation has done for its artificial humans—created a fiction of time and history, encapsulated in/as photographs.[19]

If memories can be produced through programming, then "reality" becomes changeable, fungible; as a function of interpenetrating perceptions and recollections, reality can be morphed. Such "reality morphing" is central to the science fiction of Philip K. Dick. For example, *Ubik's* characters are caught in an accelerating process of reality erosion; temporality reverses its valence as first the objects, then the rooms, buildings, and city blocks around them appear in earlier and earlier manifestations. Only Ubik, a product that appears to be packaged in historically appropriate forms (aerosol, ointment, elixir), can briefly restore the present—Ubik cures the heartbreak of reality morphing.

Reality morphing can be, and often is, linked to metamorphoses of textuality. William Burroughs morphed reality by cutting up, folding in or otherwise altering the layout of words on the page. Philip Dick's screenplay for *Ubik* was to end with the film bubbling and burning to a halt, and Thomas Pynchon's *Gravity's Rainbow* ended with the film breaking just before the bomb hit. Reality is as ephemeral as the paper or celluloid it's printed on. In the Pirandellian comic book *Supreme*, Alan Moore has troped the increasingly common process of superhero history revision: each revision of a superhero's universe (from Batman to the Dark Knight and so on) is experienced by the occupants of that universe as a massive reality morph. "I fought evil in Omega City until 1941," the original Supreme tells the most recent one, "which is when my whole world disappeared! I found myself alone in an infinity of blank, white space! I was in limbo. This may sound crazy, but it was just like I'd been written out."[20] Actually, a new version of Supreme had just been written in. The newest Supreme visits his "hometown" to experience his newly revised existence: "I felt a long, peculiar life well up around me."[21]

In all these examples, Proust, *Blade Runner, Supreme,* it is the world that morphs and not the body. Bergson's self, constantly "melting," morphing, *enduring* (in the richest sense of that word), is not, in these cases, experienced as a mutating, morphing body. The body of the experiencing subject tends to remain a fixed and unchanging point of reference. "As my body moves in space, all the other images vary, while that image, my body, remains invariable. I must, therefore, make it a center, to which I refer all the other images."[22] The fixed body becomes the basis for continuity in the self, especially when measured against a discontinuous world.

Bergson also points out that a "slight change" in the body has a disproportionate effect on everything else. "The problem," he writes,

> might be stated as follows: Here is a system of images which I term my perception of the universe, and which may be entirely altered by a very slight change in a certain privileged image—*my body*. This image occupies the center; by it all the others are conditioned; at each of its move-

ments everything changes, as though by a turn of the kaleidoscope. Here, on the other hand, are the same images, but referred each one to itself, influencing each other no doubt, but in such a manner that the effect is always in proportion to the cause: this is what I term *the universe*. The question is: how can these two systems coexist, and why are the same images relatively invariable in the universe and infinitely variable in perception? . . . *How is it that the same images can belong at the same time to two different systems?*[23]

Bergson wasn't considering morphing bodies but the paradoxical relations between, as Deleuze puts it, "two fundamental characteristics of duration; continuity and heterogeneity" in psychological experience.[24] Morphing exploits this seeming paradox by *turning* one into the other (a literal troping): continuity *becomes* heterogeneity. Continuities of perception and body image melt and dissolve into kaleidoscopic mutabilities. So, as with time-lapse photography, a spectacle of continual transformation produces, at the same time, the continuity of a perceiving subject.

But time-lapse photography also reveals and explores the world that lies beneath the perceptions of the unaided human sensorium while morphing tends toward an obfuscating manipulation of surface; in a sense, morphing is a parody of time-lapse images. I would like to argue an analogy: perhaps as time-lapse images once revealed the underlying processes of the natural order, morphing now reveals invisible processes of electronic manipulation to our increasingly informed gaze. I would like to argue something like that, but I can't. For one thing, the special effects sequences of contemporary horror and science fiction may indeed be bursting with mighty morphing bodies galore, but in most cases it is an other who morphs and not (my) self. I'm fixed, I'm OK—you're not. Subjectivity is hardly reconfigured. In its most familiar examples, morphing is too seductive, too glossy, literally too empty. Through the literalism of morphing, as used in Jackson's "Black or White" or *The Mask*, difference is erased—heterogeneity becomes continuity. And even when it does produce some surplus "knowledge effect" regarding digital image manipulation, at this point the pervasive complexity of the society of the <www.spectacle.com> calls for something more than simple reflexive gestures to explain or encompass it.

Morphing Liberation: Movement of World

In an evident reference to Bergson's notes on the cinema, Proust distinguished between the smooth movement of a horse running from the isolated "successive positions of its body as they appear upon a bioscope" (7). *Biomorph Encyclopedia*, a 1994 CD-ROM by Nobuhiro Shibayama, confuses this distinction by using morphing technology to reanimate and reinterpret some of Muybridge's photographic sequences. The original sequences were, of course, produced with multiple cameras triggered in sequence to follow a movement, and so they divided motion into a series of discrete moments; within nature's continuity, Muybridge produced—seemingly *discovered*—images of discontinuity and division. His images were published, and often exhibited, in a sequential array of discrete steps that seemed to demonstrate time's divisibility. It was this false demonstration of discrete temporal steps that led Bergson to refer to the "cinematographic effect" in negative terms. Following the invention of cinema, Muybridge and others reanimated the images, restoring an experience of temporal flow from disconnected parts.[25]

By morphing Muybridge, creating new space and time between the original images (connecting the dots, one could say), Shibayama has produced something different from the stills or a cinematic reanimation. The original images have become a source for further experimentation rather than irreducible records of experience—they are somewhat devalued, their aura somewhat removed. Fabulously enough, Shibayama's morphing program can misinterpret what were once the stable elements of measurement within the image, such as background grid lines or some of the accidental irregularities of the ground or the movement—all these "stable," grounding elements now also warp and undulate. Shibayama also allows the user to morph chains of Muybridge sequences, bridging the gap between animal species and human genders. And so the sequences are continuous yet unstable: this is hardly a "natural" order of movement.

Morphing produces a more constant movement, more melting and transformative than discrete and intermittent. There is a continuity here, but also a marked, computer-programmed artificiality that preserves the discontinuity of the original images. The morph occurs as a real-time performance that doesn't need to be outputted to photographic stills, film frames, or any other "permanent" medium. Minor tweaking of the programming parameters can greatly alter the results. So the morph, as demonstrated by Shibayama, is repeatable, reversible, and variable as well as—forgive me— polymorphously polysemic. But because of all this it is also highly artificial, easily distinguished from the mundaneness of lived space-time and bodily grounding, which is probably why it has been reserved for the fantastic, the alien, and the illusionist. Somewhat like the cinema, but uniquely, morphing is both very like and unlike human perception.

This new movement is as different from Muybridge's original profilmic event as from his series of discrete photographs or their reanimation. The text that accompanies the *Biomorph Encyclopedia* argues that "Shibayama's experiments . . . reinvest a Bergsonian sensuality into Muybridge's analyses — remapping them into a continuous flow, a pulsing world. The effect is completely different than cinematically animating them. The same time, but a very different space is regained. Fluid space. Erotic and intensional."[26]

The *Biomorph Encyclopedia* is a beautiful illustration of Deleuze's writing about cinema and the "movement of world." In its articulation of duration, "cinema does not give us an image to which movement is added, it immediately gives us a *movement-image*. It does give us a section, but a section which is mobile."[27] Central to his understanding of movement are, among other things, musicals and the films of Jerry Lewis, which leads to an emphasis, rare in film study, upon performance and the movement of the body. Cinema constructs worlds of profound instability that constantly undergo transition and reconfiguration. "The shot, that is to say consciousness, traces a movement which means that the things between which it arises are continuously reuniting into a whole, and the whole is continuously dividing between things." Cinematic worlds, for Deleuze, are morphing worlds, in which movement itself is "decomposed and recomposed."[28]

In musicals, the motion of the dancer and the corresponding movements of camera, sets, and subsidiary players produce a participatory kinesis for the viewer but also a thoroughgoing sense of movement of and through and between worlds. The musical produces "a mystery of memory, of dream and of time . . . a point of indiscernibility of the real and the imaginary"[29]

What Deleuze observes in musicals is extended in his encounter with Jerry Lewis, a figure who emerges from the aesthetics of burlesque and musicals: "his smallest sketched or inhibited gestures, and the inarticulate sounds he comes out with, in turn resonate, because they set off a movement of world which goes as far as catastrophe . . . or which travels from one world to another, in a pulverizing of colors, a metamorphosis of forms and a mutation of sounds."[30] Deleuze further describes how with Lewis a new age is inaugurated: "This is no longer the age of the tool or machine, as they appear in the earlier stages, notably in the machines of Keaton. . . . This is a new age of electronics, and the remote-controlled object which substitutes optical and sound signs for sensory-motor ones."[31] Lewis's "new way of dancing" is involuntary, and this "movement of world on which the character is placed as if in orbit" produces Lewis's unique themes: "the 'proliferations' by which the burlesque character makes others swarm together, or implicates others who are absorbed; the cases of 'spontaneous generation' of faces, bodies, or crowds; the 'agglutinations' of characters who meet, join together, and separate."[32]

Elsewhere, I have argued that dance is where Lewis's grace and control emerge in fantastic balance.[33] Movements that first seem spastic become signals of emancipation; a precarious but exhilarating equilibrium is attained. Deleuze makes a similar point, although for him the brilliance of Lewis lies in the way he continues to function as a new sort of electronic automaton: "even the way he walks seems like so many misperformed dance steps, an extended and recommenced 'degree zero', with every possible variation, until the perfect dance is born."[34] More than any single figure, for me (and apparently for Deleuze) Jerry Lewis anticipates the electronic technology of morphing, going so far as to allow himself to be endosmotically absorbed in everything around him. He, too, is polymorphous and polysemic—locked in a spastic struggle between the twin containments of narrative and the body and the multivalent possibilities offered by cinema and performance. The indivisible fluidity of Lewis's camera movements and his play with music and movement are always accompanied by constant divisibility: the division of self into multiples and "agglutinations" and "swarms" (combining morphing and cloning), the staccato rhythms and failed improvisations, the lack of punch lines and effective narrative resolutions. In the complexity and irresolution of Jerry Lewis, the fluid and the discrete, the indivisible and the divisible, coexist in an uncomfortable electronic "circuit," what I once referred to as "paralysis in motion."[35] No wonder Deleuze notes: "It is here for once, that it can be said that Bergson is outstripped."[36]

"Black or White"

Morphing is a mode of performance that certainly puts the world into movement, but it is also a performance mode that depends on ideas of masquerade and mimicry. It is almost impossible to miss the connection between morphing and ethnicity in a world that has given us Michael Jackson and *The Mask*. Morphing allows a performance of ethnicity that at the same time defines *ethnicity* and reduces it to performance.

It's not about races / It's places . . . faces. "Black or White," Michael Jackson's fascinating music video (directed by John Landis), features morphing

Figure 10. Michael Jackson works the alley in "Black or White."
(Courtesy of Photofest.)

on every level and remains a highly unsettling, unsettled work. After a peculiar suburban prologue the scene changes to Africa, where we see Jackson in black and white—black hair, light skin, open and loose white shirt over a white V-neck and T-shirt, black belt, black pants, and black shoes with white socks (socks by Jerry Lewis?)—who lets loose with a Tarzan yell. Surrounded by "natives," he dances exuberantly and plays a little air guitar. He and his troupe run into an undefined grey area: an arbitrarily placed ladder connotes "backstageness." Jackson begins to dance with some Thai women. A cut puts him amid some Native Americans, and suddenly we're way out west, with dancers in celebratory garb surrounded by trick-ridin', gun-totin', war-whoopin' Injun riders. A few more transitions bring Russian dancers into a sequence that resembles Jackson's own Pepsi commercial and Pinocchio's stage debut, where he sang "There Are No Strings on Me" to demonstrate his near human status.

Soon Jackson appears on a Vegas-y, Disney-ish set of world landmarks: Statue of Liberty, Parthenon, Big Ben, Eiffel Tower, Sphinx, Taj Mahal. Then comes the utopian climax, as a series of GORGEOUS people of different races, genders, and apparent sexual preferences morph into each other as they lip-synch, concluding with the cry of CUT! ("That was perfect—how do you *do* that?" the director asks.) The pull-back that reveals the camera recalls the end of Jerry Lewis's *The Patsy.*

But it's not over yet. The camera cranes through the studio to a black panther, which wanders from the studio onto a street before morphing into Michael Jackson (now wearing black jacket and a lovely rose lip gloss). He moves into a superbly edited tap solo, reminiscent of Fred Astaire and Savion Glover, but the street set especially evokes Gene Kelly's double-exposure "solo" in 1944's *Cover Girl.* As in the Kelly number, significantly titled "Alter-Ego," a deserted street becomes a site for self-confrontation and an enraged vandalism that seems primarily produced by an unbearable self-loathing. Jackson dances, grabs himself, and, using a crowbar, repeatedly smashes the windshield of an abandoned car. There is no music, only the scuffing of Jackson's feet, assorted yells and screams, the occasional panther's roar, and the shattering of glass. Finally, Jackson morphs back into the black panther, which glances (glares?) at us and stalks off.[37]

In light of Jackson's subsequent legal problems, continued and increasingly scary surgical reformation, and growing reclusiveness, "Black or White," and especially the final solo sequence, take on added, and very real, poignance. The crotch-grabbing, glass-smashing violence so alarmed parents that Jackson apologized and removed it, leaving the "it's a small world," "family of man" morphing sequence as the finale. He never again attempted anything so risky, in which all the contradictions of his character were so nakedly, tormentedly, displayed. As I once remarked about the many endings of Jerry Lewis's *The Nutty Professor* (1963), the multiplicity of solutions reveals, finally, that there is no solution to these issues of racial and personal identity. The utopian morphing of all the pretty people is as enchanting and irresistible as the world beat riff that plays behind them, but its sunny message of hope is at least complicated by Jackson's dance. By dramatizing what seems to be a furious rejection of a benign, assigned role, by reclaiming a masculine, black, urban identity, Jackson unexpectedly performs a frightening *pas d'un* of isolation, entrapment, and refusal.[38]

Two passages from Deleuze, intended to discuss Vincente Minnelli musicals, have uncanny applicability to "Black or White." "Dance," Deleuze writes, "arises directly as the dreamlike power which gives depth and life to these flat views, which makes use of a whole space in the film set and beyond, which gives a world to the image, surrounds it with an atmosphere of world."[39] The dynamism of Jackson's performance indeed gives depth and a kind of life to the Disney-fied versions of ethnic cultures on exotic display, and the video certainly uses the space of the set and the space of the world. But morphing remains metaphorically pervasive: in a kaleidoscopic set of substitutions, world becomes set and set becomes world.[40] Meanings and identities are unfixed but in conflicting ways. While the dance joyously surges through locations and ethnic barriers, creating a homogeneous globalism, the heterogeneity of the entire video's structure, with its nine sections, produces at the same time a more tentative, uncertain set of positions. Not even the song creates a unity—it's absent from the prologue and the extended solo dance. Not even Jackson creates a unity—he's absent from prologue, epilogue, and morphing sequence.

The initial dance provides a great, clear example of the movement of the dancer that extends to a movement of world. Jackson's presence is both disruptive (he rarely dances in unison with the others) and unifying (his music and moves bind sequence to sequence, race to race). Deleuze writes that "what counts is the way in which the dancer's individual genius, his subjectivity, moves from a personal motivity to a suprapersonal element, to a movement of world that the dance will outline. This is the moment of truth in which the dancer is still going but already a sleepwalker who will be taken over by the movement that seems to summon him."[41] Jackson's trancelike behavior in his solo section does recall the figure of the sleepwalker (consider Cesare, *The Cabinet of Dr. Caligari's* pallid somnambulist). Yet what occurs via Jackson's dance is almost exactly the opposite of what Deleuze describes: the movement of world (through dance and morphing) loses its suprapersonal element and returns instead to a personal motivity. Something is being refused and regained in the final sequence and with a deeply emotional ambivalence. It's not impossible to believe that this was what was truly disturbing about it rather than Michael grabbing his penis.

Morphing Ethnicity: Masquerade, Minstrelsy, and *The Mask*

The morphing of Michael Jackson (in videos as in life) and in *The Mask* demonstrate that morphing carries to a logical (if irrational) extreme some long-standing traditions of appropriation, masquerade, and disguise. Michael Rogin has discussed the use of morphing technology on a 1993 cover of *Time* to create an ideal woman, an "All-American synthesis" that reflected the nation's racial makeup in proper proportions. The software program Elastic Reality has the user practice morphing between two head shots: one of a white man and the other of a black woman. Even in these examples, morphing presents racial identity only to neutralize it.[42]

The history of blackface performance reveals what fantasies of morphing are at least partly all about.[43] Robert Toll argues that elements of black culture infiltrated white culture via the minstrel show.[44] Philip Boskin concurs, noting that the minstrel show paved the way for ragtime's acceptance at the turn of the century. He further states that, "Within its humorous confines, whites could peer into black culture without much anxiety, subject their stereotypes to some skepticism, cope with ambivalent racial feelings, and appreciate the nuances of the black experience."[45]

Michael Rogin's view of blackface minstrelsy is rather less benign, and he convincingly links it to American frontier mythology, a mythology of domination. While the Indian conveniently disappeared from mainstream American (especially urban) life, the presence of blacks and unassimilated immigrant groups was increasingly part of quotidian existence.[46] Black-white relations became more central and strained, but they were consequently also more repressed: meanwhile, frontier mythology was sustained through Westerns, which luxuriated in portraying the noble (not to mention defeated and unthreatening) savage. Through gestures of inclusion (the "white man who knows Indians" or the infusion of black dialect and musical styles into

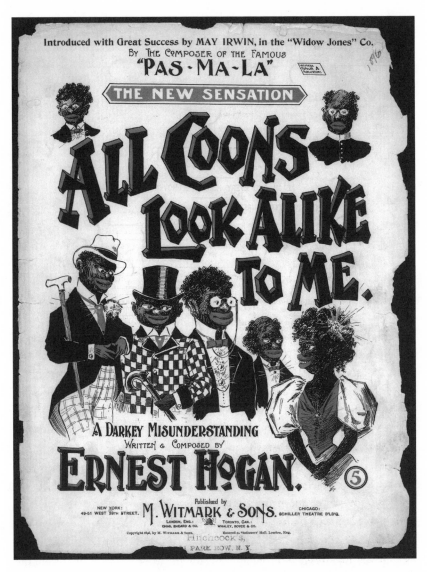

Figure 11. Sheet music for an 1896 "coon song."
(Courtesy of the Music Division, New York Public Library for the Performing Arts,
Astor, Lenox, and Tilden Foundations.)

white performance) blackface and the frontier myth brought together different races and ethnicities, but to Rogin they exemplified, in fact created, "the
distinctive feature of American multiculturalism: racial *division* and ethnic
incorporation."[47]

There is no denying white fascination with black performance styles as
blacks moved northward, into urban areas and increasing contact with
whites. Blacks were seen as exotic but attractive, their "vibrantly expres-
sive" mannerisms quite at odds with prevailing social conventions imposed
upon the "civilized" white citizens.[48] Blackface gave license to greater emotive
range in performance. But if "the minstrel expanded the white view of black
culture and comedy," it "did so within a preconceived formula,"[49] (The jeal-
ousy that whites directed toward their own stereotypes of the black man—his
characteristic erotic "abandon" and "primitivism"—turned into a continual
performance of mockery and emasculation. Here, too, the furor over Jackson's onanistic crotch-grabbing has its history.)

The rhetoric of primitivism that informed both modern art and Harlem
hotspots in the 1920s and 1930s increased black culture's visibility but kept
the condescension. "Almost without exception, popular-culture writing in
the 1920s treated Negro primitivism as the raw material out of which whites
fashioned jazz. Savage, not polyphonic, rhythm, was heard in black music."[50]
And this appropriation slash rescue extended to performance: "Burnt cork,
so the minstrel claimed, gave Apollonian form to the Dionysiac African,
making art from his nature."[51] There was indeed an "appropriative identification" at work; blackface became a means of participating, cross-dressing, in
black "experience." But note, as Rogin does, that this is identification as containment, and it is also blackness without blacks, ethnicity without race—
what James Snead called an "exclusionary emulation."[52]

Following the nativist lead, Irish and later Jewish immigrant entertainers
virtually took over blackface performance. By mocking the African American,
as white performers had throughout the nineteenth century, more recent immigrants aligned themselves with dominant culture, outdistancing their own
pariah status. Blackface furnished an opportunity to be both American and
outsider, or, Rogin adds, to become American by mocking the outsider. By
1910, Jews dominated blackface entertainment, and attention was deflected
from one stereotype (anti-Semitic) onto another (antiblack): in the 1920s,
"the black mask of deference enforced on one pariah group covered the ambition attributed to the other."[53] Yet Irving Howe finds something more than
mockery at work: "When they took over the conventions of ethnic mimicry,

Figure 12. "One woe speaking through the voice of another,"
Al Jolson in *The Jazz Singer*. (Courtesy of Warner Bros.)

the Jewish performers transformed it into something emotionally richer and more humane. Black became a mask for Jewish expressiveness, with one woe speaking through the voice of another. . . . Blacking their faces seems to have enabled the Jewish performers to reach a spontaneity and assertiveness in the declaration of their Jewish selves."[54]

Gilbert Seldes, writing on Al Jolson and Fanny Brice, found qualities of "daemonic" abandon and heat in their performances—they were possessed: "In addition to being more or less a Christian country, America is a Protestant community and a business organization—and none of these units is peculiarly prolific in the creation of daemonic individuals." Jolson and Brice, and we can add Eddie Cantor and the Marx Brothers, "gave something to America which America lacks and loves. . . . Possibly this accounts for their fine carelessness about our superstitions of politeness and gentility . . . [and their] contempt for artificial notions of propriety."[55]

This more generous, even heroic, view of blackface performance is easily aligned with Marjorie Garber's analysis of transvestite perfomance. The self-aware flamboyance of the cross-dressed figure is central to her analysis: "Excess, that which overflows a boundary, is the space of the transvestite."[56] The transvestite marks a "category crisis" for culture, "disrupting and calling attention to cultural, social, or aesthetic dissonances."[57] The most obvious disruption is to "the categories of 'female' and 'male,' whether they are considered essential or constructed, biological or cultural," but what is really at stake are all such "easy notions of binarity."[58] "Transvestism is a space of possibility structuring and confounding culture: the disruptive element that intervenes, not just a category crisis of male and female, but the crisis of category itself."[59] Michael Jackson, with his confounding of the categories of male/female, black/white, child/adult is exemplary (but, thank God, also unique). While Garber includes material from a broad range of Western cultural history, she wants to emphasize "an underlying psychosocial, and not merely a local or historical effect. What might be called the 'transvestite effect.'"[60] Her intentional ahistoricism is precisely what Michael Rogin writes against,[61] reminding us that "far from being the radical practice of marginal groups, cross-dressing defined the most popular, integrative forms of mass culture. Racial masquerade did promote identity exchange . . . but it moved settlers and ethnics into the melting pot by keeping racial groups out."[62]

Rogin astutely unmasks minstrelsy's fetishistic face. "There is a primal scene in every blackface musical: it shows the performer blacking up. The scene lets viewers in on the secret of the fetish: *I know I'm not, but all the same.* . . . What remains hidden, however, are the historical crimes embedded in the fetish's invidious distinction; here white over black parallels man over woman."[63] He echoes the case made by bell hooks regarding the suppression that ethnic citation, even politically correct ethnic citation, can entail: hooks argues that the attempt by nineteenth-century white women's rights advocates "to make synonymous their lot with that of the black slave was aimed at drawing attention away from the slave toward themselves."[64] Analogy did not produce an equivalence: as Rogin remarks of the corked-up performer, "it was whites in blackface, not mammies, who were allowed to perform the *separation* of self from role onscreen."[65]

Morphing as a mode of performance shares much with blackface performance: both work through analogy. But analogy marks a similarity (this is like that) as it also affirms a distance (but it is not that). Ortega y Gasset described analogy as a "mental activity which substitutes one thing for another from an urge not so much to get at the first as to get rid of the second. The metaphor disposes of an object by having it masquerade as something else."[66] Blackface is already a caricature, but one at least complexly informed by specific ethnic histories and incursions. Morphing, the latest incarnation of this

Figure 13. Zoot-suited Cab Calloway leads the band in *Stormy Weather*.
(Courtesy of Photofest.)

performative mode, disposes of even that already repressed history. By "rendering" everything as surface, and all surfaces as equal, morphing becomes a caricature of blackface. Morphing, a celebration of endlessly transmutable surface, becomes a sign only of itself, hardly even alluding to the complexities of history and ethnic culture behind its digital gloss.

Blackface, transvestism, and morphing all participate in analogy's subtle suppression (this is both but also neither), but morphing brings with it a new literalism (this *becomes* that; it *takes* shape). Appropriation becomes an act of complete erasure. Morphing confirms the validity of Rogin's arguments in the way that it literalizes the suppression that blackface had realized with more subtlety but less thoroughness.

The Mask provides an excellent example of Rogin's "ethnicity without race," as ethnicity itself becomes a mask to be donned and doffed with surprising facility. In the film, shy Stanley Ipkiss, played by the extraordinarily white Jim Carrey, finds a "primitive" wooden mask, which, when worn, transforms him into a green-skinned, zoot-suited parody of African American performer Cab Calloway. The film offers an explicit and misleading interpretation of its own themes before the plot even begins, as the author of *The Masks We Wear*

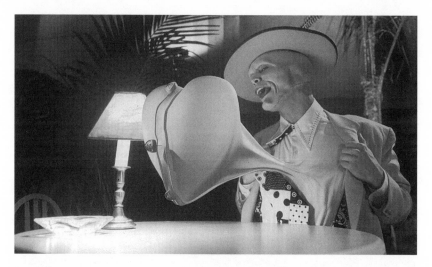

Figure 14. Greenface trumps blackface. (Courtesy of New Line Cinema.)

is interviewed on television explaining that masking is a means of suppressing the id; in the film, however, masking becomes a means of *releasing* the id. This is only the first of many recuperations or suppressions the film uses against more liberating slippages of self.

Calloway has himself been seen as a caricature, playing the fool for white audiences. In the all black Fox musical *Stormy Weather* (1943), for example, Calloway struts his considerable stuff while performing in an outrageously exaggerated zoot suit topped with massive shoulder pads and a bowtie at least a foot wide. The zoot suit was, by this time, fully associated with primarily Latino and black gangs in Los Angeles and other integrated urban areas. With its generous tails, wide lapels and baggy trousers, the zoot suit was a literal gesture of defiance in times of cloth rationing, and in the Hearst press and elsewhere zoot suiters were portrayed as subversives at war with (invariably) white servicemen. On Calloway, however, the zoot suit became just another costume.[67] Thus, the *outrage* of white readers of yellow journalism directed against ethnic subcultures was transformed into the more benign and harmless posing of the comically *outrageous*. Calloway, his hair flying in all directions, is easily seen as a parody of the ethnic wild man, an unrestrained id playing—this time—for laughs. Whether or not this view of Calloway is legitimate—and it ignores his skills as bandleader, composer, and singer—it is true that he served as quite the deracinated icon of "hep" in the 1930s and 1940s.

Calloway's own impersonation of the ethnic other is even more interesting in light of his appearance (in both senses of the word) in three Fleischer Brothers cartoons from the 1930s. The Fleischer cartoons are significantly funkier, and vastly more surreal, than the product from other studios such as Disney or MGM: things are continually transforming, or coming to life; they exist in uneasy but wondrous states of trembling impermanence. I've got to say it: they morph. In the Betty Boops in which Calloway performs, he appears first as "himself" and later as a rotoscoped, animated figure (rotoscoping, whereby photographic footage is traced, is an obvious kind of protomorphing). Max and Dave Fleischer were proudly Jewish New Yorkers—their cartoons are rich in ethnic flavor—and in the context of Jewish identification with black performance styles it's not difficult to see these acts of rotoscoping in relation to blackface as yet another entry in the history of cinematic minstrelsy. (In another Betty Boop cartoon, Koko is pursued by the disembodied head of Louis Armstrong. The Hebrew word for "kosher" appears on a speedometer that emerges from Koko's *tuchus*.)

So a remarkable trajectory is described: Carrey's white Stanley Ipkiss becomes an animated parody of the self-parodic Cab Calloway, who had himself already been transformed into a cartoon version of himself in the 1930s. In *The Mask*, however, morphing works to downplay the film's evident racial subtext. Carrey's character is not presented as a jazz aficionado but as a cartoon buff, with animation cels on his bedroom wall and a statue of Tex Avery's (again) zoot-suited Wolf character all too prominently displayed. When he morphs, the film's comedy depends on a level of exaggeration usually reserved for, and associated with, cartoons: the mask bounces off walls, floors, and ceilings, his eyes and tongue bug way out of his head, his heart pumps visibly (and is visibly heart shaped). Etcetera. In an altogether classic example of Freudian displacement and fetishism, the prominent cartoon references hide, or at least downplay, ethnic associations. Greenface trumps blackface.

The greenface/blackface masquerade of *The Mask* should also be juxtaposed with the Joker's whiteface/blackface in Tim Burton's first *Batman* film (1989). Actually, there are two blackface figures in the film: the Joker, with his pained and painted frozen Sambo smile and purple zoot suit (*again* with the zoot suit?), is once more a parody of a parody—the tragic clown, the blackface performer who can no longer remove the mask—while the more mysterious, darkly muscled figure of the Batman summons (and contains) the anxiety surrounding the Mandingo figure of black sexual power.

Based on a comic book from Dark Horse Publications, *The Mask* is also a kind of superhero remake of *The Nutty Professor*, but it is devoid of that film's unsettling ambiguities of identity. *The Mask* instead supplies an endless rhetoric of authenticity and sincerity: it's all about finding *the real you*. As an unchanged Ipkiss embraces an improbably attractive blonde, the finale manages to simultaneously reject ethnicity, the unconscious, morphing, *and* narrative plausibility. Unlike the more challenging and agonized works by Jerry Lewis and, indeed, Michael Jackson, *The Mask* entirely reifies the "authentic" self. In this light, Carrey's non-Jewishness is as important a suppression here as his alter ego's nonblackness: ethnicity and history are morphed out of existence on both sides. Here lie the limits of the "category crisis" that Garber emphasizes: erasure presents a category crisis but also its resolution.

Performance and Possibility

The endlessly regenerative self-creation of morphing thus permits history's elision and repression. We are not trapped by that history, but we do ourselves no service by denying it. Garber's utopian vision of category crises must contend more fully with the mythology of American self-invention and reinvention, a history that denies history's determinism, but she is hardly wrong in defining the crisis. Resolution and closure are hardly as totalizing as they pretend to be; pluralism and diversity are never entirely subsumed.[68] If containment is the goal, then there are areas of excess that require containing, and attempted containment is hardly tantamount to successful containment.[69]

Garber further argues that the "mechanism of substitution, which is the trigger of transvestic fetishism," is "also the very essence of theater: role playing, improvisation, costume, and disguise."[70] Theatrical performance is a licensed but still unsettling transvestism: "all of the figures onstage are impersonators."[71] The both/neither is fundamental to the demarcated spaces of performance and spectatorship. In *S/Z*, Roland Barthes muses on the radical potentials of narrative language, a potential almost invariably denied and suppressed by particular readings of inherently pluralistic texts: "the slash (/) confronting the S of SarraSine and the Z of Zambinella has a panic function: it is the slash of censure, the surface of the mirror, the wall of hallucination, the verge of antithesis, the abstraction of limit, the obliquity of the signifier, the index of the paradigm, hence of meaning . . . to choose, to decide on a hierarchy of codes, on a predetermination of messages, as in secondary-school explications, is *impertinent* since it overwhelms the articulation of the writing by a single voice."[72]

The text becomes a sustained performance of mis-taken identities: multiple valences and unstable analogies constantly edge up on (or transgress) the limits of assigned meaning. "Furthermore, to miss the plurality of the codes is to censor the work of the discourse: non-decidability defines a praxis, the performance of the narrator: just as a successful metaphor affords, between its terms, no hierarchy and removes all hindrances from the polysemic chain (in contrast to the comparison, an originated figure), so a 'good' narrative fulfills both the plurality and the circularity of the codes."[73]

Morphing melts through the "panic function" of the slash—it is mutable and repeatable and variable and reversible. All codes become potentially plural; they disappear at the moment they emerge. Garber writes that the transvestite performance is "always undoing itself as part of its process of self-enactment,"[74] but *S/Z* indicates that this might be true of all performance, albeit in less explicit ways. The duration common to semic chain, time-lapse sequence, morph, and performance provides "plurality and circularity" rather than a unidirectional and unchallenged telos.

The Mask, for all its morphological play, denies this dual valence of enacting and undoing. Here, transformation reinstates the slash of censure and repression, enforcing a tyranny of decision, hierarchy, and predetermination. Compare *The Mask's* tedious univocalism with, arbitrarily enough, someone like Carmen Miranda (not a cross-dresser, but certainly a muse for transvestite culture). Shari Roberts has demonstrated the conflict between reading Miranda as a sign of any actually existing ethnicity and the camp appropriation of her as a tutti-frutti Technicolor explosion of polysemic artificiality (her voice overwhelms by means of its hilarious incomprehensibility).[75] Miranda's playful masquerade points up the limitations of *The Mask*, in which narrative containment and fixed ideas of identity, authenticity, and ethnicity work together to suppress the more polymorphous phenomenologies of morphing and masquerades. The delirious, kaleidoscopic movement of the world is limited by predictability, stasis, and reification. The sense of denial that seems to be working overtime in *The Mask* is what makes it an immature, inferior work. Where Jerry Lewis and Michael Jackson put more of themselves into play than they can ever possibly contain and Barthes and Deleuze recognize polysemic richness, *The Mask* "settles" self and world within an unchallenging and ahistorical haze. "Black or White" provides something similar, at least until Jackson smashes that neat little fantasy with a crowbar.

But ideological determinism should not blind us to morphing's performative, durational aspect. Like musical sequences, they are extranarrative: more or less "justified" by the story but also more or less uncontained. While some film theories suggest that such heterogeneity, especially pronounced in the musical, is inevitably "contained" by some dominating structure (frequently the narrative), a distinction should be made between the *re*-presentation of already circulating cultural "meanings" and the dynamism of a self-aware and playfully fluid performance. Performance can become a highly pleasurable sign of its own constructedness, revealing all identity to be partly nonidentical—an at least somewhat artificial construction. Musical sequences, Betty Boop cartoons, time-lapse imagery, Marcel's nocturnal awakening, and the burlesque excess of Jerry Lewis all produce and perform "world as movement": they vibrate with possibility.

Through its fundamentally cinematic blending of heterogeneity and continuity, morphing can become a shimmering performance of unresolved transformation. Since our existence depends on our moments of self-definition "melting into one another," transformation is fundamental to continuity. We are never fully ourselves, never fully resolved. Morphing provides a profound illustration of our own irresolution without requiring that we accept its conditional instabilities as ahistorical absolutes. Transformation is not unbounded, ahistorical, or absolute, but neither is it simply an illusion lacking in truth or reality.[76]

This Is Not a Conclusion

There is something symptomatic in my simultaneous desire to embrace and reject morphing. Much of my writing has been about morphing in some form or another. Jerry Lewis morphs into multiple selves, on-screen and off, in a jerky dance of simultaneous liberation and repression. Superheroes, with their secret identities, morph, and some, like Plastic Man or Mr. Fantastic, are even shape shifters. And the terminal identities of cyberculture promise a liberation from space, time, flesh, and history.[77]

Looking back, I can see my own desire to accumulate identities without settling down into any one—I'm always ready to morph. But in its most familiar versions, in countless sci-fi movies and TV commercials, the hollowness of morphing—its literal hollowness, the fact that there's nothing inside—offers surprisingly scant room for fantasy. Morphing is an inadequate, overly literal gesture toward change without pain, without consequence, without meaning. There is something comforting, perhaps, about the stability of unstable identity, but morphing holds out empty arms.

7

Syncopated City:
New York in Musical Film (1929–1961)

What belongs to a metropolis? Anything amusing, surprising,
exciting, sensational, intensified stimulation, temptation renewed daily.
Arthur Eloesser

George and Ira Gershwin's "Fascinating Rhythm" was originally going to
be called "Syncopated City," and New York by the early part of the twentieth century was exactly that. In 1924, Irving Berlin remarked that ragtime
was a "new rhythm" for the new age of automation and mechanization:
the times "demanded new music for new action" because "the country had
speeded up."[1] Musicals, whether from Broadway or Hollywood, understood
the same thing. This is a wondrously paradoxical genre: panoramic yet integrative, exemplary of Siegfried Kracauer's "mass ornament" (his example
was the Rockette-like Tiller Girls) but filled with individual virtuosity by
performers, songwriters, choreographers, and directors. Its debts to theater,
popular song, painting, and dance are most evident, but musicals can feel
more "purely" cinematic than any other genre. This most artificial of forms
is among the most "moving," emotionally and physically, and perhaps, Jane
Feuer notwithstanding, musicals are even the least duplicitous of genres.[2]

With the advent of synchronized sound in the late 1920s, musicals became a primary vehicle of delirious urban celebration. Musicals are largely
about integration on formal and narrative levels: formally, camera movement, choreography, montage, and set design all function together within
what Gerald Mast has called "diversity within unity." The films also produce
images of utopian reconciliation and a forging of community. "Formal self-
consciousness, the shapes of individual energy, and the definition of the ideal
community are the basic themes of musicals," wrote Leo Braudy, and Richard

Dyer notes that musicals show us what utopia would *feel* like.[3] Film musicals order urban density through set design, commercial aesthetics, the structure of popular song, and especially through the virtuosity of physical and perceptual performance, rehearsing a fantastic cohesion of body with world or self with city.

I want to look at a number of musical sequences from American films that feature New York City in a prominent role. What began for me as a simple descriptive overview set at the intersection of Broadway and Forty-Second Street quickly turned out to present a significant intersection of its own—of Times Square, colored lights, and the aesthetic of commercialism, of New York as polyrhythmic, dynamic, and culturally pluralist, with driving ensemble work, soulful soloists and elegant, balletic encounters, and of musicals as paradigmatic of cinema's panoramic, kaleidoscopic euphoria. These sequences present both an escape from the city's managerial rationalities and a reconfiguration of the city as a delirious space of possibility and becoming (see color fig. 8). They may be hegemonic and assimilationist in their overall strategies and ideologies, but these are also sequences about tactical negotiation—the power represented by "walking in the city," in Michel de Certeau's language, only becomes more pronounced when the movement completes its trajectory toward dance.

The sequences will, with few exceptions, not be considered in the context of the surrounding narrative. Musicals encourage browsing. Vaudeville and cabaret, and hence the musical onstage or on film, epitomized the fragmentary yet abundant character of modern life: "impressions of commercial diversity and plenitude, to which young and old succumbed, helped fashion the metropolitan spirit from which cabaret was born."[4] The relationship between number and narrative is less flexible in a film than in a vaudeville revue, cabaret, or Broadway show, but it's still true that most of these songs proved to be eminently detachable from their original settings; some of the songs predated their use in a particular show or film and many became pop and jazz standards. More than a few of these sequences have become even more familiar from revue compilations of the *That's Entertainment* genre (where in very rare instances they can become even more effective).[5] And, as with Times Square, Broadway, or the movies themselves, the numbers represent an oasis within which spectacle can be indulged, consumed, and played with.

Furthermore, the musical numbers were often supervised by someone other than the credited director (Busby Berkeley, Jack Cole, Fred Astaire, or

Hermes Pan, for example) and feature a different aesthetic. The camera takes on less of a narrative function than in the "dramatic" sections and is fixed less upon the trajectory of a single protagonist. Note, for example, how the staging of "42nd Street" separates the two (weakly) romantic protagonists until the final shot—and, further, how the formation of the couple at the end of "42nd Street" is immediately superseded and undermined by Warner Baxter's isolation and exhaustion at the end of *42nd Street*.

New York works well as the setting for this overview; it's a real place but also, and especially in American silent drama and early sound film, it's a major site of cinematic fantasy. It was, of course, the major setting for the early Hollywood musical: music, and the business of creating music, were already associated with New York through the existence of Tin Pan Alley and Broadway, while Harlem permitted an engagement with urban ethnicity, smart set sophistication, and racist exoticism. The city sat poised between America and Europe; it exemplified the pace of modernity and also the edge of modern art. New York was equally defined by the pluralism of immigrant cultures and the awesome, hegemonic power of the financial district.

Musicals give us a New York that is innately pluralist as well as antihierarchical; populist and democratic. Pluralism is figured through ethnicity, the mass, congestion. Stereotyping, the sign of a kind of social consensus, is hugely common, and many of these numbers feature easily recognizable, benign "types" coexisting comfortably. Violence punctuates a surprising number of these sequences, while sexuality is far more evident in these New York interludes than in, say, *Oklahoma!* with its acres of gingham. Jazz rhythms define the city, from the ragtime of 1929's "Broadway Melody" to Bernstein's Latino-inflected score for *West Side Story*. Overall, these sequences are both contemporary and sensual—to the point of suggesting some fundamental causal relation between urban stimulus and embodied response.

"A Revel of Recreation"

New York musicals turn what outsiders might have considered most negative about New York City—its noise, violence, ethnic pluralism, and vulgarity—into a positive, rhythmic, democratic experience. A democratic space, yes, and even the site for the overturning of hierarchies—this is a place where, as they say in "42nd Street," *side by side they're glorified. . . . Where the underworld can meet the elite (42nd Street!)*. This coincides with the popular image of New York that emerged with its increasing popularity as a tourist destination. Neil Harris has written that "the imaging of New York [in the late nineteenth and into the twentieth century] and the effort to define its special personality were stimulated by the heady experience of becoming the country's major tourist center."[6] Cinema certainly inherited from, and contributed to, that history of representation. The sailors of *On the Town* have twenty-four hours to see the sights and experience what New York has to offer. Fortunately, the lovable gobs aren't restricted to New York's actual topography: the rhythm of Bernstein's "New York, New York" permits a new, liberating, and joyous creative geography. The real world becomes a set of backdrops, a stage set, a department store, an amusement park, a playground.[7]

One of the first things to note is the prominence given to Broadway and Times Square (this was not limited to film musicals—ask a George Cohan fan). Times Square has an evident synecdochic function: Harris observes that, beginning in the late nineteenth century, "New York was on stage, and Times Square had become the centerpiece."[8] Harlem, Coney Island, and Times Square all figured in the common imagination of the twentieth century as amusement zones of vibrancy, electric and vaguely threatening, but while Harlem and Coney lay on the outskirts Times Square occupied the city's heart, indeed, its center.

Times Square as a realm of leisure, spectacle, and display mirrored and distilled developing tendencies in the imaging of New York at large. While the Statue of Liberty, the Woolworth Tower, Grants Tomb, and the Stock Exchange drew their visitors and sold their postcards, plenty of tours visited the tenements of the Lower East Side as well as burlesque houses, Barnum's American Museum, and Harlem hotspots. In *On the Town*, the native New York taxi driver played by Betty Garrett mocks Frank Sinatra's young *naif*'s touristic desire to see the Hippodrome, Tobacco Road, and the Woolworth Tower with the libidinal refrain of "Come up to my place!"

Centering on Times Square, the New York musicals present a self-consciously touristic view of the city, at once panoramic and integrative.[9] *Broadway Melody*, the first all-sound musical film, provides an easy example: a panoramic overview of the city is followed by a movement through the window of a Tin Pan Alley music publishing company. But rather than the intrusive and unlicensed voyeurism that marks the formally similar opening of *Psycho*, this is simply a stop on a sightseeing tour: the cast promptly and conveniently gathers to sing a new song. The panoramic has moved into something more participatory. I love the cacophony of the office, the impromptu verve of the musical performance, the overall density of the sound environment. The city *is* the song: *that's* the Broadway melody!

Harris cites Dean MacCannell's theorizing of the position of the tourist:

Figure 15. Creative geography in *On the Town*.
(Courtesy of Photofest.)

"The act of sightseeing is uniquely well-suited among leisure alternatives to draw the tourist into a relationship with the modern social totality. As a worker, the individual's relationship to his society is partial and limited, secured by a fragile 'work ethic,' and restricted to a single position among millions in the division of labor. As a tourist, the individual may step out into the universal drama of modernity." [10] This is remarkably apposite to any number of musical sequences. *Broadway Melody* and *42nd Street* begin with panoramic views of the city, displaying the social totality of New York through aerial shots and a multitude of views before moving down to the city's leisure district. In these films, as in *On the Town, It's Always Fair Weather, 42nd Street, Guys and Dolls, The Band Wagon,* and even *West Side Story,* the individual indeed "steps out" into an integrated, syncopated, and carefully synchronized environment in which work is either replaced by play or transformed into a kind of play. [11]

The opening of *Guys and Dolls* exploits Times Square as a panorama populated by the colorful characters of its Runyon-derived imagination and presented in the widest of Cinemascope formats. The wide-screen format allows a more "panoramic perception" while it also mimics the large-scale spectacle of the Broadway extravaganza (see color fig. 10). Times Square is defined through an elaborate choreography of criss-crossing trajectories, of conmen, tourists, sweater girls, and racing touts. In style this is not so different from the Paris of Jacques Tati's *Playtime* (1967), another film that uses a large film format (65mm) to convey urban density. The only possible view, explicitly figured in *Guys and Dolls* and most clearly in *On the Town* (not to mention *Playtime*), is touristic.

The tourist's view was incorporated in the amusement parks and expositions that distilled the essence of the modern city at the turn of the century. Wordsworth described the urban fair ("true epitome / Of what the mighty City is herself") in exactly these terms in Book 7 of *The Prelude.*

> What a shock
> For eyes and ears! what anarchy and din,
> Barbarian and infernal—a phantasma,
> Monstrous in colour, motion, shape, sight, sound!

Foregoing Wordsworth's virulent aversion, several musical sequences transform the city into an amusement park, a carnivalesque site of informal collision and healthy chaos. Three soldiers go out on the town for a celebratory binge in *It's Always Fair Weather,* and the city is theirs. Beneath the tracks of the elevated train, New York's yellowest taxicab becomes something to play with and climb around and through, and trash can lids become cymbals and tap shoes. New York in *On the Town* is a giant rollercoaster (the ride lasts for twenty-four hours), while the arcade in *The Band Wagon* features classic Coney-style amusements. Rem Koolhaas reminds us that Coney Island was only "a fetal Manhattan," its fantastic architectures and spectacular nature not an escape from New York but an anticipation of its mature form and the key to decoding its innate irrationalism.[12] While John Kasson and others have described Coney Island as a safety valve for those living an intense urban existence,[13] Koolhaas emphasizes the carnivalesque character of urbanism itself, a condition revealed, but not created, by Coney.

Coney Island figured in a surprising number of films in the late silent era; 1928 and 1929 alone brought Harold Lloyd in *Speedy*, King Vidor's *The Crowd*, and, most sublimely, Paul Fejos's *Lonesome* and the archetypal urban amusement area of F. W. Murnau's *Sunrise*. But with synchronized sound Times Square instantly becomes New York's new cinematic playground: it beats with what they archly refer to in *It's Always Fair Weather* as "The Throb of Manhattan." These musicals present the heart of the city as a permanent carnival, and they become another way of laying bare the potential sensuality and pleasure that the urban environment only seems to hold in check.

Production design added to the evocation of a dream world aesthetic of leisure and pleasure. In all these sequences the city is abstracted and formalized, usually—with the significant exceptions of the openings of *On the Town* and *West Side Story*—through set design. Deco gave us a city of machinic elegance, mass produced but placed in the service of leisure, borrowing from the styles of the future for a little pleasure in the here and now. At the same time, the perfection of the sets offered a settled refuge from Depression realities—they combined aspiration and enclosure.[14] The stage setting of Deco produced the city as a glittering, organic machine, its very artificiality a kind of reassurance.

The forced perspective of the dance floor in *Swing Time* (1936) allows the elite to glide transcendentally above the city in a giddy, elegant, lofty trompe l'oeil. The onstage city in *Broadway Melody of 1938* is a backdrop of nearly abstract, upward-thrusting neon shapes, distant and decorative. The miniature limousines and carriages moving laterally across this cool machine remind me of the anachronistic roadsters that dot Le Corbusier's precise drawings of Radiant City.[15] In "42nd Street," the dancers become the Deco skyscrapers of New York, only two years after New York's most prominent architects had

Figure 16. Dancing above the city in *Swing Time,* set by John Harkrider
(Courtesy of Photofest.)

attended the Fête Moderne ball dressed as their own buildings. The city is an object and a performance, a costume and a world.

It was the astonishing lighting that marked Times Square as a uniquely recognizable "other space." While this aesthetic had already taken hold "at world's fairs and in American advertising and merchandising," William Leach argues that "it was the formation of commercial districts like Times Square, where commercial light and color were gathered into one spot to an unusual degree, that pushed the commercial aesthetic to the visual forefront of American urban life."[16]

That commercial aesthetic is innately connected to the aesthetics of American cinema. Leach cites an advertising industry spokesman who proclaims that "Electrical advertising is a *picture medium.* Moreover, it is a *color* medium; still again, electrical advertising is a medium of motion, of action, *of life, of light,* of compulsory attraction."[17] And Leach's description of the window displays favored by L. Frank Baum—"moving electrical displays of revolving stars, 'vanishing ladies,' mechanical butterflies, revolving wheels, incandescent lamp globes"—evokes the nearly concurrent film work of Georges Méliès rather directly.[18] But American commercial display differed from French. While Europeans constrained the level of vulgar display, Leach writes that "The American way was to concentrate or confine such activity to a limited space, while at the same time *liberating* it to an unparalleled degree.[19]

American cinema was surely another place to "concentrate or confine" such vulgar displays of spectacular light and color (even in black and white), and one could further see musical sequences as yet another neat containment within the carefully delimited space and time of the narrative. Delimitation again brackets an aesthetic liberation, as with the camera movement and expressionist set design of "42nd Street" and in the creative geography of "New York, New York." It's also rampant in the sets, color, lighting, and choreography of the Deco musicals of the 1930s, *On the Town's* central ballet, *The Band Wagon's* "Shine on Your Shoes," and perhaps even the prologue to *West Side Story*, as the bodily movements of Sharks and Jets establish the very conditions of being in the world.

For some recent historians, a celebratory commercial aesthetic encouraged some sense of the self as a fluid construct. Jackson Lears writes of the tendencies in American culture that moved against systems of rational control—not the least of which was market capitalism itself: "The magic of the marketplace was fragmentary and attenuated; it had less to do with a coherent cosmology than with a developing world of free-floating, shape-shifting selves. But under certain circumstances, it held out a vision of transcendence, however fleeting."[20] The self-definition that emerged in reaction to this discourse of secular satisfaction was notably rigid. "Middle upper classes in the antebellum United States, turning to their own Protestant ethos . . . created an ideal of unified, controlled, sincere selfhood—a bourgeois self—as a counterweight to the centrifugal tendencies unleashed by market exchange."[21]

There were, meanwhile, plenty of cultural forces tending "toward a more dynamic conception of mind-body relations than the static dualisms enshrined in rationalist and orthodox Christian tradition."[22] Amusement parks and Times Square seemed designed to confound those "static dualisms." The brilliant designer of Coney Island's Luna Park was Frederic Thompson, who built the Hippodrome right in the theater district (it opened in 1905). William Register writes that it was "a theatrical amusement park, a commercial dreamworld of pleasure, abundance, insouciant youth, fluidity, fantasy and magic."[23] All this depended on orchestrated movement and release, elements that also came to figure prominently in the cinema and noticeably in the film musical: "Amusement architecture . . . had to affirm human desires and encourage release, freedom, and spending instead of admonishing people to deny themselves pleasure and to restrict their desires. Above all, the amusement park had to manufacture the carnival spirit by insuring energetic movement instead of rest and stasis in the park's attractions as well as in its architecture."[24] Movement reconnected self to body, and the mobilization of desire reestablished one's presence in the metropolis. (In this regard, it's worth drawing a distinction between the unbounded informality of the amusement park and the hypercontrolled environment of the theme park. As Koolhaas wrote of the Disneyfication of Times Square in the 1990s: "The bottom line is: 42nd Street was utterly authentic, a throbbing Zone of flickering, stroboscopic liveliness and energy, of invention and exploitation.")[25] In the New York musical, music and dance initiate a connection between mind, body, and world.

Lears notes the preponderance of fantastic imagery and allegories in nineteenth-century advertising (recall Baum's window displays). Clearly, some elements of the fantastic moved directly into the cinema via unreal subject matter as well as the metamorphic nature of the medium. The musical became an evident site of fantasy in the sound cinema. The Broadway musical had nearly defined phantasmagoria in its way, and in fact cinematic spectacle must have seemed pretty impoverished next to the luxuriant art nouveau designs (by Joseph Urban) for the Ziegfeld Follies.[26] Film was censored, framed, and delimited, with poor sound reproduction and black and white imagery, but there were ways to compensate for its limitations.[27] Incorporating live entertainment helped preserve the color associated with theater and commercialism, and the décor of the picture palace also supplemented cinematic fantasy with color, depth, and tactility. And nearly every film revue in 1929 and 1930 featured a sequence in two-strip Technicolor.

So musicals, in their depiction of a modern, bustling New York, represented a commercial aesthetic and gleefully participated in it (Vincente Minnelli and Norman Bel Geddes—who would later create the urban phantasmagoria of Futurama—first worked as commercial window designers). And, if we accept Lears's argument, this commercial aesthetic had the value of resurrecting the idea of the body in a culture that privileged mind and self-control: "Maybe the most coherent conclusion one can draw about the ferment of fantastic advertising during the late nineteenth century is that it played counterpoint to the dominant culture's celebration of mind over body."[28] The phantasmagoria of consumption and advertising might have served market forces and economic principles, but the rhetoric used to sell products relied on older, more atavistic, even repressed iconographies and discourses. Advertising tapped into antirational impulses, which doesn't mean those impulses were thereby contained: G. K. Chesterton saw the dark side to these bright lights, through which everything was trivialized, desacralized, and made subject to the power of capital, but his exuberant regard for the city temporarily forestalled all else: "If a child saw these colored lights, he would dance with as much delight as at any other coloured toys; and it is the duty of every poet, and even of every critic, to dance in respectful imitation of the child. Indeed, I am in a mood of so much sympathy with fairy nights of this pantomime city, that I should be almost sorry to see social sanity and a sense of proportion return to extinguish them."[29]

By the 1930s, the colored toy of the Times Square area was no longer primarily a legitimate theater district; it had evolved into a much more broadly based entertainment center—the movies were one new element—and a far less genteel area.[30] Ward Morehouse, the Broadway critic, commented on the "decline" of 42nd Street in the 1930s.

> Broadway itself, once the street of Rector's and Churchill's and Stanley's, was now cheapened and nightmarish. It was offering palm readings and photos while-U-wait, live turtles and tropical fruit drinks, sheet music, nut fudge, jumbo malteds, hot waffles, ham and eggs, hot dogs, and hamburgers. A screeching amusement park bedlam that was somehow without a Ferris Wheel and a roller coaster, but that presented shooting galleries, bowling alleys, guess-your-weight stands, gypsy tea rooms, rug auctions, electric shoeshines, dance halls—fifty beautiful girls—chop suey, beer on draught, wines and liquors, oyster bars, bus-barkers, and right there at the curb was the man with the giant telescope, ready to show you the craters of the moon for a dime.[31]

One can almost see Fred Astaire weaving through all of this, asking "What's happened to Times Square!?"—I mean, this is the arcade in *The Band Wagon*, isn't it? Astaire briefly laments the past of "legitimate theater . . . strictly carriage trade," before getting into the rhythm of the new city. Neil Harris observes that

> The strident pace, electric atmosphere, life under tension, scurry for space, towering skyscrapers, and ethnic neighborhoods that constituted

so much of New York's tourist appeal did not fit the 'city beautiful' recipe that true believers in municipal destiny had composed. Their vision of an imperial capital, graced by magnificent buildings, squares, broad avenues, unhurried promenaders, celebrated cultural institutions, resurfaced from time to time in architectural competitions and planning proposals. But it was not the consensual image of the city.[32]

Musicals like *The Band Wagon* extended the consensual touristic desire to see the city in all its glorious squalor (don't forget the screams, shootings, and knifings in "42nd Street," "Slaughter on Tenth Avenue," and *West Side Story*). The city is exotic, a distillation of life in modern times, in the very way that Coney Island and the 1893 World Columbian Exposition distilled modern urbanism. In fact, one journalist wrote around 1910 that tourists "stare at New York as a New Yorker stares at Coney Island. For New York is, after all, the Coney Island of the nation."[33]

The Syncopated City

Times Square was Coney Island set to music, and usually that music was rhythmic, urban, and heavily syncopated. Jazz, or at least jazz-inflected popular song—elaborate amalgams of English ballad, informal diction, urbane sophistication, colloquialism, twelve-bar blues structures, and ragtime syncopation—defines Broadway and, to only a slightly lesser degree, Hollywood musical songs. A good example is "42nd Street," featuring Ruby Keeler, who goes out there a youngster and comes back a star. The film constantly cuts to the company rehearsing the title song, as dozens of feet heavily stamp out its syncopated, ragged rhythms in what Jim Hoberman describes as a Depression era fantasy of full industrial production.[34]

Ragtime, beginning in the mid-1890s, mixed syncopated beats in the treble with an even bass rhythm; the piano became a percussive instrument. The influence of African instrumentation and rhythm was combined with the popularity of society verse, as published in the later teens and 1920s in places like *Vanity Fair*, Franklin Pierce Adams's "Conning Tower" column, and later the *New Yorker*. The result came to be known as the New York style of lyric, demonstrated in the work of Lorenz Hart, Ira Gershwin, Dorothy Fields, Irving Berlin, and Cole Porter. Philip Furia sees the form as "characterized by 'ease' and 'playful spontaneity,' 'the conversational key.' The rhymes are 'frequent' and the rhythm 'crisp and sparkling.' The tone should be 'playfully malicious,' 'tenderly ironical,' or 'satirically facetious.'"[35] Furia's exemplary lyric

is for Rodgers and Hart's "Manhattan," which might be said to have chris-
tened the syncopated city.

> We'll take Manhattan
> The Bronx and Staten
> Island too
> It's lovely going to
> The zoo.

Rhymes break up the colloquial phrases (*Staten/Island*), and appear in mid-
line or elsewhere, in twos and threes (*too/to/zoo*). A proudly ironic regional-
ism prevails: "And tell me what street / Compares to Mott Street / in July?"
The city is dispersed and united, informally casual but formally rich, rhythmic and relaxed, familiar but newly surprising.

The sources of this urbane colloquialism were many and included the appropriation and exaggeration of speech patterns of urban African Americans
in the wave of "coon songs" that first amused and later even moved audiences. Ann Douglas also points to the 1920s vogue for the urban slang that
originated with entertainers and gangsters and found written expression in
the work of Damon Runyon, Walter Winchell, Ben Hecht, Dashiell Ham-
mett, George S. Kaufman, Dorothy Parker, Zora Neale Hurston, and Langston
Hughes (novelists, journalists, screenwriters, dramatists, and poets mostly
living in New York). This was "creative slumming," Douglas argues: "Slang
was deliberate disguise and pretense."[36] (Witness the faux Spillane narration
in *The Band Wagon's* "Girl Hunt Ballet": "She came at me in pieces.") Furia further observes that the New York lyric often features a character ("I"): "This
thoroughly American rainbow-chaser would become the perfect 'voice' for
wittily turned lyrics that balance nonchalance and sophistication, slang and
elegance." The casual urbanity of Fred Astaire exemplifies the type—and I'd
further argue that this stylistic blend of high and low urbanity marks the
structures and plots of the musicals as much as the individual songs. The "I"
that Furia refers to was ideally suited to play all these different rhythms, to
improvise identities that could partake of, and negotiate, the city's spontaneity and contemporaneity.[37]

One could offer the usual argument that these hijackings of ethnic and
class-defined languages represent an appropriation and silencing of other
voices and proffer a strategy of hegemonic control over the dangerous free-
doms of the urban environment. But is responding to the city tantamount
to its mastery? These songs present a ludic field of give and take, call and

response, a realm of parody and irony (see, e.g., Dorothy Fields's lyric for "A Fine Romance," which describes anything but). This is hardly to say that music publishing, performance, or hiring practices were equitable across class and ethnic boundaries—who got to sing these songs or make money or gain recognition from them? I'm only suggesting that the discursive positions offered by these songs were hardly as fixed, as some theories might suggest, and it's worth remembering the number of Jewish and gay songwriters who were able to find voice, to pass, within a highly discriminatory culture.[38] One recent documentary referred to small, homely Irving Berlin as Cyrano to Astaire's Christian. Masquerades are complicated affairs that involve as much improvisation as preparation.

Improvisation is fundamental to the urban style of jazz. Paul Berliner's massive, extraordinary book, *Thinking in Jazz*, argues that improvisation arises in part from the dynamic interactions of itinerant musicians working from a book of familiar American "standards"—often building, by the way, on the very songs that had originally "appropriated" African American stylings, as with, for example, Harold Arlen's "Stormy Weather." Berliner describes a process at once scholarly and responsive: "Amid the dynamic display of imagined fleeting images and impulses—entrancing sounds and vibrant feelings, dancing shapes and kinetic gestures, theoretical symbols and perceptive commentaries—improvisers extend the logic of previous phrases, as ever-emerging figures on the periphery of their vision encroach upon and supplant those in performance."[39] He goes even further to claim that "jazz improvisation is not merely a process by which musicians create a record album or an evening's performance. It is a particular artistic way of going through life."[40]

Film musicals are usually the occasion for introducing the standards rather than the site of their exploration and deconstruction. Still, one could certainly argue that the dancer, acutely attuned to the possibilities presented by the urban environment, is the soloist and improviser in several of these numbers. One study of Hollywood musicals notes that "Dancers' musicals are more likely, like the majority of the Astaire-Rogers vehicles, to be light, fast and modern in their setting; singers' musicals are more likely, like the majority of the MacDonald-Eddy vehicles, to look back nostalgically to glamorous and romantic periods and to the more expansive world of the operetta as opposed to the slick and jazzy musical comedy."[41] The dancer's musical is modern, more attuned to contemporary styles.

Joseph Delameter has described Astaire's work process as one of improvisation and counterpoint.

Having established expectations for a certain kind of choreographic interpretation of the music, Astaire would change his approach and purposely work against the music. Choreographing to the accompaniment rather than the melody; speeding up where the music seems to call for slowing down—and the opposite; doing simple movements where the drama of the number, as well as the orchestration, seems to call for complexity; and, in general, building his routines without the customary repetition of movement to accompany musical repetition all serve as approaches to Astaire's choreographic style.[42]

"Shine on Your Shoes," from *The Band Wagon,* perfectly illustrates Astaire's technique and the strategies of the musical. At first, Astaire, bewildered and displaced by the shifting demographic of Times Square, wanders through the arcade, testing the various apparatuses and interacting uncomfortably with the denizens of this new world. But gradually, as he continues to experiment, and to an increasingly prominent jazz sound, Astaire learns to "play" the arcade. When he reads a fortune he doesn't care for, he gets another that's more to his liking (reacting both times with proper conviction). When the Pokerino table fails him, he jiggles the appearance of five aces. By the time he trips over the despondent shoeshiner (LeRoy Daniels), Astaire has begun to figure this place out. After singing the song, a Howard Dietz and Arthur Schwartz number (once a part of Ethel Waters's repertoire), Astaire begins his dance solo (a moment long delayed in the film, whose opening movements are an elaborate tease).[43] The arcade now becomes the setting for Astaire's improvisations of sound, color, light, and movement. He "picks up" the spirits of the shoeshiner, but also wins his approval, and they appear together for the entire finale. While the narrative represents the fundamental difference in their social positions in grotesquely explicit fashion, the number presents Astaire's assimilation into the pluralistic city through jazz improvisation and its embodiment in the African American shoeshine.[44]

For Ella Shohat, on the other hand, the sequence functions through the erasure of the very ethnicity it purports to celebrate. Astaire's performance, she argues,

> inspires the otherwise nonexistent or dormant dancing talent of the African-American shoeshine . . . who is merely used as a kinetic object, a device reminiscent in its objectification of Busby Berkeley's depersonalizing rhetoric of gender. Daniels as the shoeshine "boy" (kneeling) literally shines Astaire's shoes and brushes his clothes during the musi-

cal number. Just as images of women beautifying themselves in *Dames* yield their quantum of spectacle, the African-American shoeshine servant status in *The Band Wagon* is deployed to form part of the esthetic dynamics of the number.[45]

But I think more is being enacted here than mere social subservience and cultural obscurantism. There is stereotyping at work here—it's obviously hard to stomach Daniels at Astaire's feet. But Astaire simply does not hide the black influence in his work. Citing a blackface performance may seem strange, but "Bojangles of Harlem" (*Swing Time*, 1936) is, after all, an explicit homage to Bill "Bojangles" Robinson, while "Slap That Bass" (*Shall We Dance*, 1937) has Astaire doing a jazz tap accompanied by the African American stevedores (alluding to the combination of African American and mechanico-industrial rhythms in the development of jazz).

Ann Douglas describes Manhattan of the 1920s, when Astaire (with his sister Adele) was making his mark on Broadway along with Gershwin, Rodgers and Hart, and others, as a "mongrel culture." This was a period of fierce interpenetration of white and black Manhattans—Broadway, Tin Pan Alley, the Cotton Club, and the Harlem Renaissance were not so easily separated. But for Douglas this is not simply a period of white appropriation of black styles but also the reverse, and she points to Ethel Waters's incorporation of white influences while still performing exclusively for black audiences: "Blacks imitating and fooling whites, whites imitating and stealing from blacks, blacks reappropriating and transforming what has been stolen, whites making yet another foray on black styles, and on and on: this *is* American popular culture."[46] The interpenetration of cultures, rather than a unilateral appropriation, was everywhere on display. Astaire himself described his style as an "outlaw style" rather than something strictly defined as purely this or that.

In "Shine on Your Shoes" and "Slap That Bass," the presence of black performers serves to recall (and reenact) the provenance of these steps and this music, not hide it. An attempt, ultimately a provisional and failed attempt, is made to team Astaire and Daniels: the most dramatic, emotional cut in the sequence occurs at the end, when they are joyously "reunited" for the finale. Some critics are perhaps overly quick to identify a totalizing operation of containment and displacement in a sequence that is, at the very least, a clear illustration of what Eric Lott has called the dialectic of "love and theft" that characterizes white engagement with African American cultural motifs.[47] Astaire is the one assimilated here, and, while that kind of hipster ethos

Figure 17. Fred Astaire teamed with LeRoy Daniels in *The Band Wagon*.
(Courtesy of Metro-Goldwyn-Mayer.)

carries its own racial fantasies, to dramatize—indeed, to dance—that assimilation seems less obscurantist than dialectical, although crudely so. The dual contexts of Astaire's career and the film's narrative reveal "Shine on Your Shoes" to be a problematic number but maybe not wholly so.

Most of the more recent *Tap* (1989) is set around Times Square, an area that has, again, begun to lose its past, this time a past of of black hoofers and per-formers (represented by Sammy Davis Jr., Sandman Sims, Harold Nicholas, and others).[48] Gregory Hines leads an ensemble of annoyingly "hip" club patrons on an exploration of the sounds of Times Square, its rhythms and noise. As in Clair's *Sous les toits de Paris* (1930) or Mamoulian's *Love Me Tonight* (1932), the city is defined as a sonic environment (*Paaaa-ris haaas to seeeeeng*, Maurice Chevalier informs us). When *Tap* begins, Hines is in prison, and he defeats impending panic by improvising a frantic dance around the sounds of his cell block at night. Improvisation becomes a means of alert, dynamic response, as it was for Astaire—less a means of putting something on than of getting inside of it, living it. *The Band Wagon* gives us a character beginning to respond to the new life of the district and of the city itself. Improvisation does indeed begin to seem like a "particular" and legitimate "way of going through life."

The syncopated city depends on the stylization of the everyday; in ragtime and tap (and *musique concrete* and techno) the sounds of machinery and urban congestion are sampled, replayed, and returned to the environment, and the musical does this in other ways, too. Oliver Smith's urban sets for *The Band Wagon* and *Guys and Dolls* abstract the commercial milieu. In the latter, the overlapping billboards, electric signage, flat buildings, and angular costumes explicitly evoke Fernand Léger and Stuart Davis (see color fig. 9). The "Girl Hunt Ballet" gave Smith license to indulge in a poster art sensibility of vivid, saturated colors. The surreal red fire escape extending into infinity, the nega-tive silhouettes of skyscrapers, and the generally expressionist colors all par-take of a "dream ballet" aesthetic (by then an old standby) but here with wit rather than pretension and a proto-Pop sensibility (quoting the lurid book covers of 1950s pulp fiction) replacing interiorized, psychological fantasy (see color fig. 11).

Michael Kidd's choreography in both films furthers the assimilation and abstraction of the everyday. The finger-snapping, trucking gangsters of "Girl Hunt Ballet" metamorphose into the balletic gamblers of *Guys and Dolls*. The beginning of *Guys and Dolls* is nothing but a modernist assemblage of urban activities, as the city becomes a grand performative space: tourists gawk, pickpockets pick pockets, athletes train, girls preen, hucksters hustle, and so forth. In the phenomenal sewer sequence, a craps game becomes an exuber-ant, muscular ballet that must have been even more impressive onstage—Mankiewicz doesn't quite know how to bring the cinematic spectator into the dance the way Donen and Minnelli do. In these films, as in *Seven Brides for*

Seven Brothers, Kidd choreographs masculinity, competition, and ritual (it's difficult to imagine *West Side Story* without Kidd's work as a precedent). But while the rural aesthetic of *Seven Brides* sent Kidd toward the forms of Russian folk dance, *The Band Wagon* and *Guys and Dolls* are fiercely urban—jazzy and slick.

The musical sequences that I'm describing don't present a city symphony in the more limited sense of the city as an ensemble swelling to greatness above its constituent instrumentalists.[49] Rather, in these sequences, the ensemble of urban actors and chorines yields to a soloist or two, improvising on or playing off the city. These are jazz ballets, or something very like that, and they comprise a significant engagement with everyday New York as an aural environment, marked by surprise and diversity and complexity. Berliner recounts how jazz musicians "in New York City sometimes practice outside in deserted areas or near bridges where their performance is partially masked by late-night traffic, adopting the city's collective sounds—the rhythmic clatter of cars and trains, the mixes of honking horns and sirens—as their accompaniment to improvisations."[50]

The Splendid Mirage

What possibilities emerge for the individual within this kaleidoscopic and kaleidophonic array?[51] How does the individual exist in the phantasmagoria of the syncopated city? As the discussion of improvisation already suggests, the cinematic synchrony of bodies and cameras becomes a primary vehicle of urban integration in the New York musical. Such synchrony extends the formal abstraction of everyday life found in set designs, rhythms, lyrics, and choreography to the body of the spectator. Choreography of dancers and cameras creates a movement both with the city and against it, forging a position that is independent of, yet buried deeply within, the rhythms of the city, of America, of modernity. In 1903, Georg Simmel emphasized the complex richness of sensation in the city. "The individual's horizon is enlarged," he wrote, but he was already ambivalent, for the instrumentalism of commercial relations produced alienation rather than an enhanced subjectivity. Simmel saw that "the self-preservation of certain types of personalities is obtained at the cost of devaluing the entire objective world, ending inevitably in dragging the personality downward into a feeling of its own valuelessness."[52] But the musical presents another image of self-preservation, one that balances group unity and individual counterpoint.

The movement of chorines presents the clearest example of Siegfried Kra-

Figure 18. Busby Berkeley: mass ornament meets kaleidoscopic perception.
(Courtesy of Warner Bros.)

cauer's "mass ornament" in the cinema. The group moves with the city, in unison with its dominant, mechanical rhythms. For Kracauer, the mass ornament was unitary, not a community; the individual performers in The Tiller Girls were "component parts" of a larger composition.[53] The goose-stepping entertainers of Busby Berkeley's "Lullaby of Broadway" remain jaw-droppingly, Springtime-for-Hitler exemplary, but they aren't unique. All the chorus lines in all the films are variations on the mass ornament—but as the American dancers' musical evolves, the chorus line increasingly exists to set off the individual performance of the star (a phenomenon that culminates in the reflexive examination of *A Chorus Line*).

Berkeley's sequences might not showcase individual dancers, but the camera is imbued with a presence that certainly individuates the spectator.[54] The camera's passage is less determined by narrative and character; it becomes more participatory than descriptive. The "42nd Street" number begins with Ruby Keeler onstage singing and doing one of her heavy tap routines, but suddenly she's scrabbling over a taxi on a larger set (which connotes a "real

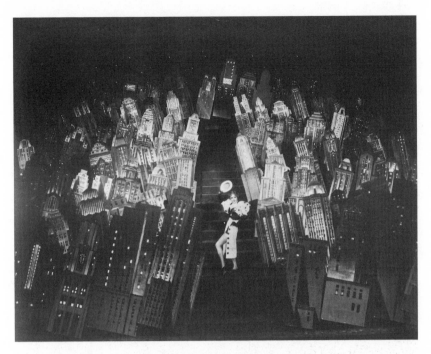

Figure 19. The dance of the skyscrapers, Ruby Keeler in *42nd Street*.
(Courtesy of Photofest.)

street"). The music begins to compete with klaxon horns and policemen's whistles, and the camera tracks along the street as doormen, drunks, and nannies do their thing—this is very like the panoramic opening of *Guys and Dolls*. The camera finds a drunken domestic brawl on an upper floor; when the woman jumps from the window she immediately becomes part of the dance, but that doesn't stop her from getting a knife in the back. Dick Powell, looking on, sings a refrain, and the street is filled with choristers tapping away. The camera is less interested in the protagonists than the panorama, the multiplicity of people and events that the "big parade" of life in the city has to offer. The camera had never worked in such narrative terms during a musical sequence, but the narrational structures are very different from the rest of the film.

"Lullaby of Broadway" is pretty clearly modeled on the city symphony films of the 1920s and 1930s. It begins with a long, slow movement in on Wini Shaw singing—swathed in black and posed against a dark background, only her face is visible. A graphic match links her silhouette to the outline of Manhattan, and (via a dissolve) the camera continues its movement. There's some similarity to *West Side Story*, which begins with an abstract Saul Bass graphic against a monochromatic background that dissolves to a photographic view of lower Manhattan. In both, abstract visual patterns yield to a familiar image of the urban environment. This is not so different from the opening of Walter Ruttmann's *Berlin: Die Sinfonie der Großstadt* (1927), in which the approach to the city is marked by the kinetic abstraction of railroad ties, telegraph wires, and bridge supports.

"Lullaby" continues with typical city symphony stuff, structured around a single day's labor and leisure in the metropolis: people going to work, crowded subways, revolving doors, coffee counters, office buildings, and street vendors. "Lullaby" is a little different, since this rather sinister cautionary tale climaxes with the nightclubbing protagonist's fall from a skyscraper balcony (King Kong had met a similar fate two years earlier),[55] but many city symphonies featured the violence of breakdown—the suicide in *Berlin* and similar moments in Vertov and in Steiner and Van Dyke's *The City* (1939). Afterward, the song (or symphony) continues, and life goes on as it was; the loss of one person is worth a momentary look, but it scarcely affects the city at large. Such breakdowns come with the territory, these films say. (*The City* predicts a similar fate for all urbanists without a decisive shift to effective city planning.) The climax of "Lullaby" presents the obverse of the finale of "42nd Street" in which the camera zooms up the side of a skyscraper to a gaily waving Dick Powell and Ruby Keeler (which itself anticipates the phallic delirium at the end of *The Fountainhead* [1949]). The sequences reveal the simultaneous attraction and anxiety that the city could engender in Depression America as in Weimar Germany.

Anton Kaes argues that city movement and silent film spectatorship were closely aligned.[56] The absence of language in silent films increased the signifying weight of architecture and sets, as interior impulses were translated into exteriorized forms. The city wanderer had a similarly restricted access to language, explanation, and denotation and had to "read" the city through its visible signs. Paradoxically, perhaps, the musical is the genre with the strongest ties to the silent aesthetic.[57] Peter Wollen writes that the body in musicals is a gestural body, recalling the physical expressiveness of Chaplin, Gish, or Fairbanks.[58] Musical sequences, from about 1930 onward, were filmed using playback systems so the camera could again possess the unfettered mobility of the silent cinema. And an exaggerated studio aesthetic remained central— the sets had to distill New York, changing it enough but not too much. Kaes

Figure 20. Dance attuned to the real space of the city in *West Side Story*.
(Courtesy of Photofest.)

writes of the *Straßenfilm* (Weimar street film) that "The artificiality of the studio sets only enhanced the magic of the street as a site of wonder and adventure."[59] This was certainly also true in the musical, in which, again, the lack of spoken language and the amplification of the set design similarly evoke what Henry Roth once called "the kaleidoscope of passage" through the city.

Is there a better synthesis of bodily movement, location shooting, and editing than "The Jet Ballet" that begins *West Side Story*? The most panoramic of cameras provides an overflight of a New York that is recognizable but unfamiliar. The eerily stable camera moves north past the tourist destinations of lower Manhattan, the Empire State Building, and the United Nations to the less visited neighborhoods of the Bronx. A cut to a lower height and a zoom in on a group of kids, Bernstein's jazzy score swells, and suddenly the huge screen is filled with snapping fingers. In the sequences supervised by Jerome Robbins, including this one, cutting, choreography, and scoring work in superb unison. The dancers' physicality seems perfectly attuned to the real space around them, as the cutting constructs a virtual geography that owes much to, but goes well beyond, the montage that begins *On the Town*.[60] Robbins and codirector and editor Robert Wise cut and resynthesized movements with a power that approaches the boldness of Maya Deren. The streets are transformed, as in "New York, New York," but the sequence retains a strong sense of a specific neighborhood. Most of the rest of *West Side Story* is staged on Boris Leven's sets, with mixed results, but "America," danced on a tenement rooftop, is among the most joyous New York sequences of all.[61]

While "42nd Street" and "The Jet Ballet" are cinematic by any definition of the term, the more restricted space, intimate performance, and long takes of "Dancing in the Dark" (by Minnelli, Kidd, Astaire, and Charisse) shouldn't lead us to mistake its aesthetic for a simple transplanting of the theatrical. The camera rarely pans, which would reproduce the fixed positionality of the theater spectator. Instead the camera tracks laterally (here and in many numbers filmed by Minnelli or Donen); it follows the dancers, but it also mimics their movements to a greater or lesser degree. In "Dancing in the Dark" the camera also cranes toward them and away but never moves closer than a full body shot.

The viewer becomes both a spectator and an integrated part of the dance, a kinesthetic participant in its graceful mobility. The identification is powerful and entirely bodily. The choreography mirrors this increasing integration. At first Astaire and Charisse maintain a watchful distance from one another, but their dance brings them into increasingly intimate contact. Astaire takes on an uncharacteristically supportive role, in deference, perhaps, to the balletic background of Charisse's character, but their interaction becomes increasingly intricate, precise, and deeply erotic. They are integrated with each other and with the world, the city visible behind them, and the spectator is integrated in a dreamlike synthesis of bodies, perceptions, world, and representation.

The subjective is sacrificed to a complex, physical integration with the world—here dancer and spectator discover a delicate, embodied relation to the overwhelming fact and fantasy of New York. Gilles Deleuze has written that dance in cinema "gives a world to the image" by imbuing it with movement—the image partakes of a movement that "surrounds and suffuses it."[62] At the same time, the dancer "will be taken over by the movement which seems to summon him."[63] Dance brings both self and world into being and unites them. "The dancer's individual genius, his subjectivity, moves from a personal motivity to a supra-personal element, to a movement of world that

Figure 21. The intimate communion of dancers, camera, and a dream of
New York in *The Band Wagon*. (Courtesy of Metro-Goldwyn-Mayer.)

the dance will outline."[64] The New York musical is thus panoramic and integrative. The camera is unfettered, whether flying over the city or constructing a montage of postcard views, but the camera is also strongly linked to bodily movement, whether choruses, couples, or soloists. The city is distant and proximate, spectacular and lived—"a splendid mirage" is how F. Scott Fitzgerald referred to it from the vantage point of memory.[65]

Ironically, as the film musical emerged, much of New York's opulence and dynamism had already gone into hiding. An elegiac despair hovers over Fitzgerald's 1932 "My Lost City," an essay contemporaneous with many of the celebrations of New York and "42nd Street" and "My Broadway and Your Broadway." The city in 1919 "had all the iridescence of the beginning of the world," he recalls. Fitzgerald's reverie helps us to see the musical sequences as something other than new, progressive, and modern—they actually become nostalgic in their very moment of becoming. "I remember riding in a taxi one afternoon between very tall buildings under a mauve and rosy sky. I began to bawl because I had everything I wanted and knew I would never be so happy again."[66] Isn't this a description of the raucous binge from *It's Always Fair Weather*, danced by army buddies Gene Kelly, Michael Kidd, and Dan Duryea just before their separation and descent into jaded adulthood? And when Fitzgerald recalls "a moment of utter peace in riding south through Central Park at dark toward where the façade of 59th Street thrusts its lights through the trees" can one not recall "Dancing in the Dark"?[67] Fred Astaire and Cyd Charisse find sublime, wordless communion beneath that very facade as they negotiate their differences through that intimate combination of dancers and camera.[68]

Of *Die Straße* (1923) in particular and the *Straßenfilm* in general, Anton Kaes writes that "The film's contradictory reactions to urban experience encapsulate the whole range of emotions associated with the big city throughout modern history, running the gamut from idolization to condemnation, from intoxication and elation to feelings of anxiety and apocalypse."[69] All of this is found in the New York musical sequences as well, although in *Die Straße* the urban experience is ultimately figured negatively; Grune's film finally rejects the power of the street, of the public sphere. The New York musicals are simpler and less blocked by contradiction, yet they, too, articulate the gamut of emotions that Kaes describes. The musicals are more open to the possibilities of the public sphere—their very aesthetic speaks to integration and resolution—but, finally, *living* in New York isn't the issue. From a musical perspective, New York is a nice place to visit.

Musicals are too controlled to fully attain the state of the Dionysian, the bacchanal, the carnivalesque, whoopee, or whatever, but they do suggest something perhaps mildly Dionysian, spaces at least set apart from normal life that remain safely contained by a multitude of formal and social structures. If there is no permanent transcendence here, there is still a sense of the city as something to be lived, a celebration of leisure, sensual discovery, and bodily response. When Fitzgerald considers the "splendid mirage" of New York, he acknowledges the artificial abstraction that his memory has made of the real metropolis, and when he refers to his internalized "movie of New York" he recognizes the mnemonic function of cinema, which is very different from its mimetic function.[70] Cinema is the medium of the "splendid mirage," and the New York musical permits an integration with the spaces of New York and the Broadway stage and the reflecting screen, the present time of performance, and the past of narrative representation and personal memory.

I became serious about musicals when I left New York City for the deserts of New Mexico. Channel surfing one night brought me to *On the Town*, and I felt my absence from the city more keenly than before. I'm writing this coda in Berlin, a few days after the death of Frank Sinatra, and last night *On the Town* played again—accompanied this time by a different and more permanent feeling of loss. What all these sequences present is, of course, only an image of New York, but it's one of which I'm very fond. The world remains willfully open to the body's embrace. "The essence of the musical," according to Leo Braudy, "is the potential of the individual to free himself from inhibition at the same time that he retains a sense of limit and propriety in the very form of the liberating dance. . . . The cop who stops Kelly's exuberant dance in *Singin in the Rain* asserts the reality of the streets and the rain and the lamppost Kelly is holding on to—a reality that is in opposition to what dance would like to make of the world."[71] Seen in the fading light of "My Lost City," these sequences and all the others become signs of loss themselves— they knowingly perform an ephemeral and fantasied, but necessary and real, urban synthesis.

The Boys in the Hoods:
A Song of the Urban Superhero (2000)

> There is a city. a glorious and singular place.
> Old and yet pristine, ornate and yet streamlined.
> A metropolis of now and then and never was.
>
> *Starman* #1

In the stories they come straight at you, in bold, blurred streaks of color against the ground of the great metropolis. At first glance they are terribly crude—especially in their first decades of existence—but familiarity and developing history endow them with copious nuance. Cloaking themselves in vibrant tones, they come straight at you in a blur and streak across the panel, the page, the city, the mind, and then they stop: wondrous polychrome monuments, somehow intimate and solid and untouchable as the sky.

I find it fascinating, or at least noteworthy, that superheroes, many of whom could, let's face it, live anywhere they want, invariably reside in American cities.[1] Other comics bring us to the 'burbs (*Archie*) or beyond known space (*Star Wars*), but superheroes are homebodies as much as homeboys: Superman is generally content to operate in and around Metropolis, Batman's name is synonymous with Gotham City, Opal City is Starman's official place of residence, and, for a strange while, all the Marvel superheroes jostled for room (and, presumably, apartments) in—where else?—New York. Crime remains at the level of heists and elaborate capers, the crowd exists only to gawk, and an anticorporatist populism marks the sole intrusion of a realpolitik. In the mid-1980s, creators began to explore the relation between heroic figure and urban ground, and the city became something more than a generic background for superheroic derring-do.[2] The superhero-city link has become increasingly explicit in such recent comics as Kurt Busiek's *Astro City* and Alan Moore's *Top 10* (see color fig. 13).

Let me propose that American superheroes encapsulated and embodied the same utopian aspirations of modernity as the cities themselves. Superhero narratives thus comprise a genre that joins World's Fairs, urban musicals, and slapstick comedies in presenting urban modernity as a utopia of sublime grace. These comics dream impossible figures in ideal cities. Even if those cities themselves were hardly individuated in the first decades of superhero comics—Coast City and Central City served as backdrops more than fully felt environments—still, they were cities, and while superhero comics don't produce an urban analysis that city planners can use, they nevertheless provide a compelling iconography of a rich urban imaginary, unfettered and uncanny.

Because the audience for superhero comics largely consisted of adolescent and postadolescent males (as any visitor to a comics shop can attest), explanations of comics' appeal have stuck to well-worn paths mostly trodden by Oedipus. Superheroes have been regarded as power fantasies for boys who have not yet acclimated socially (as with kids' fascination with less-than-human/more-than-human dinosaurs). Superheroes are also said to embody the displacement of sexual energy into aggression (which is why comics are profligate with property damage and evenly matched opponents locked in nonlethal slugfests). And of course superheroes are authority and order incarnate, innately fascist at their core (especially Superman, our homegrown *übermensch*). Still further, superheroes negotiate dichotomous roles: the child (the orphaned Bruce Wayne) and the father (Batman), the servant of law (crime fighter) and the autonomous outsider (vigilante) are condensed into a single, titanic, figure. Displacement and condensation are the real superpowers. Thus have superheroes been reduced to a standard set of psychoanalytic and sociological maneuvers. No wonder they were neurotic by the 1960s.

The stories themselves generally tell it this way (and creators and fans alike generally concur): the superhero is a figure of great independence who chooses to serve the laws and moral values of our society. He is an urban dweller because that's where the criminals are; he operates beyond the strict parameters of the law the better to enforce its values; he supports the status quo but remains uncorrupted by the constant corruption he encounters. As comics creator Howard Chaykin observed, not inaccurately, "The comic book reader has very proscribed ideas about how comic book heroes behave. It comes back to Raymond Chandler's line about Alan Ladd: 'A small boy's idea of a tough guy.'"[3] The superhero is Philip Marlowe in tights.

I would say that as avatars of law and order and justice and authority go, superheroes are a trivial and unconvincing lot. For the most part, nothing really changes through their actions. Their enemies are only marginally freakier than they. The battles leave the "real" problems of society sporadically acknowledged and hardly addressed. Further, if ideas of preserving order are present at all, it is only at the level of narrative: the sequence of images, with their candy-colored costumes, dynamic and irregular layouts, movement beyond the boundary of the frame, fragmented temporalities, sound effects, and further abstractions, insist on a pervasive and appealing chaos, more Midway than White City. The hyperbolic spectacle of the color comics page easily undermines and, yes, subverts, thin fantasies of social order.

Superhero comics present something other than, or apart from, aggressive fantasies of authority and control; something more closely aligned with fantasy and color but at the same time specific to the urban settings that pervade the genre.[4]

Grids and Grace

To ensure a more rational system of urban growth in New York, in 1811 a gridded projection dividing the entire territory of the island into a system of 155 streets and 12 avenues (a total of 2,028 blocks) was superimposed on the topography of Manhattan: "a blueprint for the island's manifest destiny," the architect Rem Koolhaas wrote in *Delirious New York*. The system was at once totalitarian (only Broadway, cutting a broad diagonal swath across the grid, was allowed to deviate from the system) and democratic (a leveling of irregularities, an erasure of difference), an order that would permit expansion and prosperity. With the advent of the grid, rationalist order ruled the city, or at least that's how the story goes. Koolhaas, on the other hand, views the two-dimensional array as little more than a blind for the irrational fantasies that lay at the heart of Manhattan, "the neutralizing agent" that structured the "subutopian fragments" of the city upon which urban planning never completely foreclosed. Horizontality was balanced, perhaps even contradicted, by the upward thrust of the city into vast skyscrapers, each disconnected block and each building, every separate floor and room defined by its own unique and grandiose designs and imaginings. "Through the establishment of enclaves such as the Roman Gardens—emotional shelters for the metropolitan masses that represent ideal worlds removed in time and space, insulated against the corrosion of reality—the fantastic supplants the utilitarian in Manhattan."[5] The irrational dreams of the city only *seemed* constrained by the even tempos of the urban grid.

The urban newspaper was also characterized by the regularity of its columns and the compaction of vast amounts of information within a limited space. In Pulitzer's and Hearst's wooing of New York's vast immigrant and laboring population, the newspaper, once a source of dry information central to the mercantile economy of the nation, became a conduit for fantasies of urban existence. With the introduction of illustrations and multicolumned headlines, the organization of the page owed more to the grid, but this was a grid characterized by new, more open spaces that broke from the strict constraints of even columns. Illustrations and headlines were the signs, lights, and marquees of Broadway and perhaps, too, the invigorating expanse of Olmstead and Vaux's Central Park or sometimes even the playground of Coney.

Newspaper comics, whether in their initial single-panel incarnation or later horizontal sequences, also offered entertainment and respite for eyes regulated by columnar precision, although their legibility also depended on the grid's regularity. In his *New York Journal*, William Randolph Hearst pushed sensational stories, multicolumned headlines, and plenty of multicolumned illustrations. The papers increasingly reflected the kaleidoscopic experience of life in the city, and the Sunday color comic supplements gave readers a fantasia of familiar urban types in sumptuous settings. While newspapers established their centrality as a set of information discourses through reportage, advertising, and editorials, comics remained distinct: aesthetically, through their color and varied organization; and in their content, which generally stressed fantasy, if not outright metamorphosis. Comics were the most conspicuous noninformational feature, or at least the only one that had no pretensions about uplifting the masses. In their deployment of color and fantasy, they were a deliberate departure from the rest of the paper.

The most visually striking strips luxuriated in the space of a full page, and artists frequently played with (and, in the case of one memorable Winsor McCay strip from 1905, exploded) the grids and boxes that dominated the rest of the paper.[6] The fluid metamorphoses that mark nearly all of McCay's *Little Nemo* pages introduce the reader to built environments of surprising yet inevitable complexity. *Nemo* summons thoughts of visionary architecture, but the pages are also reminiscent of the ornate and singular facades on the apartment buildings of the *belle époque*. In contrast, the compressed and formulaic pages of early comic books suggest the overcrowded tenements—democratic, graceless, and durable—that defined immigrant neighborhoods.[7]

The superhero city is founded on the relationship between grids and grace. The city becomes a place of grace by licensing the multitude of fantasies that thrived against the "constraining" ground of the grid. Grace is a function of elegant precision but also implies a virtuostic transcendence of the purely functional, and the city thus possesses a grace of its own. Superheroes are physically graceful, but they are also graced through their freedom, their power, and their mobility. Superhero comics embody the grace of the city; superheroes are graced by the city. Through the superhero, we gain a freedom of movement not constrained by the ground-level order imposed by the urban grid. The city becomes legible through signage and captions and the hero's panoramic and panoptic gaze. It is at once a site of anonymity and flamboyance. Above all, soaring above all, the superhero city is a place of weightlessness, a site that exists, at least in part, in playful defiance of the spirit of gravity.

Part One. The Phenomenology of Superhero Cities

The twentieth-century city put new concentrations of information into increasingly rapid circulation, coincident with new modes of perception and social definition. The now familiar litany of modernist tropes usually includes the problem of mapping an urban space that had become so big, complex, and dynamic as to evade easy comprehension by both its residents and its ostensible controllers. There were anxieties about urban concentration and the concurrent impact of new technologies on mundane life. The city was a contradictory field; the humans within it were reduced to economic units of undifferentiated labor value, and yet, as Georg Simmel famously argued, liberation might lie within this anonymity. The city was its faceless masses, but it was also the new opportunities to make (or remake) a self (or selves). Cities were hardly panoptic spaces of total control: the perfect gaze of the authorities worked most efficiently in fiction that still seemed to posit an amateur sleuth as the last, best, hope.

In fiction, journalism, and cinema, the uncentered city appeared as a dark maze or labyrinth, a site of disappearance and murky invisibilities, a giant trap for the unwary, but it was also a stage for spectacular, kaleidoscopic experience. The city was described in a set of clichéd but not inappropriate dichotomies: the familiar and the strange, the sunlit and the shadowed, the planned and the chaotic, the sublime and the uncanny. This was the poem of the city, so compelling that one can almost see the crosswalks filled with bedazzled, entranced citizens, all struggling to retain their balance on the mesmerizing streets of modernity. Flying over the horizon relatively late in this history, superheroes nevertheless inherit and embody many of these paradoxical tropes. Some define perceptual paradigms and tactics of negotiation appropriate to city life.

Flying in the City

The experience of the city (and the comic book) is less one of static order than dynamic negotiation. "Within the network of its rectilinearity, movement becomes ideological navigation between the conflicting claims and promises of each block," writes Koolhaas.[8] The city, in his seductive view, is not the logical place of business that it pretends to be; it is instead a multitude of fantasies projected in three dimensions. The superhero, in his costumed extravagance, muscular absurdity, and hyperkineticism, superimposes the fantastic on the face of the utilitarian, bringing the city back to the fact of its fantasy. First of all, superheroes negate the negation of the grid—they move through space in three dimensions, designing their own vehicles, choosing their own trajectories. To be a superhero, you've got to be able to move. Superhero narratives are sagas of propulsion, thrust, and movement through the city.

New York is a city of intense circulation. Vivian Gornick finds comfort in its incessant turbulence: "The street keeps moving, and you've got to love the movement. You've got to find the composition of the rhythm, lift the story from the motion, understand and not regret that all is dependent on the swiftness with which we come into view and pass out again. The pleasure and the reassurance lie precisely in the speed with which connection is established and then let go of. No need to clutch. The connection is generic not specific. There's another piece of it coming right along behind this one."[9] But while it might be a city of intense circulation, it also quickly became a place of blocked circulation. The grids of Manhattan imposed regularity on the traffic but channeled it into narrow streets that worked against the flow as well as the logic of the island's narrow, hilly topography.[10] And so, not surprisingly, nearly every superhero worthy of the name has enhanced powers of motion. Superman, Green Lantern, Mighty Mouse, and Captain Marvel can fly, Wonder Woman has an invisible airplane, The Flash has superspeed, and Batman swings on a rope, drives the Batmobile, flies the Batgyro, and so on.[11] The Spectre can walk through walls, Iceman can ride an ice slide, the Fantastic Four have a hovercar, Hawkman and the Angel have wings, and Daredevil and Spiderman leap and swing. Some of them can teleport, but I can't remember who.

Plastic Man is perhaps the most urban of them all—maybe because he

Figure 22. The frantic perspectival shifts of Jack Cole's *Plastic Man*.
(Courtesy of DC Comics.)

doesn't seem to own a car. When Plastic Man needs to be somewhere, he runs, and Jack Cole's art deploys an enormous array of such forms of urban clutter as lampposts, subway entrances, cobblestoned streets, peeling posters, and moldering brick walls. We are often placed so low to the ground that even the curbs loom menacingly. Cole continually varied perspectives on a single page as Plastic Man's body snaked from panel to panel, his stretched body itself linking the spaces of the panels, the city.[12]

The best of them move with more than swift efficiency, their poise and elegance also speaking a kind of poetic appropriation of space. Batman's eloquent cape, Green Lantern's slightly arched back, Daredevil's acrobatic virtuosity, and Superman's vibrant coloration all speak to more than the business at hand.[13] Alan Moore's "imaginary" last Superman story finds Lois Lane describing one of her innumerable rescues: "What happened next had all the familiarity of a recurring dream. I was falling, and a violet comet was falling alongside me. The reds and blues ran together, you see, so that's how he looked when he flew . . . a violet comet."[14] In the consciously mythic *Superman for All Seasons,* Tim Sale represents Superman's blurred superspeed with a thick patina of crayon (see color fig. 13).[15] There is an appealing childlike wonder in these kinetic views. Superheroes preserve the order of the city but need not submit to it. What they must do, however, is partake of its movement.

The Legible City

Cities were also "word cities," as Peter Fritzsche calls them, spaces to be literally and continually read. Newspapers, magazines, and comics helped to constitute the word cities of the United States, as did a wealth of private and municipal signage.[16] Comics superimpose text on the space of the city.[17] In signs, labels, captions, word balloons, and sound effects, words become a fundamental aspect of urban space. Captions are placed in colored boxes, sound effects are depicted in BRIGHT! BOLD! FORMS! These texts compete for the eye's attention, but the overall effect is usually to guide the eye through the complex space. The reader simultaneously juggles words that are part of the landscape (signs), words that are constitutive of narrative (captions, word balloons), and words that produce sensational impact (sound effects). In the later 1970s, such artists as Walt Simonson and Howard Chaykin refined the interplay of image and text: in *American Flagg!, Time²,* and *Manhunter,* reading and looking overlapped as they hadn't before.

The city's many layers are also made legible in the superhero city. Superman tunnels through the city, and the reader is given a cross section of buildings, streets, substructures, and even the rocky substrate. The Hulk shoves The Thing down a manhole, and Jack Kirby divides the panel to show both the street above and the embarrassin' space below. Otomo Katsuhiro's *Akira* is set in a postapocalyptic Neo-Tokyo rendered in meticulous detail. Broken slabs of steel-reinforced concrete, jumbled slabs of asphalt, and the dense underpinnings of the city are all newly exposed to harsh light.

Further, superhero comics are filled with schematic diagrams, like the one of the Fantastic Four's high-rise headquarters. Everything is carefully labeled, from the Giant Map Room and the Hidden Elevator to the Fantasticar Hangar, Trophy Room, and Weapon Collection and the Long Range Passenger Missile (able to reach any point on Earth in minutes). These schematics provide a way of reading the city and are great instances of skyscrapers as both rational and fantastic spaces. The Baxter Building is the Fantastic Four's place of business. The labels are signs that this is a working environ-

Figure 23. The urban battleground, art by Jack Kirby.
(Courtesy of Marvel Comics.)

Figure 24. Substructures exposed, art and text by Will Eisner.
(Courtesy of Will Eisner and DC Comics.)

ment (they're also a further set of signs in the legible city), and they also provide some tantalizing clues as to how the environment works. But, while my childhood mind could well imagine that skyscrapers contained Conference Rooms and Computers, did they also have Missile Monitoring Rooms? The Hidden Elevator ran up and down the length of the building, which the Fantastic Four shared with other, presumably less fantastic, tenants, and another label explained how "Rocket exhaust travels down these pipes to expend its heat in fire pits beneath the city surface." Fire pits beneath the city surface? Wow! So labeling gave me a rational city that was really anything but, while cutaway views showed me high-tech hiding places nested within the modern spaces of adulthood.

The superhero city is experienced in a rush but opened to contemplation: it is distinguished by this dialectic of exuberent motion and a legible stasis. By exposing and labeling the multiple layers of the city, superhero comics enact something equivalent to the superhero's panoramic and panoptic gaze, just as the dynamic organization of figures and panels enact something of the city's constant hustle.

The City in Our Grasp

Before there was a Giant Man, an Ant Man, or an Atom, McCay's Little Nemo grew to the size of Manhattan's rising skyline, as he and Flip stepped over the buildings like toy blocks. Decades later, Bill Watterson's Calvin underwent

Figure 25. The Fantastic Four's secret headquarters.
Courtesy of Marvel Comics

Figure 26. The city on life support. (Courtesy of DC Comics.)

a similar metamorphosis.[18] In the comic strips, fantasy and dreams explicitly licensed the transformation; superhero comics relied on radioactivity or Red Kryptonite to do the same job. Whatever the cause, scale is constantly refigured in the superhero's city.

Bill Finger, a Batman cocreator, was fond of battles at trade exhibitions, where the Caped Crusader and Boy Wonder would hop along the keys of giant typewriters. The expanding list of Kryptonian survivors included the entire city of Kandor, which had been shrunk, bottled, and stolen by Brainiac before the planet exploded. The citizens of Kandor live their normal, albeit tiny, lives on a shelf in Superman's Fortress of Solitude, apparently undismayed by the giant faces of Superman or Lois Lane peering down at them. The most uncanny aspect of Kandor was not simply its portability, although that was pretty interesting, but the notion that a city could be detached, isolated, and removed from its surroundings. The city was a clearly bounded, self-enclosed, self-sustaining environment, something like Manhattan Island without the outlying suburbs. Who feeds the people of Kandor, and how do they dispose of waste? Do these people have jobs? What do they *do* in there? While these are the kind of questions that earthbound urban planners might well ponder, Kandor's secrets remain its own. Susan Stewart reminds us that the miniature erases labor and cause and effect; it also arrests time.[19]

Humans loom above Kandor, a display city, Krypton's Futurama. In a recent Batman animated film, the Joker and Batman do battle at the abandoned site of the Gotham City World's Fair in a Futurama-style exhibition space.[20] The antagonists are the size of buildings. The Joker even wears the spire of the Chrysler Building, just as its architect, William Van Allen, did at a 1931 masquerade ball. The city, then, becomes a toy, a pocket city, a dream house. The body of the child, as with Nemo and Calvin or the ostensible adults of the superhero comics, becomes adequate to the size of the city. The city moves from sublime unknown to marvelous object, its blocks now children's blocks to be rearranged at will. These shifts of scale put the body into a fundamentally different, more tactile relation to the city. "The hand is the measure of the miniature," Susan Stewart writes.[21] Enlarging the body or diminishing the city permit one to "grasp" the city as a whole. "To toy with something is to manipulate it, to try it out within sets of contexts, none of which is determinative."[22]

The city is shrunken and distilled in the superhero comic in ways that recall the distilled urbanism of world's fairs. The World of Tomorrow, in the guise of the 1939 New York World's Fair, had opened to the public only one year after the appearance of the Superman, the Man of Tomorrow. Fairs organized the city into a set of panoramic views, with ample opportunities to see it all from the air. Towers and Ferris wheels and parachute jumps swept the visitors aloft to experience a "fiction of knowledge" and to satisfy "this lust to be a viewpoint." And the fair was the city reduced in scale, open to view, an educational, sensational, but nonlinear immersion in an ideal urban experience. They were progressive and nostalgic in exactly the ways that superheroes were. They humanized the future in terms of the past. Two issues of *World's Fair Comics* appeared, with Superman and Batman sharing the covers, and the fair marked the first public appearance of a "live" Superman (played by Ray Middleton) as part of 1940's "Superman Day." And then there was a short-lived superhero called The Fantom of the Fair, who lurked in utopia's basement (OK, its substructure), fighting crime at, well, world's fairs. In the last decade, a striking number of superheroes have managed to visit the 1939 fair: The Squadron Supreme, Superman, the citizens of Terminal City, and Batman all return to this locus of American urban utopian aspiration as if they recognized their ideological complicity in producing a distilled, controllable urbanism.[23]

Part Two: Superhero City Tours

Superman's Metropolis

Superman was inevitable. Jerry Siegel and Joe Schuster had already tried the name out on a mad villain, which made some kind of sense against the background of an incompletely grasped Nietzschean philosophy and the growing sense of impending war in Europe. Even two midwestern lads could sense a change in the air. America needed a Superman of its own, an American Superman—a boy's Superman. Actually, they gave us a pretty good one.

Superman entered a substantial tradition of hero AS America. With his ability to fly and his inhuman endurance, he became a worthy successor to Lindbergh, while he was also, like Babe Ruth, a power slugger. He was a fine and willing celebrity, frequently sighted by ordinary citizens ("Look! Up in the sky!"). For consumers he incarnated the dreams of personal flying machines, and he was always comfortingly collectible. In a country dedicated to propositions of progress and the "new," Superman appeared with his invulnerable body: the body that retains no marks, on which history cannot be inscribed.

Superman's city, Metropolis, was named for the darkly modern urban center in Fritz Lang's 1926 film, but our Metropolis is more democratic and far less decadent. Its vertical lines cut cleanly to the sky. Our Metropolis is soaring lines and vivid colors. Superman belongs here. Kryptonian skyscrapers tumbled like dominoes in the first panel of Superman's first daily strip. Jor-El bundled his only begotten son into a prototype rocket and aimed it toward Earth. The little rocket, streamlined and slightly bulbous, resembles Siegel's skyscrapers, and the little baby, of course, becomes something of a skyscraper himself. The icon of Superman and the icon of the modern American skyscraper are closely associated. (Superman is raised in the Midwest by Jonathan and Martha Kent before setting out for Metropolis. Immigrant Kryptonian orphan *and* rural American: Superman comes to the city from both directions.) Shortly after his arrival in Metropolis (which went unnamed until 1939 and *Action Comics* #16), Clark Kent took a job at the *Daily Planet,* whose building probably wasn't designed by Raymond Hood but might have been.

Superman *is* a skyscraper, "able to leap tall buildings in a single bound," as I just mentioned: a monument of the modern city, to be gawked at as part of the landscape. He is blessed with panoramic perception, a magisterial gaze upon a known and controlled urban landscape. His body is clothed in a skintight uniform, ornamented only by a functional *S* and a red cape cum banner. There are no hidden secrets to his power—he just hovers there, a Super-Every-Man. Light informs him, from his brightly colored togs to the yellow sunlight that endows him with strength and the beams of heat vision that he can direct at will. No mask hides his face with false ornament: his features are clear, his focus direct. The magisterial gaze becomes democratic, and the "inhuman" skyscraper is mastered by a visibly human body.

There were some precedents. In 1931, the world watched the construction of the Empire State Building, and the photographs taken by Lewis Hine celebrated the young American men who lived and worked in the sky. One figure straddles a guy wire, his right arm stretched above him, his left curved against his body. The city is visible in the distance far below his strikingly casual body. Seven years later, on the cover of *Superman* #1, a smiling Superman rises above the city in a similar pose, the buildings again arrayed below. And people could climb the Statue of Liberty, or be lifted to the top of the Empire State itself, attempting "to find the machinery hidden in the god and approach a transcendent view of the city himself or herself."[24]

If there is a tectonic honesty to this so-called Man of Steel, let's note that he represented, in 1938, a kind of Corbusierian ideal. Superman has X-ray vision: walls become permeable, transparent. Through his benign, controlled authority, Superman renders the city open, modernist, and democratic; he furthers a sense that Le Corbusier described in 1925, namely, that "Everything is known to us." Knowledge depended, for Corbusier, on the mass media, but for Superman "knowledge coincides with sight"—natural sight, I'd add.[25] His X-ray vision imposes transparency, and it manages to reinvent and undermine the city as a private space. There are still secrets behind the old stone walls, but Superman punctures the walls with his gaze and fists and brings the secrets to light.

The aerial perspective provides a powerful liberation. De Certeau wrote of riding to the top of a New York skyscraper that it is "to be lifted out of the city's grasp. One's body is no longer clasped by the streets that turn and return it according to an anonymous law; nor is it possessed, whether as player or played, by the rumble of so many differences."[26] Superman is, as much as anything else, a magisterial view of Metropolis, a way of seeing and negotiating the space of seeing. "The exaltation of a gnostic and scopic drive: the fiction of knowledge is related to this lust to be a viewpoint and nothing more."[27]

Superman seems to be an incarnation of Corbusier's panoramic authority based on perfect transparency, control, and knowledge. He is democratic, open, and idealistic, carving a space for the little guy. A walking, flying figure of utopian progress, Superman prefigures in his mode of perception and spatial negotiation the development of the city of tomorrow. But fantasies of urban planning were rarely so nobly realized, especially in America, and

Figure 27. Sky Boy, Lewis Hine, 1931. (Courtesy of the Avery Architectural
and Fine Arts Library, Columbia University, New York.)

Figure 28. *Superman* #1, 1938, art by Joe Schuster.
(Courtesy of DC Comics.)

Figure 29. Sky Boy, Lewis Hine (detail) (Courtesy of the Avery Architectural and Fine Arts Library, Columbia University, New York.)

by the latter part of the century Corbusier's vision seemed myopic, overly centralized, and terrifyingly corrupted. Highway systems had displaced the centrality of the metropolis, and the emergent configurations were as distant from the Radiant City of Corbusier as from the Broadacre City of Frank Lloyd Wright. The Metropolis of To-Morrow had become the Suburbia of To-Day. Urban "renewal" tended toward the obliteration of both history and nature, demolishing neighborhoods, air quality, and ethnic pluralism in short-sighted obeisance to the engorged networks of automobile circulation.

Eight years before Superman appeared above the streets of Metropolis, Corbusier polemicized against modernity's assault on the human sensorium. Using language that first recalls Benjamin, Kracauer, and other nascent critical theorists of the early twentieth century, his shock polemic abruptly turns toward severe social realignment: "man lives in a perpetual state of instability, insecurity, fatigue and accumulating delusions. Our physical and nervous organization is brutalized and battered by this torrent; it makes its protest, of course, but it will soon give way unless some energetic decision, far-sighted and not too long delayed, brings order once more to a situation which is rapidly getting out of hand."[28] Superman was the New Man, the Man of Steel, the Man of Tomorrow, a "far-sighted" fellow, "not too long delayed" (*faster than a locomotive*) who could suffer the brutalizing shocks of modernity with neither broken bones nor neurasthenic breakdowns. Superior senses and a body so strong that "nothing less than a bursting shell could penetrate his skin" made him the first perfect citizen of the modern Metropolis. But if Superman is its perfect citizen, Lex Luthor is its perfect manager. Lex was retooled in the 1980s and 1990s as the flip side of Superman's democratic radiance. He emerged as the Master of Metropolis—a corporate city planner discontented with this unpredictable individualist sailing through his skies. Luthor, not Superman, best personifies Corbusier's call to order and energetic decision. "Metropolis was nothing until I rebuilt it according to my vision," he ruminates. "All in all, it's a perfect picture of order." But Superman, "an alien with freakish powers," threatens the control of "me, the true Master of Metropolis." Luthor combined the instrumental reason of Corbusier, the independent bureaucratic clout and self-aggrandizement of Robert Moses, and the ruthless baldness of Edward Arnold in *Meet John Doe*. And so Metropolis, whether operating under the gaze of Superman or Luthor, remains primarily Corbusier's turf.

Batman's Gotham

Gotham City, it hardly needs to be said, has no master. It is a city askew, defined by angular perspectives, impenetrable shadows, and the grotesque inhabitants of its night. The screenplay for Tim Burton's 1989 film sums up what Gotham City had become through the 1970s and 1980s: "stark angles, creeping shadows, dense, crowded, airless, a random tangle of steel and concrete, as if Hell had erupted through the sidewalk and kept on growing."[29] Batman's nemesis is the id figure of the Joker rather than Luthor's cool capitalist. Gotham is a city of massed solidities: heavy stone and thick fog cloak its goings-on. The physiognomies here are as warped as the perspectives (Chester Gould's *Dick Tracy* was a precursor) but as solid as the buildings. The city became a "backdrop which was sometimes a mood-setting frieze, sometimes an enveloping or even choking atmosphere that mirrored the twisted preoccupations of villains."[30] Here, as in the detective fictions of the Victorian era and the American pulps and early narrative cinema, crime links the spaces of the city—high and low, penthouses and sewers. All of the city's sunshine and shadow dichotomies are knitted together, and every place is equally susceptible to criminal infection and infestation. Frank Miller's *Dark Knight Returns* was central to bringing this version of Gotham City to the fore, with doses of *Blade Runner* and *Road Warrior* compounding the sense of nihilistic gloom. Gotham became an even more grotesque, gothic, claustrophobic environment (see color fig. 15). The bird's-eye view—Superman's magisterial, panoramic perception—is insufficiently panoptic. Gotham is a city defined more by its underworld. It's a concatenation of hidden spaces, corners, and traps. This city needs to be read, deciphered, made legible, and the one to do it lives among the bats in his own subterranean hideout.

Tom Gunning has shown how around the turn of the century surveillance and counter-surveillance structured the urban detective story. Disguise became a major weapon, and acts of deception and unmasking increasingly structured the narratives.[31] Superman's X-ray vision is too natural, its world-view too rooted in transparency, to get to the bottom of things. Superman's naturalism yields to the dark ratiocinations and high technologies of Batman. Batman inherits from the urban pulp tradition of The Shadow and The Spider, and there is more than a little Holmes and Dupin in his ratiocentrism. His effects are carefully considered, and his endless training has made him a self-made fighting machine—perhaps more steely than his Metropolis counterpart. He is rational, if monomaniacal, but throws fear around him. Superman, appearing in *Action Comics*, inspired wonder, curling across the sky like

Figure 30. The weight of Gotham City,
art by Frank Miller,
from *The Dark Knight Returns*, 1986.
(Courtesy of DC Comics.)

Figure 31. Nothing is mysterious to the
mysterious figure of Batman,
art by Bob Kane.
(Courtesy of DC Comics.)

Figure 32. The Joker, replete with green hair, purple zoot suit, and bad attitude.
(Courtesy of DC Comics.)

a rainbow. Batman summoned a more sublime terror. But both figures, all of these figures, are lingeringly uncanny—childhood anxieties and desires granted crudely concrete form.

Terry Castle has argued that the rise of the Enlightenment was inevitably accompanied "like a toxic side effect" by its uncanny underside, and it is indeed striking how quickly the nocturnal gothic figure of the Batman followed the vivid blur of Superman onto the world stage.[32] Metropolis and Gotham City were variations on New York, but Gotham was the dark side while the sun tended to shine a whole lot more brightly on Superman's city. Recent Superman/Batman teamings, beginning with Frank Miller's *Dark Knight Returns*, have emphasized the dichotomous nature of these two heroes and their two cities. While Luthor and the Joker have their admirers, many revisionist writers have become increasingly intent on exploring the evident (and all too often mechanistic) dualism of these two.[33]

The Joker serves as another double, a psychotic funhouse mirror image of the somber and obsessed hero.[34] He first appeared in *Batman* #1, only a year after the Caped Crusader's own debut: a grotesque figure with a permanent maniacal grin ripped from the posters for Coney Island's Steeplechase Park, chalk-white features and a green shock of slicked-back hair, all dressed up in a purple flat-brimmed hat and zoot suit. The eerie whiteness of the Joker's face signals its opposite; it's the "dark" version of Batman's removable disguise, even more unnatural against the prevailing gloom. Tim Burton's film updated him as a jive pimp, but the Joker was always racial ambiguity incarnate—the original "white Negro."

Spiderman in New York

In an early issue of *Spiderman*, Peter Parker decides he needs a study break and sets off, as his arachnid alter ego, to swing around the city for awhile. It's hard to imagine Batman or The Hulk making the rounds for the sheer joy of moving, but Spiderman is after all a healthy teenager with a need to grandstand.[35]

Spiderman is something of an all-around pariah. Parker began as a nerd's nerd, overly fascinated with chemistry class and oblivious to embodied subjectivities. A bite from a radioactive spider gave him proportionally great strength, the ability to climb walls, and enhanced "spider-senses." But the police suspect him, the press is waging a vendetta against him, and the public perceives him as a menace. While Batman courts his vigilante status, Spiderman has it thrust on him. His first impulse was not to fight crime but to become a TV star, and his self-centeredness led to the death of his beloved uncle. Guilt, rather than righteous vengeance, provides his primal motivation. Not surprisingly, given the level of self-torture involved here, Spiderman's main foes have turned out to be his own doppelgangers. As the theme song for the Spiderman cartoon show once jauntily summed it up: "To him, life is a great big hang-up!"

All this high-flying neurosis would have been impossible to take without the exuberant depictions of Spiderman swinging through New York City. New York: not Metropolis, not Gotham City, not Coast City. Real neuroses demand a real city (or vice versa, I'm not sure which). And New York is a complex organism that, especially by the 1960s when Spiderman and the other Marvel Comics heroes appeared, defied easy apprehension. Superman's magisterial gaze and Batman's profound urban knowledge were revised by Spiderman's more improvisational, sensational style. When his spider-sense tingles, something's up.

Spiderman, particularly as drawn by original artist Steve Ditko, is a more tactile hero than Superman or Batman. He clings to buildings, and Ditko clearly relished the opportunity to further skew the perspectives of the city. Ditko's other creation was Dr. Strange, a mystic master who lived in a great Greenwich Village brownstone. Ditko rendered Strange's ectoplasmic conjurings with peculiar solidity, while in *Spiderman* the physical space of the actual city became utterly unstable. Walls became floors and verticality was close to being entirely lost in his swirling circular forms. One small Ditko panel gives us a rear view of Spiderman in the air over the city. His artificial web snakes slackly through his hands: this is movement in progress, not an arrested bat pose. Two buildings flank his body in the lowest part of the frame, no more than jutting corners against the open space. The superhero's body is marvelous and sinuous, as curved as the web but poised and muscular. No wonder he likes to get out of the house.

More than other heroes, Spiderman makes me reach for de Certeau's "Walking in the City." [36] "To walk is to lack a place," de Certeau argues in a famous passage. "It is the indefinite process of being absent and in search of a proper. The moving about that the city multiplies and concentrates makes the city an immense social experience of lacking a place." Spiderman indeed lacks a place. Superman and Batman are guardians of the urban space, but Spiderman is a trespasser. He is not the master of Metropolis, as is Superman or Luthor; he is not a part of the city's power elite, as is Bruce Wayne. He is not as omnipresent as Batman, and he doesn't own a skyscraper like the Fantastic Four. What de Certeau calls the strategies of institutional control (by governments, for example, or corporations) are not his to command. He is, at best, an interloper, making his own path across the spaces controlled by others (The Kingpin, for example). [37] The tactics of spatial trespass, de Certeau reminds us, constitute the art (the essential art) of the weak. [38]

That same early issue that began with Peter's study break ends with Spiderman standing, alone, on an isolated chimney, wishing he could simply let everyone know who he really is. "To walk is to lack a place," Certeau writes, but the anonymity implied by one's lack of place is precisely what permits that trajectory across the range of positions that only the city allows. [39]

Crusaders for the City

William Randolph Hearst was more than just a maverick millionaire, publisher, and comics devotée; he also cast himself in the role of social crusader.

Figure 33. Skewed perspectives in *Spiderman,* art by Steve Ditko. (Courtesy of Marvel Comics.)

Figure 34. A more tactile relation to the city, art by Steve Ditko. (Courtesy of Marvel Comics.)

From an 1887 editorial in his first paper, the *San Francisco Examiner: "Examiner* reporters are everywhere; they are the first to see everything, and the first to perceive the true meaning of what they see. Whether a child is to be found, an eloping girl to be brought home or a murder to be traced, one of our staff is sure to give the sleepy detectives their first pointers . . . the *Examiner* reporter is a feature of modern California civilization. His energy, astuteness and devotion make him the one thing needed to redeem the community from the corruption that seems to have selected this period as its peculiar prey." *His energy, astuteness, and devotion*—Hearst's reporters were already superheroes, redeeming the community from corruption (and San Francisco was probably a pretty good place to start).

In a way, then, Superman and his alter-ego, crusading journalist Clark Kent, are fighting the same fight using the same methods: ubiquity, speed, enhanced powers of vision and comprehension, and incorruptibility. Early Superman stories often began with Clark tackling a major social problem— corrupt politicians, slum clearance, racketeering in the taxicab industry— with Superman on hand to confront the danger and solve the problem. Here's an example from *Action Comics* #12.

> *Panel 4.* "Clark telephones the city's mayor—" [a diagonal split-screen effect]:
> *Clark:* Why has our city one of the worst traffic situations in the country?
> *Mayor:* It's really too bad—but—what can anyone do about it?
> *Panel 5.* "Later, in the privacy of his apartment, Clark Kent dons a strange uniform, transforming himself into the dynamic SUPERMAN—"
> *Superman:* I, for one, am going to do *plenty* about it!

It was almost inevitable that Clark would reappear in the final panels to receive the accolades, get caught in traffic, or strike out with Lois Lane. In a strong sense, Superman *is* the mighty newspaper.

And now we have Spider Jerusalem, the hero of Warren Ellis's postcyberpunk *Transmetropolitan*. Spider is a crusading journalist of another kind— more Hunter S. Thompson than William R. Hearst. He'd been hiding out on a mountain for five years ("Five years of shooting at fans and neighbors, eating what I kill, and bombing the unwary"),[40] but circumstances necessitate his return to the City, a crackling environment of shrill media, downloaded personalities (foglets), revived citizens from the twentieth century (nobody cares), and all manner of streetwise creatures. "This city never allowed itself to decay or degrade. It's wildly, intensely *growing*. It's a loud bright stinking mess. It takes strength from its thousands of cultures. And the thousands more that grow anew each day. It isn't perfect. It lies and cheats. It's no utopia and it ain't the mountain by a long shot—but it's alive. I can't argue that."[41]

It's Spider's endless regard for the noisy plurality of the urban environment that made *Transmet* one of the most romantic comics around (despite its, and Spider's, surface nihilism). The covers repeatedly posed Spider against the background of the city—Geoff Darrow's cover for issue #22 is a particularly fine example: a slightly oblique, somewhat high-angle view of Spider sitting on the edge of a huge electric marquee, laptop ready, a cigarette smoldering between his fingers, toasting us with his second bottle of whiskey, his two-headed cat by his side, smiling out at us. Behind him the city simply exists through the incredible density of detail that is Darrow's hallmark—bumper to bumper traffic, mounds of bagged trash and scattered litter, graffiti on every street-level surface, radioactivity warnings, jumpers, advertisements, and, in one open window, a guy on a couch with his pants open, empty beer cans and leftover pizza strewn about him. This isn't Metropolis, and Spider Jerusalem, armed with his effective "bowel disruptor," is no mild-mannered reporter, even if he sometimes refers to himself as one.[42] His column may be called "I Hate it Here," but he is deeply proud to serve as the voice of "the new scum," the underclass created by The City's new economies, technologies, and moralities.

What is best about *Transmet*, and what it lifted from the best cyberpunk, is its refusal of the city as a totalitarian site of control. Despite the constant mass media bombardment, there is always something more to see, and whenever Spider feels trapped by his new position as crusader, "media element and TV celebrity," he knows just what to do. "Do what I always do. Get the city under my feet. Become alive." In other words, he takes a walk. Michel de Certeau would be proud. I see them strolling the city together, sharing their thoughts: "I only ever experience the city properly on the street," Spider says. Michel agrees: "The act of walking is to the urban system what the speech act is to language. . . . Walking affirms, suspects, tries out, transgresses, respects, etc., the trajectories it 'speaks.' All the modalities sing a part in this chorus, changing from step to step, stepping in through proportions, sequences, and intensities which vary according to the time, the path taken, and the walker. These enunciatory operations are of an unlimited diversity." Spider answers, yeah, I know what you mean: "It only ever speaks to me here. . . . Just let it talk, in all its languages."[43] Michel continues: "the relationships and intersections of these exoduses . . . intertwine and create an urban fabric . . . placed under the sign of what ought to be, ultimately, the place but is only a name, *the City.*"[44]

Journalists aren't the only crusading superheroes. In the early 1980s there was Mr. X, architect of the now-corrupted psychetecture in the city of Somnopolis.[45] "The subtleties of my psychetecture . . . *destroyed,*" he laments, as he tries to restore his creation. The shaved head and tinted shades of Mr. X prefigure Spider Jerusalem's basic look; both are outsiders returning to the cities that mark their principle obsessions, becoming what de Certeau called "foreigners at home," trying to negotiate a barely contained chaos.[46] "This city was not meant for people," moans one Radiant City dweller. As an avenging superhero, Mr. X is on a crusade to repair the city, but in *Mr. X* and *Transmet*, such fantasies of megalomaniacal control have become self-evidently outmoded, damaging, and useless, especially in light of Spider Jerusalem's enunciation of urban diversity.

Part Three: Of Masks and Capes

(Secret) Identities

Superheroes are all about multiple identities and so embody the slippery sense of self that living in the city either imposes or permits. Simmel, of course, set the tone for a pervading ambivalence in his recognition that the quantification of the urban population in terms of productive labor power represented only a very partial accounting of the men and women in the crowd. The city was a place of aspiration and anonymity, a site of failure and rebirth. "It is the function of the metropolis to make a place for the conflict" between a definition of the city dweller as an object of economic relations and as an autonomous, free, and unique being.[47] In the city, "the individual's horizon is enlarged": the crowd becomes you, and you wend your way through the crowd.[48] The instrumentalities of individual capitalism define the human with precision but not completeness. As a place of being, the city offers room to move.

Who reveals this better than the superhero? Whether in their "true identities" as a mild-mannered reporter, a bored millionaire playboy, a crippled paperboy, or a policeman or incarnated in their more spectacular forms, superheroes play a continuous game of deception and duplicity that could only be played in the city. Admittedly, none of these characters approach the ambiguity of The Shadow of the pulp magazines; his identity as "Lamont Cranston" was itself only another disguise (perhaps). The city is a haven for imposters: by the early nineteenth century, physical mobility had made a mockery of social standing. "One cannot mingle much in society here without meeting some . . . mysterious individual, who claims to be of noble birth," James McCabe observed in 1872.[49] The city attracted them all: false noblemen, deceptive charity workers, strange and disguised visitors from other planets.

Clearly, it is the potential for hubristic comeuppance, and nothing else, that forces Superman to don a pair of spectacles, comb his hair, and thereby transform himself into Clark Kent, mild-mannered reporter. In later years, they tried to convince us that Superman made his face vibrate ever so slightly, which was why nobody twigged to his looking a lot like Clark Kent. Yeah, sure. We know that Clark's anonymity was a function of a sturdy pair of eyeglasses and, mostly, the very nature of life in the city. Perhaps, by the twentieth century it no longer mattered who you really were as long as the mask fit. The Spirit, the resurrection of the seemingly deceased police detective Denny Colt, dons a small black mask and no one seems the wiser—no one even seems to care.

The perfect urban hero is, again, probably Plastic Man, a one-time crook who can remold his face and body at will (something to do with some acid). He has used his power not only to forsake crime but to fight it (something to do with a monastery). One could certainly, in the cities of Poe, Doyle, and Batman, imagine the reverse effect. Plastic Man is really more of an "India Rubber Man!" as his own comic calls him, but "plastic" is more appropriately modern, more descriptive of a personal malleability: a new man for a new city.

The secret identity of the superhero depends on the mask he wears. In Moore's *Watchmen*, superheroes are generically referred to as "masks." The mask is the perfect synecdoche for the superhero, the mysterious totem that makes everything possible. Masks have their place in the history of modernity, as they do in so many other histories. Bakhtin has labeled it the most complex theme of folk culture, but it accrued still more meanings in Western cultures during the Enlightenment and still more within mass culture in the twentieth century. Terry Castle has observed the "ambiguous philosophical and ethical meanings" so prevalent in narrative appearances of masks in the eighteenth century, but these ambiguities may not be as thoroughly forgotten as she might think.[50] The mask had found its place within the elegant, deca-

dent recreation of the masquerade, a carefully delineated realm of compara-
tive abandon. In the novels of, say, Fielding, things happen under cover of
the masquerade: intrigues, scandals, and a refusal of prevailing social mores
are all played through. Castle notes a conflation of mask functions in these
tales. Bakhtin and Caillois wrote of an "old mask" of "shamanistic ritual and
medieval carnival, [that] embodied 'the joy of change and reincarnation'—
the spiritual and organic union of opposites," and of the "mask of modern
times," which was "no more than a screen, a disguise or 'false front,' evoking
new and sinister realms of alienation." Castle continues: "Instead of working
marvelous transformations, the mask now 'hides something, keeps a secret,
deceives.' "[51]

In English novels of the eighteenth century, these two ideations of the mask
intertwine without resolution. The masquerade permits an uncanny return
to an earlier animism. Identity is hidden, but upon this act of disguise something of the earlier talismanic power of the mask can again emerge. In Fielding, "the masquerade is that charged topos around which forgotten or subversive possibilities cluster."[52] The mask of the modern superhero is also both
a "new" mask of disguise and an older mask of "marvelous transformation."

For Bakhtin, the mask could never be "another object among objects"—it
was simply too charged with meanings and functions, whether erotic, magical, or fashionable. In earlier or non-European cultures, masks marked social
identity, while the modern use of the mask in the West is intended to conceal
difference, protect identity. Castle points out that only after the emergence of
a particular notion of the self as unique, individual, and distinct does the con-
cealment of identity take on social significance. To protect the self in modern
times, then, modern man had to don the mask, join the crowd. "Whereas the
primitive mask expressed an identity to the outside, in fact constructed that
identity, the modern mask is a form of protection, a canceling of differences
on the outside precisely to make identity possible, an identity that is now
individual."[53] Thus, the mask is invisible: for it to function, one cannot be
seen to be masked.

I dwell on these ideas of masking and modernity because it seems to me
that superheroes partake of some of the ambiguity that Castle ascribes to
eighteenth-century English narrative as well as twentieth-century urban concerns with anonymity and the mask that cannot be seen. In their secret identities, superheroes all hide in plain sight. Superman sets the stage but also
remains somewhat unique. As Jules Feiffer was among the first to observe,
while all the other heroes adopted their colorful alter egos, Superman grew

up hiding his true abilities.[54] Superman is disguised as Clark Kent, while Bruce Wayne disguises himself as Batman. Clark Kent, mild-mannered, blue-suited, earnest, hardworking, dolefully dweeblike for most of his history, is a perfect embodiment of the masked figure of modern man. One can read so much into this particular masquerade: Superman's adolescent creators, recognizing the repression endemic to the world of adulthood; Jewish young-sters fantasizing of being both uniquely superhuman and invisibly assimi-lated; American Everyman as Superman. Meanwhile, Superman is the hero without a mask, his "true" face revealed to the world, at once monumental and generic. Superman becomes us, goes among us, and we might be him. But Clark is about more than assimilation and even about more than geek dreams of godhood. This Everyman in a dependable suit depends on invisi-bility, the anonymity permitted by a great metropolis. He cannot be visible, and he has a secret. And so Superman and Clark subvert one another: the man who sees everything meets the man who is not seen.

But most of the others hide their faces: they can't wait to pull on the tights, don the masks, and streak out into the bright life of the city. Here masks once again mark a social identity—the costume of the burglar becomes, follow-ing Zorro and the Lone Ranger, a sign of the vigilante hero. In their first ad-ventures, Superman and Batman battle ordinary, uncostumed foes. Batman's rogue's gallery moves decidedly toward the grotesque with such villains as the Joker and Two-Face, figures who are never permitted the luxury of hiding what they are (although Two-Face, acid scarred on one side, normal on the other, carries a LOT of symbolic weight). Soon, however, with the advent of costumed and masked villains, the mask becomes less a sign of ethical status than a morally indeterminate "superness."

Both masked heroes and villains tapped back into the history of the mask in "shamanistic ritual and medieval carnival"; in comic books, the mask once more embodied something of "the joy of change and reincarnation." Many of these characters are literally or figuratively reborn into their new identi-ties. Jim Stark is a cop gunned down in the line of duty, but he returns as the domino-cloaked Spectre, a figure of unyielding vengeance. The animistic underside of the rational space of the city is exposed in bold, bright colors.

The Vigilante and the Dandy

The city is a permanent costume party, Koolhaas and Jonathan Raban re-mind us, and superheroes have the brightest costumes. Their outfits are streamlined amalgams of the machinic, the historical, and the organic, but they always emphasize the (increasingly exaggerated) human musculature beneath. An Alan Moore character of recent vintage actually wears no costume; she simply adjusts her pigments to superheroic patterns. When people find out she's "really" naked, they no longer know quite where to look, but Moore's little joke reminds us that superhero bodies have always been naked bodies exhibited to a very public gaze.

Superheroes are acrobats: their colorful tights are the garb of circus performers. Dick Grayson was a circus performer, one of the Flying Graysons, but he was orphaned when gangsters doctored the trapeze ropes (that damn acid again!). After a little training by Batman (another orphan—these cities attract them) he takes on a new role as "that astonishing phenomenon, that young Robin Hood of today—Robin the Boy Wonder!" Deadman is a reincarnated circus acrobat out to find out who had him assassinated in midperformance, but really they're all circus performers. There are strong men (Superman, The Thing), aerialists (Batman, Daredevil), clowns (the Joker), acrobats (Nightcrawler), ringmasters (Lex Luthor, The Ringmaster), hypnotists (Mysterio), wild beasts (Catwoman, Wolverine, Hawkman et al.), contortionists (The Elongated Man, Mr. Fantastic), fire acts (The Human Torch), escape artists (Batman, Mr. Miracle), sideshow freaks (Bizarro, The Geek, the X-Men), magicians (Mandrake, Dr. Strange), sharpshooters (Green Arrow), half-men/half-beasts (The Hulk, Swamp Thing), and a big finish (The Human Bomb).

In *Sex and Suits,* Anne Hollander describes several shifts in the history of "civilized" attire. At some point dress began to mark differences of gender, and not simply of class, and the neoclassical moment "put a final seal of disapproval on gaudy clothes for serious men."[55] While the man's suit was a dynamic yet subtle manifestation of bodily power—flexible and flowing, closely shaped to torso and mobile limbs—men's clothing also moved away from flamboyant color and excess. The superhero costume marks a return to earlier modes of male self-presentation by combining Rococo ornamentation (with its flashing colors, flowing capes, epaulets, and talismans) with a classical ideal in which "the hero wore nothing but his perfect nudity, perhaps enhanced by a short cape falling behind him (see color fig. 17). The nude costume was the one most suggestive of perfect male strength, perfect virtue, and perfect honesty, with overtones of independence and rationality. The hero's harmonious nude beauty was the visible expression of his uncorrupted moral and mental qualities" (87). Purity and performative flamboyance were thus uniquely combined in the superhero's costume. And, if Batman eschewed color to embody instead his heart of darkness, Robin the Boy Wonder was right by his side, accoutered in red tunic, yellow cape, and green booties.

The appeal of classical purity speaks for itself, but flamboyance is the real issue here. Alongside the image of an idealized, classical self, superheros further embody a male fantasy of flamboyant, performative intemperance, something blocked by the pragmatic, self-controlled economy of a historically constructed masculine cultural identity signified by the visual drabness of his closet. But many of those closets have secret doors opening onto a broader sense of what is appropriate for the boy or man. Our costumed vigilante is perhaps something more of a dandy, a flamboyant, flamboyantly powered, urban male, who, if not for his never-ending battle for truth, justice, and the American Way, would probably be ordered to "just move it along." What battles against "crime" and "corruption" really do, it seems, is license the donning of the superhero garb, legitimate the movement out of the home, through the window, and into the secret magic of the urban night. The fantasy, then, is one of dressing up—superheroes don't wear costumes in order to fight crime, they fight crime in order to wear the costumes.[56]

Here it seems that I'm edging up on a homoerotic reading of buff closet queens escaping the mundane world to mingle in secret places with their even more flamboyantly subversive enemies/allies/doppelgangers. But that's been done. Instead, I'd like to soften that reading and spin it somewhat differently by suggesting that the superhero raids *several* closets before swinging out on the town, indulging in the flamboyance of urban fashion, desiring to perform anonymously but in full view, fantasizing of a *present*ness usually assigned to ethnic others. The superhero heads for marginalized sites, sites of nonproduction or spectacular destruction, not to impose order but to participate in, *belong to,* the chaos.

Perhaps the concern with "law and order" should be reconstrued to remove it from a narrow, legalistic definition. After all, the "laws" of physics and biology are more inverted than affirmed by these free-flying figures, and what role can "order" serve with regard to flamboyant contents of the superhero's closet? Baudelaire referred to dandyism as "an institution beyond the laws," and despite its association with effeminacy Sartre found it more exhibitionist than homosexual at its core. Dandies operate on "their own authority" and, with "the help of wit, which is an acid, and of grace, which is a dissolvent, . . . manage to ensure the acceptance of their changeable rules, though these are in fact nothing but the outcome of their own audacious personalities." While superheroes, especially those who wisecrack while in the very midst of battle, seem more witless than witty, their universe is a kind of self-referential and solipsistic realm centered on an audacious performance by a flamboyant figure who is permitted to slip the bonds of conventional behavior and being. In Superman, the transcendent imperatives of the *über-mensch* are tempered by the dandy's unseriousness: *Look, up in the sky! Is it a bird?*

Baudelaire connected the dandy to the modern urban landscape, although his analysis of a more self-alienated observer, the flaneur, has received more attention of late than the seemingly blasé but relentlessly committed performance of the dandy. Barbey noted Brummell's "air of elegant indifference which he wore like armor, and which made him invulnerable" or, Barbey quickly adds, "which made him *appear* invulnerable." (If not for my childhood reading of Superman, would I even *know* the word *invulnerable*?) The costume is the sign and source of power, the mark of *grace*.

Norman Mailer's "white Negro" tries to co-opt some of the dandy's projected grace. In Mailer's mythos the white Negro, or hipster, is a kind of racial cross-dresser, performing the perceived existential freedom of the urban black male. Rendered powerless in American society, the black man "lived in the enormous present, he subsisted for his Saturday night kicks, relinquishing the pleasures of the mind for the more obligatory powers of the body." The hipster partakes of this acceptance of death and danger, living as he is in the shadow of the Bomb and the Holocaust. His isolation is willed; Mailer calls it "the isolated courage of isolated people," a fine superhero credo.

Superheroes could be some inchoate version of the same thing. Their sagas are passing narratives—Superman's midwestern Jewish cocreators cloaking themselves not only in the power of Superman but in the metropolitan anonymity of Everyman Clark Kent. And in his multicolored, flamboyant absurdity the superhero is also a kind of hipster, seeking to swoop down and possess the life of the street. The costume still serves as a mark of difference, but now the superhero signals an abdication of responsibility rather than becoming its exemplary figure.

So this is a fantasy of blacking up—putting on the mask permits an extroversion only in the guise of the other, which is exactly Mailer's critique of the hipster. And, as Garelick argues, "All dandyism hints at a wish for male authochthony"—the woman disturbs the dandy's (and the superhero's?) perfect aesthetic self-containment. The self in motion is also a "reified, immobilized Self."[57]

The foregoing analysis is valid and important, but it is also surely too damning. The dandy, according to Barbey, combines "frivolity, on the one hand, acting upon a people rigid and coarsely utilitarian, on the other, Imagination, claiming its rights in the face of a moral law too severe to be genuine, [producing] a kind of translation, a science of manners and attitudes, impossible elsewhere." Fantasy is, after all, the place for the abdication of responsibility, a place of temporary grace.

One hesitates to play the Nietzsche card, as his name has dominated too many attempts to take superheroes seriously. Superman just doesn't cut the mustard as an übermensch. He is to the manner born, so to speak; he doesn't need to *become* a superman. Despite his power, he continues to identify with, and fight for, the values of ordinary men (hence Clark Kent), and thus he is a superman who preserves rather than sabotages the status quo. Superman is the overman domesticated, muzzled, and neutered. There have recently appeared several serious and sustained works that grapple with the Nietzchean connotations of the genre by exploring the darker relations between superhuman morality and social responsibility.[58]

But another aspect of Nietzsche's thought might be more pertinent to our friendly neighborhood superheroes. Central to *Thus Spoke Zarathustra* and *The Gay Science* is the concept of play. Independence, the position of the overman, can only be attained through new modes of thought and thus through new languages that implicitly deconstruct the assumptions of the old. A gay science "is meant to be anti-German, anti-professorial, anti-academic. . . . It is also meant to suggest 'light feet,' 'dancing,' 'laughter'—and ridicule of 'the spirit of gravity.'"[59] Poetry and play, "light-hearted defiance(s) of convention," are the means to a new spirit of investigation: a gay science.

> I would believe only in a god who could dance. And when I saw my devil I found him serious, thorough, profound, and solemn: it was the spirit of gravity—through him all things fall.
>
> Not by wrath does one kill but by laughter. Come, let us kill the spirit of gravity!
>
> I have learned to walk: ever since, I let myself run. I have learned to fly: ever since, I do not want to be pushed before moving along.
>
> Now I am light, now I fly, now I see myself beneath myself, now a god dances through me.[60]

Thus, the plumage of the dandy is quite in keeping with the playful aspects of Neitzsche's thought and language, although not, one must note, with the philosopher's asceticism, which the dandy would find tedious. The superhero does have affinities with the overman but not in the Nietzsche Lite version of transcendence that gives the hero powers and abilities far beyond those of mortal men, nor in the movement of the hero beyond good and evil, but rather through a basically light, playful, and performative dance. The superhero is our ally against the spirit of gravity: in rising brightly over our heads, he compels us to look, and look again, and then to exclaim, *Look! Up in the sky.*[61]

"Wish I Could Fly Like Superman"

The challenge in writing about comic books lies in both the dearth of scholarship and the inaccessibility of the actual objects. In many ways, the most valuable historians of the medium have been the creators themselves, in particular those writers, editors, and artists who have continuously revitalized the genre over the last twenty years, who have pushed and prodded the idea of the superhero in all directions.[62] Because of course superheroes are real; they have history and have exerted a material impact on culture for sixty years. Most of us have grown up in a world of superheroes, a world in which the original Superman, jumping his one-eighth of a mile and chucking cars about, seems, let's face it, like a bit of a wuss. Anything less than planet-shattering power isn't worth the computer-colored paper it's printed on. But some recent comics have begun to settle back to Earth, fueled by the recognition that the real power of the superhero is primarily iconic.

Hence the spate of stories about being, or wanting to be, a superhero. *Watchmen* and *Astro City* are filled with citizens dreaming of superheroes or superheroics, and James Robinson's updating of *Starman* centers on the aging hero's son, who reluctantly takes up the heroic mantle and gravity rod but won't wear the tights. In 2000, DC Comics published its *Realworlds* series, in which "fictional super-heroes influence all-too-human people to attempt superhuman things."[63] *Realworlds: Batman* gave us a youth who thinks he's Batman. He poses in his homemade costume on the cover, beneath the Bat logo from the 1960s television program, surrounded by Bat paraphernalia of every kind, including a poster of New York he has relabeled "Gotham."[64]

Alan Moore has moved from the darkness of *Watchmen*, in which the fantasy of superheroes was tinged with pathos, to work that emphasizes the playful, colorful grace of the genre. His *Promethea*, a heroine of stories, pulp magazines, and comic books, is physically manifested through those who chronicle her adventures, each time incorporating the persona of her latest "creator." To write about her is to write her into existence. In another Moore

Figure 35. Superheroes in the real world, painted art by Alex Ross for the cover
of *Astro City* #4. (Courtesy of Image Comics.)

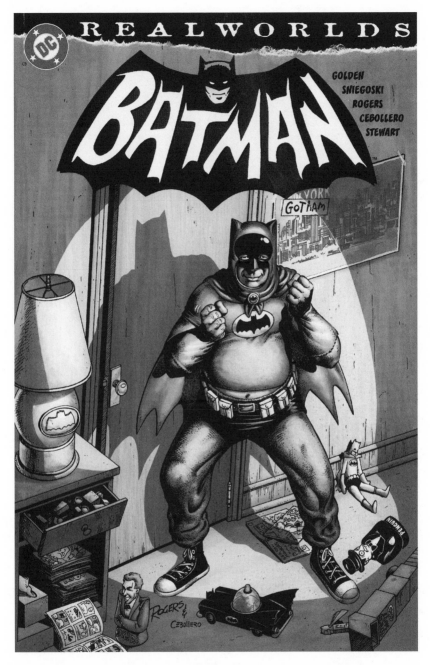

Figure 36. The real world's investment in superhero comics culture,
art by Marshall Rogers and John Cebollero. (Courtesy of DC Comics.)

Figure 37. Fantasies of flight:
T-shirt with original Superman logo.
(Collection of the author.)

comic, the character Supreme hides behind his secret identity as a superhero comic book artist who draws the adventures of "Omniman." ("I mean, you put on glasses and nobody recognizes you!" gasps his girlfriend. "Is everybody just, like, *stupid* or what?" "I've wondered about that myself," Supreme answers.)[65] In *Promethea* and *Supreme,* Moore has incorporated the comic's creator—the mythmaker—into the myth, in a movement that goes beyond postmodern parlor games of reflexivity to a deeper acknowledgment of our own imbrication in the life of our fantasies.

To Be Continued . . .

Superheroes are vehicles of urban representation; they embody perceptual paradigms. Through the vehicle of the superhero, as through cinema and sociology, one recovers the city as new and shifting ground. Urbanism was defined as a way of life by sociologist Louis Wirth in 1938, the year that also saw the appearance of Superman. Superheroes exist to inhabit the city, to patrol, map, dissect, and traverse it. They are surprisingly proper guides to these cities of change: invulnerable yet resilient and metamorphic, they hold their shape. They hold their shape as do the other skyscrapers and monuments of the metropolis, perhaps accreting some fussy ornamentation, some new functionality or relevance, but still managing to embody a dignified history that is occasionally sandblasted back into visibility.

Surely the colors should have faded by now, yet superheroes are still in the air and on the T-shirts on my chest. When I look in the mirror, I see Superman.

NOTES

Preface

1   W. G. Sebald, *Austerlitz*. Trans. Anthea Bell (New York: Random House, 2001), 19.

2   Annette Michelson, "Bodies in Space: Film as 'Carnal Knowledge,'" *Artforum* 7.6 (1969): 54–63.

3   The phrase is from James Robinson, *Batman/Hellboy/Starman* #1 (DC Comics, January 1999), 17.

4   "The unthinkable which happened was thus the object of fantasy: in a way, America got what it fantasized about, and this was the greatest surprise." Slavoj Žižek, "Welcome to the Desert of the Real!" *South Atlantic Quarterly* 101:2 (spring 2002).

5   Michael Chabon, *The Amazing Adventures of Kavalier & Clay* (New York: Random House, 2000), 575.

6   Ibid., 582.

7   Steven Millhauser, "The Little Kingdom of J. Franklin Payne" in *Little Kingdoms* (New York: Vintage Books, 1993), 107.

8   These texts present somewhat aestheticized and possibly defanged versions of William Burroughs's order to "Storm the Reality Studio and retake the universe." Chabon and Millhauser accept the hard reality of the real and the provisional quality of these escapes. Yet all three writers evoke a similar sense of reality and fantasy flickering in and out of each other's domain.

9   Cited in William Leach, *Land of Desire: Merchants, Power and the Rise of a New American Culture* (New York: Vintage Books, 1993), 346.

Introduction

1   Walken's speech patterns, often parodied by Kevin Spacey, exhibit this same combination in their quirky stresses and cadences.

2   Michel de Certeau, "Walking in the City," in *The Practice of Everyday Life*, translated by Steven Rendall (Berkeley: University of California Press, 1984), 91–110.

3   Ben Singer, *Melodrama and Modernity: Early Sensational Cinema and Its Contexts* (New York: Columbia University Press, 2001), 35.

4   Lieven de Cauter has made a similar argument. See "The Panoramic Ecstasy: On World Exhibitions and the Disintegration of Experience," *Theory, Culture, and Society* 10 (1993): 1–23.

5   And all of this was played out again around the electronic technologies of a later modernity, in theme parks, IMAX theaters, virtual realities, the magazine *Mondo 2000*, and computer games.

6   Steven Shaviro, *The Cinematic Body* (Minneapolis: University of Minnesota Press, 1993), 24.

7   David Bordwell, *On the History of Film Style* (Cambridge: Harvard University Press, 1997).

8   Ben Singer, *Modernity and Melodrama: Early Sensational Cinema and Its Contexts* (New York: Columbia University Press, 1997).

9   See the discussion of the modernity thesis in Singer, 119 (recalibration and perceptual conditioning); 121 (invigoration), 125 (impoverishment).

10 Studies of this conservativism abound in journalism, popular culture scholarship, film theory, and women's studies and can be found alongside studies proclaiming the radical subversiveness of privileged works within these media or ways of reading them "against the grain." I have benefited enormously from these studies, which were constant sources of reference in my earlier study of postmodern science fiction, *Terminal Identity: The Virtual Subject in Postmodern Science Fiction* (Durham: Duke University Press, 1993).

11 Robert Warshow, Preface to *The Immediate Experience: Movies, Comics, Theatre, and Other Aspects of Popular Culture*, enlarged ed. (Cambridge: Harvard University Press, 2001), xl (originally published in 1962).

12 Lewis Mumford, *Technics and Civilization* (New York: Harcourt, Brace, 1963), 6.

13 Bukatman, 1993.

14 See, for starters, Annette Michelson's "Bodies in Space: Film as 'Carnal Knowledge,'" *Art Forum* 7.66 (1969): 54–63; any of a number of essays by Tom Gunning, including "An Unseen Energy Swallows Space: The Space in Early Film and Its Relation to American Avant-Garde Film," in *Film before Griffith*, edited by John Fell (Berkeley: University of California Press, 1983), 355–66; Antonia Lant, "Haptical Cinema," *October* 74 (1995): 45–73; and Vivian Sobchack, *The Address of the Eye: A Phenomenology of Film Experience* (Princeton: Princeton University Press, 1992). On relations between early cinema and electronic culture, see Anne Friedberg, *Window Shopping: Cinema and the Postmodern* (Berkeley: University of California Press, 1993); and Lev Manovich, *The Language of New Media* (Cambridge: MIT Press, 2001).

15 Ann Douglas wrote that "Dorothy Parker, the city's wittiest muse, planned to entitle her autobiography . . . 'Mongrel.' Parker was presumably referring to her own mixed Jewish and Wasp heritage, but she could have been talking of racially and ethnically mixed 'mongrel' Manhattan" (*Terrible Honesty: Mongrel Manhattan in the 1920s* [New York: Farrar, Straus, Giroux, 1995], 5).

1   There's Always . . . Tomorrowland:
Disney and the Hypercinematic Experience

While much of "There's Always . . . Tomorrowland" made its way into my *Terminal Identity: The Virtual Subject in Postmodern Science Fiction* (Durham: Duke University Press, 1993), I am pleased to reprint it in its original essay form.

1 Randy Bright, *Disneyland: Inside Story* (New York: Abrams, 1987), 88.

2 Ibid., 56.

3 This execrable addition attains new heights of commodity fetishism and ideological reification—but on the other hand the notion of a simulation of Hollywood is almost embarrassingly appropriate to the era. By 2002, there was at least one more major park, Disney's California Adventure.

4 Arthur Kroker, Marilouise Kroker, and David Cook, eds., *Panic Encyclopedia* (New York: St. Martin's, 1989), 16.

5 Since the initial publication of this essay, Tomorrowland has deliberately adopted more of a retro-future tone, and Disneyland Paris features the Jules Verne inspired Discoveryland.

6 Thanks to Vivian Sobchack for this and so many other ideas.

7 H. Bruce Franklin, "America as Science Fiction: 1939," *Coordinates: Placing Science Fiction and Fantasy*, edited by George Slusser, Erik S. Rabkin, and Robert Scholes (Carbondale: Southern Illinois University Press, 1983), 119.

8 Attractions in the Magic Kingdom's Tomorrowland and EPCOT Center's Future World (ca. the early 1990s) included Horizons, The Land, Journey into Imagination, Mission to Mars, Universe of Energy, Space Mountain, The Living Seas, CommuniCore, Carousel of Progress, Spaceship Earth, Starjets, The Wonders of Life, WEDway People Mover, American Journeys, If You Could Fly, and The World of Motion.

9 William Gibson, "The Gernsback Continuum," in *Burning Chrome* (New York: Arbor House, 1986), 37–38.

10 Thomas Hine, *Populuxe* (New York: Knopf, 1986), 151.

11 Quoted in Margaret King, "Disneyland and Walt Disney World: Traditional Values in Futuristic Form," *Journal of Popular Culture* 15.1 (1981): 127.

12 Raymond Fielding, "Hale's Tours: Ultrarealism in the pre-1910 Motion Picture," in *Film Before Griffith*, edited by John Fell (Berkeley: University of California Press, 1983), 116. Even Hale's Tours was only an update of Fred Thompson's attraction at the 1901 Buffalo World Exposition, A Trip to the Moon (see Woody Register, *The Kid of Coney Island: Fred Thompson and the Rise of American Amusements* (Oxford: Oxford University Press, 2001).

13 John Clute, Introduction to *Interzone: The Second Anthology*, edited by John Clute (New York: St. Martin's, 1987), viii.

14 Bruce Sterling, Preface to *Mirrorshades: The Cyberpunk Anthology*, edited by Bruce Sterling (New York: Arbor House, 1986), xi.

15 Cyberpunk looks pretty utopian to me from the perspective of 2002.

16 Franklin, 121. While I want to demonstrate that there is more going on here than Franklin's ideological reading suggests, I largely agree with his conclusion.

17 However, Exxon's Universe of Energy pavilion was "down" one day while I was conducting research, an ironic counterpoint to the "real world" *Valdez* disaster. H. Bruce Franklin has similarly observed "deep historical ironies" at the 1939 World's Fair, an ode to technology performed in a period of rampant unemployment and stagnation (ibid., 118).

18 Richard Schickel, *The Disney Version*, rev. ed. (New York: Simon and Schuster, 1985), 23.

19 King, 1981, 127.

20 Guy Debord, "Report on the Construction of Situations and on the International Situationist Tendency's Conditions of Organization and Action," translated by Ken Knabb, in *Situationist International Anthology*, edited by Ken Knabb (Berkeley: Bureau of Public Secrets, 1981), 23.

21 Ivan Chtcheglov, "Formulary for a New Urbanism," translated by Ken Knabb, in *Situationist International Anthology*, edited by Ken Knabb (Berkeley: Bureau of Public Secrets, 1981), 4.

22 Thanks to Caitlin Kelch for this insight. This layout is identical in all versions of the Magic Kingdom, from California to Florida to Tokyo.

23 Debord, 24, my emphasis.

24 This monadism is presented and simultaneously critiqued in George Romero's witty *Dawn of the Dead* (1978), a film that plays like a pulp version of Adorno and Horkheimer's *The Dialectic of Enlightenment*.

25 Citizens, usually teenagers, of the various countries represented at EPCOT work at the park for one year.

26 William Kowinski, *The Malling of America* (New York: Morrow, 1985), 71.

27 Kroker, Kroker, and Cook, 1989, 208.

28 Kowinski, 67.

29 Schickel, 313.

30 Kowinski, 21, 18.

31 Mark Crispin Miller has noted that while Reagan was an undistinguished film actor because "his celluloid image was basically too dim and vacuous . . . this very emptiness has made him perfect for TV" (Mark Crispin Miller, "Virtù, Inc.," in *Boxed In: The Culture of TV* [Evanston: Northwestern University Press, 1988], 79–94). Reagan presided over a Disneyfied vision of America—the audioanimatronic™ president.

32 Michel de Certeau, *The Practice of Everyday Life*, translated by Steven Rendall (Berkeley: University of California Press, 1984), 35–36.

33 Research into agricultural technologies, for example, occurs at the Kraft-sponsored exhibit, The Land, at EPCOT Center.

34 de Certeau, xix.

35 Ibid., 33.

36 Richard Powers, *Prisoner's Dilemma* (New York: Collier Books, 1988), 83.

37 Umberto Eco, *Travels in Hyperreality*, translated by William Weaver (New York: Harcourt Brace Jovanovich, 1985), 46.

38 Dean Motter et al., *The Return of Mr. X* (East Fullerton, CA: Graphitti Designs, 1986).

39 Post-Mac developments in the quest for a perfect interface include voice-activated systems and touch-sensitive screens.

40 Alvin Toffler, *The Third Wave* (New York: Bantam, 1981), 186.

41 Although his work serves as invaluable reference material for the cyberpunks, Alvin Toffler's vision is pure hippie-hacker with a procapitalist slant. He is a favorite lecturer at Silicon Valley corporations.

42 James D. Foley, "Interfaces for Advanced Computing," *Scientific American*, October 1987, 129.

43 A version of the Dataglove is already available as part of the Nintendo game system for children.

44 Comments by Minsky, Leary, and the nameless developer, as well as information on the Eyephones, are from a news report on National Public Radio's *All Things Considered*, August 8, 1989. "What world am I in?" the reporter asks his guide through virtual space.

45 Sterling, xi.

46 The film—released at the time of a well-publicized transition at the Disney studios—is also unmistakably reflexive, down to the benign programmer-founder named Walter whose spirit finally "animates" the computer world with warm colors.

47 See films by Méliès, Keaton, Clair, and Vertov, as well as Kubrick and Cronenberg, for examples.

48 Christian Metz, *The Imaginary Signifier: Psychoanalysis and the Cinema*, translated by Celia Britton et al. (Bloomington: Indiana University Press, 1977), 49–51.

49 This ambiguous vision is presented effectively in David Cronenberg's film *Videodrome* (1982). See Bukatman, 1993, chap. 1.

50 Richard V. Francaviglia, "Main Street USA: A Comparison/Contrast of Streetscapes in Disneyland and Walt Disney World," *Journal of Popular Culture* 15.1 (1981): 156.

51 Friedberg, 1993, 14.

52 Ibid., 10.

53 Paul Virilio, "Cataract Surgery: Cinema in the Year 2000," in *Alien Zone: Cultural Theory and Contemporary Science Fiction*, edited by Annette Kuhn (London and New York: Verso Books, 1990), 171.

54 One might note Michelson's analysis of *2001: A Space Odyssey*, in which she compares the bodily experiences of spectators and astronauts. The curvature of the Cinerama screen mimics the shape of the space helmets themselves. Annette Michelson, "Bodies in Space: Film as Carnal Knowledge," *Artforum* 7.6 (1969): 54–63.

55 Tom Gunning, "An Unseen Energy Swallows Space: The Space in Early Film and Its Relation to American Avant-Garde Film," in *Film before Griffith*, edited by John Fell (Berkeley: University of California Press, 1983), 363.

56 Lynne Kirby, "Male Hysteria and Early Cinema," *Camera Obscura* 17 (1989): 113–31.

57 Walter Benjamin, "The Work of Art in the Age of Mechanical Reproduction," translated by Harry Zohn, in *Illuminations*, edited by Hannah Arendt (New York: Schocken, 1969), 250.

58 One peculiarity is encountered at Spaceship Earth (sponsored by AT&T). As narrator Walter Cronkite begins to proclaim the wonders of tomorrow, the cars turn around so that the guests proceed backward into the future, inexplicable yet somehow fitting.

59 de Certeau, xxiii.

60 Maurice Merleau-Ponty, *Phenomenology of Perception*, translated by Colin Smith (London: Routledge and Kegan Paul, 1962), 132.

2   Gibson's Typewriter

1 Wolfgang Schivelbusch, *The Railway Journey: The Industrialization of Time and Space in the Nineteenth Century* (Berkeley: University of California Press, 1986); *Disenchanted Night: The Industrialization of Light in the Nineteenth Century* (Berkeley: University of California Press, 1988).

2 Cited in Friedrich Kittler, *Discourse Networks, 1800–1900*, translated by Michael Metteer with Chris Cullens (Stanford: Stanford University Press, 1990), 196.

3 This is precisely how it is treated in a somewhat meager industrial history: Donald R. Hoke, *Ingenious Yankees: The Rise of the American System of Manufactures in the Private Sector* (New York: Columbia University Press, 1990).

4   Kittler, 193.

5   "We want a machine which could print as easily as we can now write" ("More Improvements Wanted," *Scientific American,* October 8, 1851, 7), cited in Hoke, 134.

6   Bruce Bliven Jr., *The Wonderful Writing Machine* (New York: Random House, 1954).

7   Hoke, 133.

8   The implications of so-called armory practice in manufacturing have been debated in economic history. The military had little reason to economize, and thus its development of labor-intensive mass production may not have been the most democratic or efficient model to apply to civilian production. The evidence seems to suggest that the Remington Company used both armory practice and new methods of organization to produce its typewriters as efficiently as possible (for a more detailed analysis, see ibid.).

9   William Gibson, *Neuromancer,* New Ace Science Fiction Specials (New York: Ace, 1984), 34.

10 Bliven, 22–23.

11 Margery Davies further argues that women could become typists because the machinery was new enough to avoid any sex-specific connotations. See *Woman's Place Is at the Typewriter: Office Work and Office Workers, 1870–1930* (Philadelphia: Temple University Press, 1982).

12 Richard N. Current, *The Typewriter and the Men Who Made It* (Urbana: University of Illinois Press, 1954), 120–21. Current notes that the typewriter, of course, was not the only such enabling technology (122).

13 Bliven, 153.

14 Cited in Kittler, 195.

15 Ibid.

16 Ibid., 194.

17 Marshall McLuhan, *Understanding Media* (New York: New American Library, 1964), 259–62.

18 Michel Chevalier, *Society, Manners, and Politics in the United States* (Ithaca: Cornell University Press, 1961), 207. This passage is cited in both Schivelbusch, *Railway Journey;* and Mark Seltzer, *Bodies and Machines* (New York: Routledge, 1992).

19 Justin Kaplan, *Mr. Clemens and Mark Twain* (New York: Simon and Schuster, 1966), 281.

20 See Seltzer, 3–4.

21 Bliven, 116.

22 Ibid., 122.

23 Ibid., 128–29.

24 Ibid., 174.

25 Jeremy Rifkin, *Time Wars: The Primary Conflict in Human History* (New York: Holt, 1987), 117.

26 Processed World Collective, "Keep Jane's Fingers Dancing," in *Bad Attitude: The Processed World Anthology,* edited by Chris Carlsson with Mark Leger (London and New York: Verso, 1990).

27 All quotations in this section are from Bliven, 176–200.

28 Fredric Jameson, *Postmodernism, or the Cultural Logic of Late Capitalism,* Post-contemporary Interventions (Durham: Duke University Press, 1991), 307.

29 Istvan Csicsery-Ronay Jr. "The Sentimental Futurist: Cybernetics and Art in William Gibson's *Neuromancer*." *Critique* 33.3 (1992): 221–40.

30 Kaplan, 283.

31 Ibid.

32 Gibson, *Neuromancer,* 115, 256–57.

33 Ibid., 256.

34 Norman Bel Geddes, *Horizons* (Boston: Little, Brown, 1932), 24.

35 Peter von Brandenburg and Marianne Trench, *Cyberpunk* (a documentary distributed by the Voyager Company [1990]; William Gibson, "Author's Afterword," in *Neuromancer,* 1st electronic ed. (New York: Voyager, 1992), 541.

36 William Gibson, *The Cyberspace Trilogy,* 1st electronic ed. (New York: Voyager, 1992).

37 William Burroughs, "The Cut-up Method of Brion Gysin," *Re/Search* 4.5 (1982): 35.

38 William Burroughs, "Technology of Writing," in *The Adding Machine: Collected Essays* (London: John Calder, 1985), 37.

39 David Porush, *The Soft Machine: Cybernetic Fiction* (New York: Methuen, 1985), 101.

40 For more on Agrippa, see Peter Schwenger's "*Agrippa,* or the Apocalyptic Book," in *Flame Wars: The Discourse of Cyberculture,* edited by Mark Dery (Durham: Duke University Press, 1994), 61–70.

41 Gibson, "Author's Afterword," 541–42.

3   X-Bodies: The Torment of the Mutant Superhero (1994)

I present this essay pretty much as it first appeared, in 1994—with some new notes and editing for greater accuracy. Image Comics has since evolved into a more varied publisher, the vogue for multiple "collector" editions has largely passed, and things have simmered down somewhat. Many of the founders of Image have moved on, dropped from sight, or otherwise lost their favored position with fans. I can't imagine updating this autobiographical essay.

1   See Scott Bukatman, *Terminal Identity: The Virtual Subject in Postmodern Science Fiction* (Durham: Duke University Press, 1993; and "Paralysis in Motion: Jerry Lewis's Life as a Man," in *Comedy/Cinema/Theory,* edited by Andrew S. Horton (Berkeley: University of California Press, 1991).

2   Bukatman, 1993.

3   Fredric Jameson, *Postmodernism, or the Cultural Logic of Late Capitalism,* Post-contemporary Interventions (Durham: Duke University Press, 1991), 54.

4   Peter Brooks, *Body Work: Objects of Desire in Modern Narrative* (Cambridge: Harvard University Press, 1993), xii.

5   Mary Douglas, *Purity and Danger: An Analysis of the Concepts of Pollution and Taboo* (1966; reprint, London: Routledge, 1984), 120.

6   DC Comics teamed up with Milestone Studios to produce a line of comics about and by minority figures, especially African Americans. One of these books, *Static,* was a very entertaining superhero comic.

7   That boom is now a severe bust.

8   The phrase "comic book masculinity" is from Alan M. Klein, *Little Big Men: Bodybuilding Subculture and Gender Construction* (Albany: State University of New York Press, 1993), 8. Both Theweleit and Douglas extend their analyses well beyond the scope of their initial researches. Theweleit's study of *Freikorps* fantasies reveals the more pervasive masculinist fantasies that underlie certain traditions in Western representation, while Mary Douglas uses her structural methodology to emphasize some broad but important connections across cultural experience: "All I am concerned with is a formula for classifying relations which can be applied

equally to the smallest band of hunters and gatherers as to the most industrialised nations" (*Natural Symbols: Explorations in Cosmology* [New York: Pantheon, 1970], viii). While I should perhaps be more interested in some of the significant differences between cultures, I nevertheless believe that these analyses retain considerable value when applied to contemporary American popular culture.

9   These are the same reasons why, despite having a solid position at Stanford University, I had to get back to superheroes in "The Boys in the Hoods" (included in this volume)—to write myself free of the responsibilities of scholarship in higher academia.

10 "*In brightest day / In blackest night / No evil shall escape my sight / Let those who worship evil's might / Beware my power / Green Lantern's light*" (this version authored by science fiction writer Alfred Bester).

11 Wolfgang Schivelbusch, *The Railway Journey: The Industrialization of Time and Space in the Nineteenth Century* (Berkeley: University of California Press, 1986), 143.

12 G. Claudin, *Paris* (Paris, 1867), 71–72. Cited in Wolfgang Schivelbusch, *The Railway Journey: The Industrialization of Time and Space in the Nineteenth Century* (Berkeley: University of California Press, 1986), 159.

13 Ibid., 156.

14 It might be worth noting that the first Mr. America contest was held in 1939.

15 Kryptonite had actually been around since 1939 and was proposed in a script from 1940. Alan Scott, the original Green Lantern, was powerless against wood. At least *that* makes sense!

16 Brooks, 21–22.

17 The overlap of golem and superhero winds through Chabon's *The Amazing Adventures of Kavalier and Clay* (New York: Random House, 2000).

18 Marie-Hélène Huet, *Monstrous Imagination* (Cambridge: Harvard University Press, 1993), 244, 239.

19 Klein, 274.

20 A contributing factor to the decline of origin stories might also lie in the repetitive nature of the genre. We already pretty much know where these characters came from.

21 Klein, 276.

22 See the first volume of Klaus Theweleit, *Male Fantasies,* translated by S. Conway, E. Carter, and C. Turner, 2 vols. (Minneapolis: University of Minnesota Press, 1977–78).

23 See volume 2 of ibid.

24 Theweleit even established a class relationship in which the working class became a flowing mass of aggressive, libidinal women.

25 The extensive illustrations that accompany Theweleit's text include several of such characters as Thor, Captain America, and Spiderman.

26 Theweleit, 1:162.

27 Hal Foster, "Armor Fou," *October* 56 (1991):94.

28 Theweleit, 1:179.

29 Schievelbusch, 152–53.

30 Will Wright, *Sixguns and Society: A Structural Study of the Western* (Berkeley: University of California Press, 1975).

31 I admit that writing about superhero comics makes me annoyingly alliterative and appallingly adverbial.

32 Further, the bickering yet supportive superhero team represents a fragmented projection of a self-contradictory subjectivity.

33 The typical superhero story is between twenty and twenty-five pages in length. Japanese *manga*, by contrast, are hundreds of pages long, and an eight-page battle, with little dialogue and few panels, would be surprisingly brief. Manga are not only longer than American comics, but they read far more quickly.

34 Theweleit, 1:192.

35 Grant Morrison et al., *Doom Force #1* (DC Comics, July 1992).

36 Characters cross over into each other's titles, creating elaborate continuities that only the most dedicated readers can unravel. The comics are lavishly produced, with heavy, glossy paper, vivid computerized color, and pinups galore. Artists' photographs and fan sketches adorn the back pages, and self-promotion for comics, caps, clothing, and cards is incessant.

37 Scott McCloud, *Understanding Comics: The Invisible Art* (Northhampton, MA: Tundra, 1993), 126.

38 *Doom Force* parodies the tone of aesthetic self-congratulation: "Our pencillers and inkers and penciller/inkers seemed inspired to artistic heights they had never previously reached. If you doubt that, go back and look again at the sheer number of lines they put into each panel and onto every figure . . . then sit there and tell me they didn't work harder than they ever have in their lives."

39 Klein, 215. See also Samuel Fussell, *Muscle* (New York: Pantheon, 1992).

40 Fussell, 55.

41 This was a major problem for Superman's creators during World War II. Superman could hardly ignore the war, but neither could he win it.

42 In Howard Chaykin's *Power and Glory* (Bravura Comics, 1994), superheroes are engineered by a U.S. government project because "*nobody* makes a hero like the U.S.A." In an interview published in the first issue, Chaykin remarks that the book "is a reaction to the emptiness of content in most super-hero comics lately. There's no action in contemporary comics, only poses." The theme of the new comic, Chaykin says, is "Why *be* a hero when you can just *look* like one?" For more on Chaykin's work, with which I feel an ongoing affinity, see Bukatman, *Terminal Identity*, chap. 1.

43 Klein, 141.

44 Ibid., 267.

45 Grant Morrison, "Musclebound: The Secret Origin of Flex Mentallo," *Doom Patrol* #42 (DC Comics, March 1991).

46 Klein, 151.

47 Ibid., 3.

48 Jules Feiffer, *The Great Comic Book Heroes* (New York: Dial, 1965), 19. In Jerry Lewis's *The Nutty Professor* (1963), Buddy Love is the hypermasculine version, the *armored body*, of the vulnerable "little man," Professor Kelp. In Richard Lester's *Superman III* (1983), Superman turns evil and ultimately battles Clark, whose morality provides its own kind of armor. The physical split between the characters makes *The Nutty Professor* analogy all the more compelling. For more on *The Nutty Professor*, see Bukatman, "Paralysis."

49 Klein, 41–42.

50 Ibid., 216.

51 Daniel Clowes, *Pussey!* (Seattle: Fantagraphics Books, 1995).

52 Since this essay was written, and thanks to Image, Frank Miller, and the inventive designs of Bruce Timm, Superman has become quite the big, big guy, and yet people *still* can't figure out that Clark Kent is Superman! See "The Boys in the Hoods," this volume.

53 And all owe something to cinema's hulking golem of 1920 as well as the Frankenstein monster of 1931.

54 Of course, the parodic *Doom Force* is on top of these tendencies as well. The villain castigates his scantily clad partner for covering herself up "like some old woman on a day trip to Alaska."

55 Klein, 191.

56 There are no prominent women writers or artists working for Image. The Vertigo titles of DC (targeted to older, nonsuperhero reading audiences) feature Karen Berger (editor), Nancy Collins (writer), Jill Thompson (penciller), Heidi MacDonald (editor), and others.

57 Paul McEnery, "The Candlemaker's Privilege: Grant Morrison Plays God," *Mondo 2000* (1993): 101.

58 My not very thorough sampling suggests that the ratio of battle to nonbattle pages in the Image titles is about three or four to one. In contrast, in Marvel's *Uncanny X-Men* #310, admittedly one of the chattiest superhero books going, that ratio was exactly reversed.

59 Klein, 9.

60 Douglas, *Purity*, 72.

61 Douglas, *Natural Symbols*, viii.

62 Ibid., 70.

63 Ibid., 70–71.

64 Douglas, *Purity*, 39.

65 Ibid., 97, 73.

66 Ibid., 98.

67 Ibid., 99.

68 Would we even know what irony is if it were not for comic books?

69 Douglas, *Purity*, 99.

70 Ibid., 125.

71 Ibid., 128.

72 Kurt Busiek and Alex Ross, *Marvels* (New York: Marvel Comics, 1994).

73 Phil recalls, "There was something in her—it *its* eyes—and I couldn't help thinking of the liberation of Auschwitz—and the look in *their* eyes."

74 Douglas, *Purity*, 121.

75 Thanks to Sarah Berry for drawing my attention to Douglas and gender.

76 Douglas, *Natural Symbols*, 162.

77 Douglas's studies are particularly relevant in relation to such rituals.

78 Douglas, *Natural Symbols*, xv.

79 Of his family, only Magneto survived internment at Auschwitz, an experience that apparently sensitized him to the issue of discrimination based on genetic difference.

80 The *X-Men* movie (1999) in fact cast Patrick Stewart (ST:TNG's Captain Picard) as Professor X.

81 At their worst, however, both ST:TNG and *X-Men* tend to wallow in overobvious emotional allegories.

82 Mary Douglas, *Natural Symbols* 166–67.

83 Bukatman, *Terminal Identity*, 243, 259.

84 Grant Morrison and Richard Case, "Crawling from the Wreckage," *Doom Patrol* #19 (DC Comics, February 1989). The first few issues of this extraordinary title have been collected in Grant Morrison and Richard Case, *Doom Patrol: Crawling from the Wreckage* (New York: DC Comics, 1992).

85 Ibid., 99.

86 The Brotherhood of Dada is featured in *Doom Patrol* #26 (September 1989) through #28 (January 1990). Flex Mentallo and Danny the Street are both introduced in #35 (August 1990), and the initial battle against The Men from N.O.W.H.E.R.E. occurs in #35–36 (August–September 1990). All issues published by DC Comics.

87 McEnery, 98. For detailed, annotated plot summaries, see Doom Patrol Online, <http://www.rpi.edu/~bulloj/Doom_Patrol/index.html>.

88 Later Alan Moore (of *Watchmen* fame) and a number of artists produced a more sustained return of those halcyon days of Marvel in their *1963* series, published by Image. The pastiche is so lovingly accurate that some readers, including myself, felt an overwhelming sense that this was how comics were meant to be. The initial *1963* series ended with the members of the Tomorrow Syndicate suddenly finding themselves in the far more brutal and textured universe of Image Comics. The homages to the comics of Lee and Kirby have continued, most evidently in *The World's Greatest Comic Magazine* (Erik Larsen and various artists, Marvel Comics, 2000–2001).

89 My terms are derived from the excellent introductory chapter of Barbara Stafford's *Body Criticism: Imaging the Unseen in Enlightenment Art and Medicine* (Cambridge: MIT Press, 1991), 5.

90 Jack Kirby, the creator of the Silver Surfer and so many other heroes, passed away in early February 1994, as I was revising this essay for its initial publication. It is to his memory and his accomplishments that this chapter is dedicated.

4 The Artificial Infinite: On Special Effects and the Sublime

This is the full-length version of "The Artificial Infinite," as it appeared in *Visual Display: Culture beyond Appearances,* edited by Lynne Cook and Peter Wollen (Seattle: Bay Press, 1995), 254–89. A much shorter version appeared in *Alien Zone II,* edited by Annette Kuhn (New York: Verso, 2001), 249–75.

1 An attempt to situate authorship around the visual designers of the film is progressive, in that it displaces the director as the sole "author" of a cinematic text, but it retains a reliance on the continuity of a single creator as a locus of textual meaning. While this latter position has been roundly criticized in recent years as outmoded in its assumption of a coherent subjectivity, it has produced an undeniably important body of textual interpretation. Authorship remains, I think, a valuable critical concept, although it is a tool to be wielded with some caution.

2 Such ontological questions are further emphasized when the technologies are alien in origin.

3 Jonathan Crary, *Techniques of the Observer: On Vision and Modernity in the Nineteenth Century* (Cambridge: MIT Press, 1990), 2.

4 Ibid., 9.

5 Ibid., 24.

6 Henri Lefebvre, *The Production of Space*, translated by Donald Nicholson-Smith (Oxford: Blackwell, 1991), 25.

7 Crary, 136.

8 Ibid., 14.

9 Ibid., 19.

10 Ibid., 103.

11 Ibid., 44.

12 All of this is elaborated in Wolfgang Schivelbusch, *The Railway Journey: The Industrialization of Time and Space in the Nineteenth Century* (Berkeley: University of California Press, 1986).

13 Crary, 24.

14 Ibid., 7.

15 Barbara Maria Stafford, *Artful Science: Enlightenment Entertainment and the Eclipse of Visual Education* (Cambridge: MIT Press, 1994), 51.

16 Ibid., xxii, 51.

17 Ibid., 32.

18 Ibid., 3.

19 Barbara Maria Stafford, *Body Criticism: Imaging the Unseen in Enlightenment Art and Medicine* (Cambridge: MIT Press, 1991), 343.

20 Susan Buck-Morss, *The Dialectics of Seeing: Walter Benjamin and the Arcades Project* (Cambridge: MIT Press, 1989), 91.

21 Ralph Hyde, *Panoramania: The Art and Entertainment of the "All-Embracing" View* (London: Trefoil, 1988), 37.

22 Tom Gunning, "The Cinema of Attractions: Early Film, Its Spectator, and the Avant-Garde," in *Early Cinema: Space, Frame, Narrative*, edited by Thomas Elsaesser (London: British Film Institute, 1990), 57; Miriam Hansen, *Babel and Babylon: Spectatorship in American Silent Film* (Cambridge: Harvard University Press, 1991), 34.

23 Hansen, 83.

24 Gunning, 57.

25 Annette Michelson, "Bodies in Space: Film as 'Carnal Knowledge'." *Artforum* 7.6 (1969): 54–63.

26 Brooks Landon, *The Aesthetics of Ambivalence: Rethinking Science Fiction Film in the Age of Electronic (Re)Production* (Westport, CT: Greenwood, 1992), 94.

27 This is not really the place to review the entire, complex history of the sublime. A very useful review is provided by Raimonda Modiano in *Coleridge and the Concept of Nature* (Tallahassee: Florida State University Press, 1985), 101–14.

28 Longinus, *Longinus on the Sublime*, translated by W. R. Roberts (Cambridge: Cambridge University Press, 1899), 65.

29 Burke, Edmund, *On the Sublime and the Beautiful* (Charlottesville: Ibis, n.d.), 106 (facsimile of 1812 edition).

30 Ibid., 120.

31 Joseph Addison in the *Spectator*, no. 420, July 2, 1712; cited in Andrew Wilton, *Turner and the Sublime* (Chicago: University of Chicago Press, 1980), 11.

32 *Brainstorm* (1983), directed by Trumbull, plays to the religious thematics of Burke's sublime.

Anticipating the advent of virtual reality technologies, the film is predicated on a device that records perceptions and feelings for playback. At the film's climax, a character jacks into the recorded death experience of another, and the effects are replete with references to after-death experiences and multitudes of Blakean angels. *Brainstorm* explicitly stages a confrontation with the terror of death that at once exalts and diminishes and offers a (somewhat romantic) portrait of greater cosmic connectedness.

33 Arthur C. Clarke, "The Nine Billion Names of God," in *The Nine Billion Names of God: The Best Short Stories of Arthur C. Clarke* (New York: Signet, 1974), 13.

34 Wilton, 30.

35 Ibid.

36 The detailed gaze of the cinematic apparatus can participate in a similar process of disclosure. In his extended evocation of a close-up, for example, Epstein recasts the physiognomic in the terms of the geologic—the human face becomes a sublime landscape, susceptible to endless contemplation. "Now," he writes, "the tragedy is anatomical." Jean Epstein, "Magnification and Other Writings" *October* 3 (1976): 9. Intimate yet distant; monumental yet minute; hypervisible yet still somehow obscure—these are the terms of the sublime and of a cinema constituted as a special effect.

37 Wilton argues that this was a careful strategy of Turner's and finds that a significant progression in his series of marine paintings (1801–10) "is one of gradually increasing involvement of the spectator in the scenes depicted" (46).

38 This remark was made in an interview with Don Shay presented on the Criterion laser disc of *CE3K*.

39 Wilton, 79, my emphasis.

40 To concentrate solely on the phallic implications of this movement of penetration seems to me unfairly and uninterestingly reductive (except, I'll admit, in the case of *Star Trek*). Annette Michelson, for example, has linked this cinematic trope to the epistemological project of works by Kubrick, Michael Snow, and Claude Lanzmann, among others.

41 Further, spectatorship is especially pronounced in the films of Steven Spielberg, whose characters spend much of their time staring upward (or downward in the case of *Jaws*).

42 Christopher Finch, *Special Effects: Creating Movie Magic* (New York: Abbeville, 1984), 180–81.

43 The film features, among other things, hyperreal effects work; a mysterious cosmic object; an extended—six-minute—docking sequence; spacewalking astronauts; and an exaggerated, willfully sublime, transcendent climax that yields an image of rebirth (the *Enterprise* emerges from a luminous, all-consuming glow above the blue arc of Earth). *Star Trek*, however, manages to miss every irony of Kubrick's film, and this is exemplified by the docking sequence, which must be the most extended scene of phallic worship in contemporary, nonpornographic cinema (as Vivian Sobchack has also noted).

44 Barbara Novak, *Nature and Culture: American Landscape and Painting, 1825–1875*, rev. ed. (New York: Oxford University Press, 1995), 198.

45 For some viewers, the *Star Trek* action figures may be an exception.

46 Note the extended sequences during which amplified breathing dominates the soundtrack, an auditory effect that often has a regulatory effect on the spectator's own respiration.

47 Alan Trachtenberg, *The Incorporation of America: Culture and Society in the Gilded Age* (New York: Hill and Wang, 1982), 59.

48 Ralph Waldo Emerson, "Nature," *Selected Essays, Lectures, and Poems,* Edited by Robert D. Richardson Jr. (NY: Bantam Books, 1990), 18–19. The connection forged between the Western landscape and American transcendentalism might help explain an odd portion of the Stargate sequence, as the cinephilic spectator suddenly recognizes the spires and pinnacles of Monument Valley. While I assumed that this was simply an obvious and rather pointless homage to John Ford, perhaps there is another explanation. Referring to the surfeit of representations of the American West in the nineteenth century, Novak has written: "For the vast expansive prairies, the immense extensions of space, the awesome mountains, the forbidding and majestic scale that characterized the varied landscape of the West could only then, as now, be called 'sublime'" (149). It is at least possible that Clarke and Kubrick's tale of a lone pioneer traveling through the "forbidding and majestic landscapes" that lie "beyond the infinite" might make some reference to these aesthetic forebears.

49 John Wilmerding, ed., *American Light: The Luminist Movement, 1850–1875* (Washington, DC: National Gallery of Art, 1980), 98.

50 Earl A. Powell, "Luminism and the American Sublime," in Wilmerding, 72.

51 Novak, 23.

52 Ibid., 27.

53 These canvasses were indeed large-scale works (Church's "The Heart of the Andes" [1859] measured about 66 × 120 inches), and Novak has noted that a consideration of these works must involve "a consideration of art as spectacle." She further notes that "this art had a clear twentieth-century heir in the film, which rehearsed many of the nineteenth century's concerns" (19).

54 Wilton, 39, my emphasis.

55 See David C. Huntington, "Church and Luminism: Light for America's Elect," in Wilmerding, 155–92.

56 Powell, 90.

57 Novak, 41–42.

58 It is also true that luminism produces a sense of distance from the carefully aestheticized landscape that differs from the immersion I am describing; nevertheless, the similarity abides in their suspended temporalities.

59 Wilmerding, 121.

60 Novak, 37, 29. One final aspect of the transcendentalist sublime needs consideration—the rigorous assertion of self. Bryan Wolf has produced a highly modernist reading of the sublime in *Romantic Re-vision: Culture and Consciousness in Nineteenth-Century American Painting and Literature* (Chicago: University of Chicago Press, 1982): "The sublime painting tells but a single tale. It repeats on each canvas the history of its struggle with older systems of meaning, which it perceives as exclusionary and prohibitive." These paintings are "records of their own composition"; their strategies involve "filling the silence of nonnarrative vistas with the clamor of self-discovery" (178). The figures of woodcutters that pepper Thomas Cole's canvases are, for Wolf, metaphors for the romantic painter, reshaping the contours of the natural for his own, human, ends (182). Trumbull's work is similarly self-referential. The special effect is inherently reflexive, especially when the narrative pauses to permit its display, but in the two films Trumbull has directed the position of the filmmaker-artist is directly alluded to. In *Silent Running,* the forests of a polluted Earth have been moved to giant spacecraft, and

an astronaut (played with neurotic zeal by Bruce Dern) is positioned as the caretaker (or director) of nature. His assistants are three robot drones, each with a built-in video camera. It's easy to consider the drones as sensitive, anthropomorphized cameras, carefully responsive to their director's needs and responsibilities. *Brainstorm*'s sensory-recording apparatus is co-opted by the military (surprise!), which wants to use it for the usual evil purposes. A fantasy of the ultimate effects technology—and its heroic inventors—turns into a nightmare of bottom-line psychic exploitation.

61 Mark Seltzer, *Bodies and Machines* (New York: Routledge, 1992), 3.

62 See Leo Marx, *The Machine in the Garden: Technology and the Pastoral Ideal in America* (New York: Oxford University Press, 1964).

63 Ibid., 206.

64 Novak, 4.

65 Rosalind Williams, *Notes on the Underground: An Essay on Technology, Society, and the Imagination* (Cambridge: MIT Press, 1990), 114.

66 Buck-Morss, 70, my emphasis.

67 Williams, 140.

68 Buck-Morss, 83–85.

69 This trajectory is completed in the cyberspace of William Gibson's novel *Neuromancer*.

70 Thomas Weiskel, *The Romantic Sublime: Studies in the Structure and Psychology of Transcendence* (Baltimore: Johns Hopkins University Press, 1976), 6.

71 "His current projects, like *Smoke*, carry the implications of these hazards farther, as even in the midst of a gorgeous abstraction of smoke and sky the viewer remembers that chemical pollution from industrial plants poses an unremitting, ongoing health threat that cannot and should not be ignored. Pfahl does not ask the viewer to indulge in mere passive contemplation, even though it must be admitted that the unbridled beauty of his landscapes is a temptation. Pfahl asks that we think" (Estelle Jussim, "Passionate Observer: The Art of John Pfahl," in *A Distanced Land: The Photographs of John Pfahl*, edited by Cheryl Brutvan [Albuquerque: University of New Mexico Press, 1990], 25).

72 Wilton, 101.

73 Novak, 97.

74 Burke, 149–50.

75 Williams, 185.

76 Novak, 157.

77 Williams, 1.

78 On the resistance to progressivism, see T. J. Jackson Lears, *No Place of Grace: Antimodernism and the Transformation of American Culture, 1880-1920* (Chicago: University of Chicago Press, 1981).

79 Weiskel, 92.

80 Patricia Yaeger, "Toward a Female Sublime," in *Gender and Theory: Dialogues on Feminist Criticism*, edited by Linda Kauffman (Oxford: Blackwell, 1989), 209.

81 Ibid., 205.

82 Harold Bloom, *Agon: Towards a Theory of Revisionism* (New York: Oxford University Press, 1982), 12.

83 Ibid., 238.

84 Ibid., 206.

85 Novak, 176.

86 Cited in Richard Slotkin, *Regeneration through Violence: The Mythology of the American Frontier, 1600-1860* (Middletown, CT: Wesleyan University Press, 1973), 525.

87 Gunning, 61.

88 Vivian Sobchack, "The Virginity of Astronauts: Sex and the Science Fiction Film," in *Alien Zone: Cultural Theory and Contemporary Science Fiction Cinema*, edited by Annette Kuhn (London: Verso, 1990), 103–15. This is especially true of *Star Trek: The Motion Picture* (directed by Robert Wise). Sobchack has noted the privileging, in SF cinema, of penetration over procreation, and penetration is, in fact, the sole plot device in *Star Trek*, which also features an array of references to the Creator, V'ger (a fascinating contraction, particularly when someone notes that "V'ger is barren"), and the Kirk unit. This most virginal of virginal astronaut films is actually a screwy masterpiece of sexual displacement.

89 See Albert Boime, *The Magestirial Gaze: Manifest Destiny and American Landscape Painting c. 1830-1865* (Washington, DC: Smithsonian Institution Press, 1991).

90 Hansen, 112.

5   The Ultimate Trip: Special Effects and
Kaleidoscopic Perception

1 Barbara Maria Stafford, *Artful Science: Enlightenment Entertainment and the Eclipse of Visual Education* (Cambridge: MIT Press, 1994), 51, 226, 58.

2 Ibid., 130.

3 Jackson Lears, *Fables of Abundance: A Cultural History of Advertising in America* (New York: Basic Books, 1994), 4.

4 Ibid.

5 Stafford, 73.

6 Ibid., xxvii.

7 Lears, 198, 194. John Kasson makes an identical point in his *Amusing the Million: Coney Island at the Turn of the Century* (New York: Hill and Wang, 1978).

8 Steven Shaviro, *The Cinematic Body* (Minneapolis: University of Minnesota Press, 1993), 41.

9 Ibid., 15.

10 Ibid., 17.

11 This idea is explored throughout Carol Clover's *Men, Women, and Chainsaws: Gender in the Modern Horror Film* (Princeton: Princeton University Press, 1992), esp. chap. 4, "The Eye of Horror."

12 Jonathan Crary, *Techniques of the Observer: On Vision and Modernity in the Nineteenth Century* (Cambridge: MIT Press, 1990), 113.

13 Ibid., 113–14.

14 This tendency continues, more or less unabated, into the late-twentieth-century rhetorics surrounding computer technologies, virtual reality, and raves.

15 Walter Benjamin saw them as a quasi-religious site of commodity fetishism: "They opened up a phantasmagoria into which people entered to be distracted" ("Paris: Capital of the Nineteenth Century," in *Relections: Essays, Aphorisms, Autobiographical Writings*, translated by Edmund Jephcott, edited by Peter Diemetz (New York: Shocken, 1986), 152.

16 Hubert Howe Bancroft's two-volume *The Book of the Fair* (1894), cited in Robert W. Rydell, *All the World's a Fair: Visions of Empire at American International Expositions, 1876–1916* (Chicago: University of Chicago Press, 1984), 60.

17 On the concentration of power and control, see Alan Trachtenberg, *The Incorporation of America: Culture and Society in the Gilded Age* (New York: Hill and Wang, 1982).

18 Terry Castle, *The Female Thermometer: Eighteenth-Century Culture and the Invention of the Uncanny* (New York: Oxford University Press, 1995), 80.

19 Ibid., 15.

20 Tom Gunning, "Phantom Images and Modern Manifestations: Spirit Photography, Magic Theater, Trick Films, and Photography's Uncanny," in *Fugitive Images: From Photography to Video,* edited by Patrice Petro (Bloomington: Indiana University Press, 1995), 46.

21 Tom Gunning, "An Aesthetic of Astonishment: Early Film and the (In)Credulous Spectator," in *Viewing Positions: Ways of Seeing Film,* edited by Linda Williams (New Brunswick, NJ: Rutgers University Press, 1997) 114–33.

22 Anne Balsamo has noted that "Hollywood representations of technological hallucinations show an amazing visual similarity over time, using out-of-focus shots, swirling images that involve a POV sequence that moves through a wormhole, rapid edits, and illogically juxtaposed shots to suggest a technologically induced subjective state" (*Technologies of the Gendered Body: Reading Cyborg Women* [Durham: Duke University Press, 1995], 205, n. 36). I would like to add, however, that these are less clichés than conventions of the genre—they're as fundamental as cactus to the Western.

23 See Roger Caillois, *Man, Play, and Games,* translated by Meyer Barash (New York: Free Press of Glencoe, 1961).

24 This "Third Law" of Clarke's is elaborated in his *Profiles of the Future: A Daring Look at Tomorrow's Fantastic World* (later more prosaically retitled *Profiles of the Future: An Inquiry into the Limits of the Possible*) (New York: Bantam, 1962).

25 On Douglas Trumbull's relation to luminism and American landscape art, see "The Artificial Infinite: On Special Effects and the Sublime," this volume.

26 Jean Epstein, *Bonjour Cinéma and Other Writings,* translated by Tom Milne, *Afterimage* 10 (1981): 18.

27 The chaos of the carnival also figures in the climax of Vincente Minnelli's *Some Came Running* (1957). The film explodes into another, more hysterical realm: the whirling, colored lights form an infernal, Cinemascope halo about the characters. Many films use amusement parks as sites of perceptual and romantic renewal: around 1928 alone, see such feature films as *Lonesome, Speedy, Sunrise,* and *The Crowd.* For unexpected explosions of color, see *Ivan the Terrible, Part 2* (Sergei Eisenstein, 1946), with its dervish-filled baccanale; and *The Wizard of Oz* (Victor Fleming, 1939) and the beginning of the trip along the kaleidoscopic, hypnotic Yellow Brick Road. For the most explicit linking of kaleidoscopic perception to color cinema this side of *2001,* see the "Polka Dot Polka Ballet" in Busby Berkeley's *The Gang's All Here* (1943).

28 Film theorists offer variant models for the spectator's response to the kaleidoscopic whirl of images. Jean-Louis Baudry stated that cinema produces illusions of transcendent control. Montage and movement are unified by the spectator's consciousness, aided and abetted by the transparency of the apparatus. Cinema produces a transcendent subject through its illusion of omniscient vision. Siegfried Kracauer argued that cinema's status is more provi-

sional: "These shows convey precisely and openly to thousands of eyes and ears the *disorder of society.*" While film is a powerful tool of reification, it also reveals the very process of ideological production. Jean Epstein's writings balance, like his films, between narrative and gesture, science and sensuality. In the 1920s, Epstein linked film to the new scientific worldview, but he is at pains to link science, in the era of Einstein and Bohr, to the breakdown of logic, causality, and linearity. Science, in Epstein's poetic ruminations, becomes an effective ally of unreason and cinema the tool that reveals the latent unreason in everyday experience. Kracauer and Epstein were responding to the cinematic revelation of complexity when the medium was still new, its potential seemingly unlimited. For Baudry, cinematic structures were numbingly familiar, and Stan Brakhage's *Metaphors on Vision* evokes a similar despair. Brakhage describes the camera eye as one "capable of any imagining," but it has been too long tethered to received structures (language primary among them). See Jean-Louis Baudry, "Ideological Effects of the Basic Cinematographic Apparatus," in *Film Theory and Criticism*, edited by Marshall Cohen, Gerald Mast, and Leo Braudy. 4th ed. (New York: Oxford University Press, 1992), 302–12; Siegfried Kracauer, "The Cult of Distraction," in *The Mass Ornament: Weimar Essays*, edited by Thomas Y. Levin (Cambridge: Harvard University Press, 1995); Jean Epstein, "Magnification and Other Writings," *October* 3 (1976): 9–25; and Stan Brakhage, *Metaphors on Vision*, 2d ed. (New York: Film Culture, 1976).

29 Nonetheless, in *2001*, as elsewhere, Kubrick's camera movement is largely determinist rather than liberatory. The Stargate sequence, however, which was at least coproduced by Trumbull, is both of a piece with the rest of the film and eminently detachable as a separate aesthetic experience playing by its own set of rules.

30 Castle, 103, 102, 107.

31 Ibid., 107.

32 Samuel R. Delany, "Some Real Mothers: An Interview with Samuel R. Delany by Takayuki Tatsumi," *Science Fiction Eye* 1.3 (1988): 5–11.

33 *A Matter of Life and Death* (1946), one of the most superb Powell-Pressburger films, conflates the materially constituted other world of the paraspace with the stylistic hyperbole of musicals or melodramas. In this deeply reflective and reflexive work, melodrama is endowed with almost metaphysical importance.

34 Castle, 11.

35 Ibid., 104.

36 Gunning, "Cinema of Attractions," 59.

37 Ibid., 57.

38 See Leo Braudy's discussion of *Singin' in the Rain* (Gene Kelly and Stanley Donen, 1951) in *The World in a Frame: What We See in Films* (Garden City, NJ: Anchor, 1976), 157. In the musical, the paraspace would be the space of performance—sometimes materially constituted (as in a backstage musical) but often not (singin' and dancin' might break out anywhere). Heightened rhetoricity takes the form of exaggerated color, costume, and performance style, perhaps augmented by elaborate cutting, devastatingly complex crane shots, or superbly sustained long takes. The paraspace of the musical number becomes a space of liberation, of masquerade, a place where, as Dyer brilliantly observes, emotional authenticity and theatricality—too often regarded as dichotomously opposed—are combined. For Dyer, this (f)act of combination is at the heart of queer responses to the genre—the musical becomes a place of resistance to a culture that continues to insist, absurdly, on dualistic oppositions. Utopia is

thus defined as a place of movement, of border crossings and crane shots, of choreographed transgressions and performances of liberation. See Richard Dyer, "Judy Garland and Gay Men," in *Heavenly Bodies: Film Stars and Society* (London: Macmillan, 1986), esp. 154; and Dyer's "Entertainment and Utopia" in *Movies and Methods,* edited by Bill Nichols (Berkeley: University of California Press, 1985), 2:220–32. I continue this discussion of musicals in the chapters that follow, especially Chapter 7, "Syncopated City."

39 Gunning, "Cinema of Attractions," 61.

40 This is an assumption almost endemic to recent, spectator-centered theories of cinematic experience. Both Castle and Delany have produced significant works of queer theory.

41 Not all narratives are so conservative. This is more than an issue of narrative versus spectacle but concerns the placement of spectacle within such reactionary narrative structures as eighteenth-century novels of social manners and twentieth-century romance films and science fiction. Other narrative structures work differently and certainly challenge causal structures as well as fixed notions of subject-definition: *2001,* which is in some ways more of a parody of science fiction narrative than anything else, can be used as an example in either instance.

42 Castle, 124.

43 Ibid. Gunning makes a very similar argument with regard to "spirit" photography of the nineteenth century in "Phantom Images."

44 Geoffrey O'Brien, *The Phantom Empire* (New York: Norton, 1993), 109.

45 See chapter 4 and Scott Bukatman, *Terminal Identity: The Virtual Subject in Postmodern Science Fiction* (Durham: Duke University Press, 1993).

46 This is not to say that SF literature didn't have its Jules Verne and Edgar Rice Burroughs, but this strain of adventure writing always coexisted with its more meditative partner.

47 Considering how strongly the utopian discourse has been aligned with scientific socialism, this was hardly the most auspicious time for its existence in the mainstream of American culture.

48 Geoffrey O'Brien writes that in 1950s SF cinema "The body was not the same size as the world. It was a bad fit, whether too big or not big enough: *Attack of the Fifty-Foot Woman, The Amazing Colossal Man, War of the Colossal Beast, Attack of the Puppet People, The Incredible Shrinking Man*" (73).

49 Louis Marin, *Utopics: The Semiological Play of Textual Spaces,* translated by Robert A. Vollrath (Atlantic Highlands, NJ: Humanities Press, 1984), 124.

50 Louis Marin, "Frontiers of Utopia: Past and Present." *Critical Inquiry* 19 (1993): 413.

51 "At the very moment that I look at the map—when I follow with my finger the route of a road, a contour line, when I cross here and not there a frontier, when I jump from one bank of a river to the other—at this moment, a figure is extracted from the map ground, the figure of a projected journey, even if it is an imaginary one, a dreamed one. With that figure a narrative begins. . . . The locus has become space: directions, speeds, travel-timing give motion to the map with the tracings of various routes" (ibid., 413).

52 Michel de Certeau, *The Practice of Everyday Life,* translated by Steven Rendall (Berkeley: University of California Press, 1984), 129. Transcendence involves a rising above and a denial of social reality; transgression is a cutting across that remains fully cognizant of, if also refusing of, ideological strictures.

53 Marin, *Utopics,* 407.

54 Again, this is emphasized when the technologies are alien.

55 Marin, *Utopics*, 412, my emphasis.

56 See Fredric Jameson, "Science Fiction as a Spatial Genre: Generic Discontinuities and the Problem of Figuration in Vonda McIntyre's *The Exile Waiting*," *Science Fiction Studies* 14.1 (1987): 44–59.

57 Marin, *Utopics*, 117.

58 O'Brien, 116. I am again reminded of the comparison Annette Michelson has made between the curvilinear Cinerama screen to the shape of the astronauts' visors. ("Bodies in Space: Film as 'Carnal Knowledge,'" *Artforum* 7.6 [1969]: 58).

59 Edward Bellamy, *Looking Backward* (1888; reprint, New York: Penguin, 1982).

60 King Camp Gillette, *The Human Drift* (Boston: New Era, 1894). See also Robert Fishman, *Urban Utopias in the Twentieth Century: Ebenezer Howard, Frank Lloyd Wright, Le Corbusier* (Cambridge: MIT Press, 1982); Howard P. Segal, *Technological Utopianism in American Culture* (Chicago: University of Chicago Press, 1985); Elizabeth Wilson, *The Sphinx in the City: Urban Life, the Control of Disorder, and Women* (Berkeley: University of California Press, 1991), 42–46.

61 Krishan Kumar, *Utopia and Anti-utopia in Modern Times* (Oxford: Blackwell, 1987), 81.

62 Gilbert Seldes, *The Great Audience* (1950), cited in Ann Douglas, *Terrible Honesty: Mongrel Manhattan in the 1920s* (New York: Farrar, Straus, Giroux, 1995), 448.

63 Ann Douglas, 448–49.

64 John Belton, *Widescreen Cinema* (Cambridge: Harvard University Press, 1992), 36–37.

65 Ibid., 38.

66 See Marx.

67 William Moritz, historical text for "Absolut Panushka: The Online Experimental Film Festival," curated by Christine Panushka, 1996, available at <http://www.absolutvodka.com/panushka/>. Additional films for the Vortex Concerts were provided by James and John Whitney among many others. The concerts continued for three years and were showcased at the 1958 Brussels World's Fair.

68 Appropriately for the themes of *The Right Stuff*, Belson's work through the 1960s was increasingly about transcendence. *Samadhi* is the Sanskrit term referring to the state of consciousness in which the individual soul merges with the universal soul. Malcolm Le Grice has uncharitably compared Belson's work to the car chase in *The French Connection* (William Friedkin, 1970), a comparison with some ironic relevance to this essay. See his *Abstract Cinema and Beyond* (Cambridge: MIT Press, 1977), 83.

69 Some of the information about Jordan Belson was found in Tom Charity, *The Right Stuff*, BFI Modern Classics (London: British Film Institute, 1997).

70 Charity writes that "the Western—a lone man on horseback—confronts science fiction. The cowboy stares at a technological future" (ibid., 37).

71 Thanks to Marion Kuschnerus for this observation.

72 And isn't this somehow typical of American epics? I think of *Leaves of Grass, Moby Dick*, and *The Wild Bunch* as also exemplary of a vast, inclusive, and hugely self-conscious incoherence: each represents another sprawling, encyclopedic attempt to encompass America both as ideal and as tainted history. Each combines minutely observed and catalogued detail with epic, panoramic sweep. In the restless movement across frontiers, each one both challenges and succumbs to mythologies of masculinist (re)generation.

73 Charity. I'd add Howard Hawks to the list, for the emphasis on male camaraderie among pilots who are "good enough"—who have "the right stuff."

74 Marin, *Utopics*, 8, 195.

75 Marx, 365.

76 Lears, 126.

77 Richard Dyer said this of entertainment, specifically in the form of the musical. His emphasis on what he terms "nonrepresentational signs" is similar to mine. See Dyer, "Entertainment," 222.

78 Gaston Bachelard, *The Poetics of Space*, translated by Maria Jolas (Boston: Beacon, 1964), xvi.

79 Ibid., xxii.

80 Ibid., xxvii.

81 Ibid., xix.

82 Ibid., xxxiv.

6 Taking Shape: Morphing and the Performance of Self

1 Annette Michelson has described the nineteenth century in this way.

2 Thus, I will not be considering still images produced through morphing technology.

3 Michael Rogin, *Blackface, White Noise: Jewish Immigrants in the Hollywood Melting Pot* (Berkeley: University of California Press, 1996), 12.

4 Ibid., 51–52.

5 Jean Epstein, "Magnifications and Other Writings." *October* 3 (1976), p. 19, 17.

6 Ibid., 23.

7 Gilles Deleuze, *Bergsonism*, translated by Hugh Tomlinson and Barbara Habberjam (New York: Zone, 1991), 37.

8 Henri Bergson, *Matter and Memory*, translated by Nancy Margaret Paul and W. Scott Palmer (New York: Zone, 1991), 33.

9 Ibid., 69.

10 Martin Jay writes that our selves should properly be identified with "the internal experience of individually endured time, the private reality of *durée*" (*Downcast Eyes: The Denigration of Vision in Twentieth-Century French Thought* [Berkeley: University of California Press, 1994], 197).

11 Henri Bergson, *Time and Free Will: An Essay on the Immediate Data of Consciousness*, translated by F. L. Pogson (New York: Humanities, 1971), 128–29.

12 Bergson, *Matter*, 67.

13 Ibid.

14 Marcel Proust, *Remembrance of Things Past*, translated by C. K. Scott Moncrieff and Terence Kilmartin (New York: Random House, 1981), 1:5.

15 Oliver Sacks, "A Matter of Identity" in *The Man Who Mistook His Wife for a Hat* (New York: Summit, 1985), 104.

16 Luis Buñuel, *My Last Sigh*, translated by Abigail Israel (New York: Vintage, 1984), 4–5.

17 Sacks, 104.

18 Sacks, "The Lost Mariner" in *The Man Who Mistook His Wife for a Hat* (New York: Summit, 1985), 41.

19 See my monograph on *Blade Runner* (London: British Film Institute, 1997) for more on this film.

20 Alan Moore, *Supreme* 2.41 (August 1996): 13, panels 3–4.

21 Alan Moore, *Supreme*, 2.42 (September 1996): 3, panel 5.

22 Bergson, *Matter*, 46.

23 Ibid., 25.

24 Deleuze, 37.

25 For Jean-Louis Baudry, conversely, individual frames admitted a Derridean difference that projected sequences denied.

26 The notes are by David D'heilly.

27 Gilles Deleuze, *Cinema 1: The Movement-Image*, translated Hugh Tomlinson and Robert Galeta (Minneapolis: University of Minnesota Press, 1989), 2.

28 Ibid., 20.

29 Gilles Deleuze, *Cinema 2: The Time-Image*, translated by Hugh Tomlinson and Robert Galeta (Minneapolis: University of Minnesota Press, 1989), 4. The films of Vincente Minnelli serve as Deleuze's extended point of reference.

30 Ibid., 65. Deleuze illustrates the first example with the destruction of the music professor's home in *The Patsy* and the second with the transformation sequence in *The Nutty Professor*.

31 Ibid.

32 Ibid., 66. Deleuze's examples here are, respectively, the six uncles in *The Family Jewels*, the three women in *Three on a Couch*, and the characters in *The Big Mouth*.

33 Scott Bukatman, "Paralysis in Motion: Jerry Lewis's Life as a Man," in *Comedy/Cinema/Theory*, edited by Andrew S. Horton (Berkeley: University of California Press, 1991).

34 Deleuze, *Cinema 2*, 65. See also Scott Bukatman, "Terminal Idiocy (the comedian is the message)." *Enfant Terrible! Jerry Lewis in American Film*. Edited by Murray Pomerance (New York: New York University Press, 2002), 181–91.

35 Bukatman, "Paralysis."

36 Deleuze, *Cinema 2*, 66.

37 Even this is not the end: an animated framing sequence gives us Bart and Homer Simpson arguing about TV.

38 There is some parallel to the monstrous, masochistic, morphosis Jackson undergoes in *Thriller*. One could also see some anticipation, in its racial anger and reclamation of African American tap culture, of the polemical stage musical *Bring in 'da Noise, Bring in 'da Funk* (1996) by Reg E. Gaines, George Wolfe, and Savion Glover.

39 Deleuze, *Cinema 2*, 62.

40 These substitutions from another link to Minnelli's aesthetic of illusionism.

41 Deleuze, *Cinema 2*, 61.

42 Rogin, 7. The computer artist Nancy Burson had been creating similar composite images at least a decade earlier.

43 James Weldon Johnson has called blackface performance "the only completely original contribution America has made to the theater" (*Black Manhattan* [1930], cited in Ann Douglas, *Terrible Honesty: Mongrel Manhattan in the 1920s* [New York: Farrar, Straus, Giroux, 1995], 76). Blackface minstrel shows dominated popular culture by the turn of the century, and nearly every city and town had its troupe, but blackface was not limited to onstage performers from

Daddy Rice through Al Jolson, Eddie Cantor, and beyond: innumerable composers, including Stephen Foster and later Irving Berlin, Oscar Hammerstein, and the Gershwins, dipped heavily into black vernacular culture for its figurative, colloquial, and erotic languages. These were primarily whites mimicking their own image of black style, but during the Civil War shortages of white performers led to blacks' inclusion—in blackface, naturally. Blackface finally waned as a tradition in the later 1920s, but it was still a big part of the Hollywood film musical (Jolson, Cantor, a faux-minstrel revue in 1943's *Babes in Arms, Holiday Inn,* and so on). Despite its seeking refuge in the cinema, the naturalistic demands of sound cinema were certainly a major factor contributing to the disappearance of this very theatrical, very conventional performative mode.

44 Robert C. Toll, *Blacking Up: The Minstrel Show in Nineteenth-Century America* (New York: Oxford University Press, 1974), 42, 51.

45 Joseph Boskin, *Sambo: The Rise and Demise of an American Jester* (New York: Oxford University Press, 1986), 93–94.

46 "American film was born in the industrial age out of the conjunction between southern defeat in the Civil War, black resubordination, and national integration; the rise of the multiethnic, industrial metropolis; and the emergence of mass entertainment, expropriated from its black roots, as the locus of Americanization" (Rogin 15).

47 Ibid., 26.

48 Boskin, 68.

49 Ibid., 78.

50 Ibid., 113.

51 Rogin, 22.

52 James Snead, *White Screens/Black Images: Hollywood from the Dark Side* (New York: Routledge, 1994), 60. In the introduction to her recent book *Black Talk,* Geneva Smitherman pointed out that "while Black *talk* has crossed over, Black *people* have not" (*Black Talk: Words and Phrases from the Hood to the Amen Corner* [Boston: Houghton-Mifflin, 1994], 30–31).

53 Rogin, 105.

54 Irving Howe, *World of Our Fathers* (New York: Simon and Schuster, 1976), 563.

55 Gilbert Seldes, *The Seven Lively Arts* (1924), cited in ibid., 566.

56 Marjorie Garber, *Vested Interests: Cross-Dressing and Cultural Anxiety* (New York: Routledge, 1992), 28.

57 Ibid., 16.

58 Ibid., 10.

59 Ibid., 17.

60 Ibid., 36.

61 "One might expect endorsements of masquerade to run aground on their largely repressed past, meeting their match in blackface. In the current excitement over popular culture, however, the direction of influence runs the other way, not disciplining present theory by past practice, but opening the past to contemporary interests" (Rogin, 35).

62 Ibid., 12.

63 Ibid., 182–83.

64 bell hooks, "Racism and Feminism," in *Ain't I a Woman?* (Boston: South End, 1981), 141.

65 Rogin, 193.

66 Cited in hooks, 141.

67 Further, since *Stormy Weather* was produced as a government-encouraged gesture of inclusion toward black servicemen stationed overseas, the zoot suit was itself impressed, shanghaied.

68 As an alternative to Michael Rogin's rather totalizing picture of white appropriation of black culture, see Ann Douglas's description of the "mongrel Manhattan" of the 1920s, which provides ample evidence of the ongoing interchange between black and white cultures in urban America.

69 Perhaps this is why the performance of cross-dressing is usually more intriguing than its narration in literature.

70 Garber, 29.

71 Ibid., 40.

72 Roland Barthes, *S/Z*, translated by Richard Miller (New York: Hill and Wang, 1974), 107, 77.

73 Ibid., 77.

74 Garber, 149.

75 Shari Roberts, "The Lady in the Tutti-Frutti Hat: Carmen Miranda, a Spectacle of Ethnicity." *Cinema Journal* 32.3 (1993): 3–23.

76 The utopianism of the musical, Richard Dyer reminds us, may be mythic, but in, say, Judy Garland's blend of theatricality and authenticity, real negotiations are made. See his "Entertainment and Utopia" and *Heavenly Bodies*.

77 Even Superman, in a fairly recent revision, shifted from the tangibly industrial to the electronically ephemeral. His costume was laced with microcircuitry to contain him within a new, cool-blue body.

7   Syncopated City: New York in Musical Film (1929–1961)

1 Cited in Ann Douglas, *Terrible Honesty: Mongrel Manhattan in the 1920s* (New York: Farrar, Straus, Giroux, 1995), 426.

2 This is something that Richard Dyer seems to aver. See Richard Dyer, "Entertainment and Utopia," *Movies and Methods* vol. 2, edited by Bill Nichols (Berkeley: University of California Press, 1985), 220–32. and "Judy Garland and Gay Men," in *Heavenly Bodies: Film Stars and Society* (London: Macmillan, 1986).

3 Leo Braudy, *The World in a Frame: What We See in Films* (Garden City, NJ: Anchor, 1976), 155.

4 Peter Jelavich, *Berlin Cabaret* (Cambridge: Harvard University Press, 1993), 16. Space prohibits me from exploring the significant overlap between Berlin and New York as strongly similar urban environments: both experienced rapid growth in young countries; both were stereotypically inhabited by jaded, cynical sophisticates; and both came of age in the late nineteenth and early twentieth centuries. It's no accident that Georg Simmel, Siegfried Kracauer, the *Straßefilm*, and Walter Ruttmann's city symphony should all be relevant to a consideration of the New York musical.

5 Andrew Sarris once remarked that he never fully appreciated Falconetti's performance in Carl Dreyer's *Passion of Joan of Arc* until Anna Karina watched it in *Vivre Sa Vie*, and my own "discovery" of Jerry Lewis was inaugurated by the excerpt from *You're Never Too Young* that's arbitrarily excerpted and reenacted in Rainer Werner Fassbinder's *In a Year of Thirteen Moons*.

6   Neil Harris, "Urban Tourism and the Commercial City," in *Inventing Times Square: Commerce and Culture at the Crossroads of the World*, edited by William R. Taylor (Baltimore: Johns Hopkins University Press, 1991), 66.

7   Jelavich writes, "the last of the Metropol's prewar shows included a scene that presented Berlin as one big department store—for material goods, as well as for culture and politics. . . . This exchange was followed by a chorus asserting that the revue itself was a department store that collected and displayed the year's fashions and events" (116–17).

8   Harris, 81.

9   Is the tourist's view already self-conscious?

10 Dean MacCannell, *The Tourist: A New Theory of the Leisure Class* (New York: Schocken, 1989), 7.

11 See Jane Feuer, *The Hollywood Musical*, 2d ed. (Bloomington: Indiana University Press, 1993).

12 Rem Koolhaas, *Delirious New York* (New York: Monacelli, 1994), 30.

13 Jonathan Kasson, *Amusing the Million: Coney Island at the Turn of the Century* (New York: Hill and Wang, 1978).

14 See Jeffrey Meikle, *Twentieth-Century Limited: Industrial Design in America, 1925–1939* (Philadelphia: Temple University Press, 1979).

15 This sequence also presents a good example of how Broadway and Times Square function as a synecdoche for New York and urbanism in general.

16 William Leach, "Commercial Aesthetics: Introductory Essay," in *Inventing Times Square: Commerce and Culture at the Crossroads of the World*, edited by William R. Taylor (Baltimore: Johns Hopkins University Press, 1991), 236.

17 Advertising spokesman cited in William Leach, *Land of Desire: Merchants, Power, and the Rise of a New American Culture* (New York: Vintage: 1993), 47.

18 Ibid., 60. Leach cites Baum as saying, 'People will always step out to examine anything that moves . . . and will enjoy studying out the mechanics or wondering how the effect has been obtained."

19 Leach, "Commercial Aesthetics," 240.

20 Jackson Lears, *Fables of Abundance: A Cultural History of Advertising in America* (New York: Basic Books, 1994), 9.

21 Ibid., 75.

22 Ibid., 177–78.

23 William Wood Register Jr. "New York's Gigantic Toy," in Taylor, *Inventing Times Square*, 249–50. He adds, "Simply stated by Thompson & Dundy's publicity department, the Hippodrome offered 'A revel of recreation at rational rates.'"

24 Ibid., 247.

25 Rem Koolhaas, "Regrets?" *Grand Street* 57 (1996). Available at <http://www.voyagerco.com/gs/gs57/koolhaas.html>.

26 Of course, many of the important directors and dance directors from the New York and Chicago stage moved to Hollywood—Minnelli and Berkeley, to name only the two best known.

27 From a Broadway perspective, musicals also had to be "dumbed down" for the mainstream American market—ethnic references reduced, rhythms simplified, rhymes censored.

28 Lears, 153.

29 Cited in Leach, *Land of Desire*, 346.

30 See Harris, 179, 180.

31 Cited in Brooks McNamara, "The Entertainment District at the End of the 1930s," in Taylor, *Inventing Times Square*, 181–82.

32 Harris, 82.

33 Julian Street, cited in ibid., 80.

34 J. Hoberman, *42nd Street* (London: British Film Institute, 1993).

35 Philip Furia, *The Poets of Tin Pan Alley* (New York: Oxford University Press, 1992). Furia is citing an essay by Carolyn Wells.

36 Ann Douglas, 374.

37 Having begun with Rodgers and Hart's "Manhattan," Furia very cleverly marks the closure of this period of songwriting with Rodgers and Hammerstein's *Oklahoma*, with its long operatic phrases, folk ethos, and an explicit, nondialectical sentimentality in keeping with its wartime production date.

38 The lyrics of these songs were hardly ever specifically gendered—*I* and *you* substituted for more specific pronouns. This strategy existed for sound commercial reasons, since both male and female singers could use the material, but this androgyny continues to have intriguing implications.

39 Paul F. Berliner, *Thinking in Jazz: The Infinite Art of Improvisation* (Chicago: University of Chicago Press, 1994), 220.

40 Ibid., 486.

41 John Russell Taylor and Arthur Jackson, *The Hollywood Musical* (New York: McGraw-Hill, 1971), 12.

42 Jerome Delameter, *Dance in the Hollywood Musical* (Ann Arbor: University of Michigan Press, 1981), 64.

43 Stanley Cavell has discussed the significance of Astaire's shoes/feet in this number, arguing that in the film's first song, "By Myself," Astaire's feet remain invisible as he walks through Grand Central Station. His alienation from New York and himself is overcome at the very moment when, after his shoes are shined, he leaps over Daniels to ground himself on terra firma. Stanley Cavell, "Identifying Praise: Moments of Henry James and Fred Astaire." Lecture, Boston University, Jan. 28, 1998.

44 As James Naremore notes of Vincente Minnelli's use of Harlem motifs, this time in *Cabin in the Sky*, this is hardly less racist, but it does possess the virtue of acknowledging some level of cultural sophistication in African American culture rather than simply evoking a "natural" primitivism. See his *The Films of Vincente Minnelli* (Cambridge: Cambridge University Press, 1993), 62.

45 Ella Shohat, "Ethnicities-in-Relation: Toward a Multicultural Reading of American Cinema," in *Unspeakable Images: Ethnicity and the American Cinema*, edited by Lester D. Friedman (Urbana: University of Illinois Press, 1991), 226. The same obscurantist tendency is discussed by Mark Winokur, who notes that "Fred Astaire, in a 1930 recording of 'Puttin' on the Ritz,' astonishes his black audience with dance steps, many of which originated in black jazz styles. As late as 1953, Astaire similarly impresses blacks at the beginning of *The Band Wagon*." Mark Winokur, "Black Is White/White Is Black: 'Passing' as a Strategy of Racial Compatibility," in Friedman, *Unspeakable Images*, 202.

46 Ann Douglas, 76.

47 Eric Lott, *Love and Theft: Blackface Minstrelsy and the American Working Class* (New York: Oxford University Press, 1993).

48 It was directed by the son of movie choreographer Nick Castle.

49 This is how Scott MacDonald describes the city symphony in "The City as the Country: The New York City Symphony from Rudy Burckhardt to Spike Lee," *Film Quarterly* 51.2 (1997–98): 4.

50 Berliner, 487.

51 Berliner refers to the "kaleidophonic array" (ibid., 148).

52 Georg Simmel, "The Metropolis and Mental Life," in *On Individuality and Social Forms*, edited by Donald N. Levine (Chicago: University of Chicago Press, 1971), 330.

53 Siegfried Kracauer, "The Mass Ornament," in *The Mass Ornament: Weimar Essays*, edited and translated by Thomas Y. Levin (Cambridge: Harvard University Press, 1995), 78.

54 See Lucy Fischer, "The Image of Woman as Image: The Optical Politics of *Dames.*" in *Genre: The Musical*, edited by Rick Altman (London: Routledge, 1981), 70–84.

55 How exactly *does* that nightclub stay in business? This set by Mark Harkrider and others like it are discussed in James Sanders's superb *Celluloid Skyline: New York and the Movies* (New York: Knopf, 2001).

56 Anton Kaes, "Sites of Desire: The Weimar Street Film," in *Film Architecture: From Metropolis to Blade Runner*, edited by Dietrich Neumann (Munich: Prestel-Verlag, 1996), 31.

57 I'll grant that horror and melodrama might have their own claims. On melodrama, see Thomas Elsaesser's "Tales of Sound and Fury: Observations of the Family Melodrama," *Movies and Methods* vol. 2, edited by Bill Nichols (Berkeley: University of California Press, 1985), 165–89.

58 See Peter Wollen's kickass book *Singin' in the Rain* (London: British Film Institute, 1993).

59 Kaes, 27.

60 When the film first appeared, several critics, including Pauline Kael and Andrew Sarris, complained about the use of real locations as inappropriate to the stylized balletic movements of Robbins's choreography. I wonder whether they would still agree with those assessments. While the initial movements seem tentative and self-conscious, making the Jets seem like they're late for ballet class, the number quickly, thrillingly, succeeds in conveying the relation between the gangs and their bodies, their streets. On the other hand, Kael brilliantly notes that "The irony of this hyped-up, slam-bang production is that those involved apparently don't really believe that beauty and romance can be expressed in modern rhythms, because whenever their Romeo and Juliet enter the scene, the dialogue becomes painfully old-fashioned and mawkish, the dancing turns to simpering, sickly romantic ballet, and sugary old stars hover in the sky. When true love enters the film, Bernstein abandons Gershwin and begins to echo Richard Rodgers, Rudolf Friml, and Victor Herbert" (Pauline Kael, "West Side Story," in *I Lost It at the Movies* [New York: Bantam, 1966], 127–33).

61 Stephen Sondheim's lyric deals forcefully with racial discrimination while the stage version was more about gender.

62 Deleuze, *Cinema 2*, 62.

63 Ibid., 61.

64 Ibid.

65　F. Scott Fitzgerald, "My Lost City," in *The Crack-Up*, edited by Edmund Wilson (New York: New Directions, 1945), 31.

66　Ibid., 28–29.

67　Ibid., 31.

68　The sequence closely follows on Astaire's complaint that while humans are the only animals gifted with speech and the ability to communicate "all we can do is snarl at each other." The communication that follows, however, is wordless. In light of Astaire's earlier assimilation or negotiation in "Shine on Your Shoes," one might now see Cyd Charisse *as* New York—if, that is, one was susceptible to such outmoded metaphorizing.

69　Kaes, 26.

70　"Even New York's proudest citizens must feel it sometimes: the sneaking feeling that the city's real life is incomplete. So much of this city exists as fabulous celluloid figments of our imagination that the actual place is bound to pale by comparison" (Janet Maslin, "On the Screen: Images of New York," *New York Times*, May 1, 1998, B1).

71　Leo Braudy, *World in a Frame: What We See in Films* (Garden City, NJ: Anchor, 1976), 140, 157.

8　The Boys in the Hoods: A Song of the Urban Superhero (2000)

1　With an occasional "good neighbor" nod toward Montreal, Mexico City, or London.

2　Four titles figured most significantly in a brief explosion of postmodern urban renewal: *American Flagg!* by Howard Chaykin, *Watchmen* by Alan Moore and Dave Gibbons, Frank Miller's *Return of the Dark Knight*, and *Mr. X* by Dean Motter and the Hernandez brothers. I discuss some of these, as well as Judge Dredd and the comics of Moebius, in Scott Bukatman, *Terminal Identity: The Virtual Subject in Postmodern Science Fiction* (Durham: Duke University Press, 1993).

3　Interview with Howard Chaykin, "The New Superhero," *Spin* 4.5 (August 1988): 49.

4　I have relied greatly on histories of comics by Jules Feiffer, Mike Benton, Jim Steranko, and Les Daniels.

5　Rem Koolhaas, *Delirious New York* (New York: Monacelli, 1994), 104.

6　They included *Little Nemo in Slumberland, Polly and Her Pals, Gasoline Alley, Krazy Kat, Tarzan*, and *Prince Valiant* (and these are only a few examples).

7　With some exceptions (Will Eisner, Harvey Kurtzman, Jack Cole, Hergé, and Carl Barks) it wasn't until the later 1960s that the panel was superseded by the page as an explicit unit of composition in comic books. Panels were increasingly fragmented into diagonal shards, incorporated into larger graphic elements, or generally organized against the grain of a strict linearity.

8　Koolhaas, 104.

9　Vivian Gornick, "On the Street: Nobody Watches, Everyone Performs," in *Approaching Eye Level* (Boston: Beacon, 1996), 15.

10　A more effective design would have used the broad avenues to link the rivers, for example.

11　Batman is the fully accessorized superhero, much like Barbie: both are outfitted with clothes, car, dreamhouse, and a useless appendage (Ken, Robin).

12　See Art Spiegelman and Chip Kidd, *Jack Cole and Plastic Man: Forms Stretched to Their Limits* (New York: Chronicle, 2001); as well as three DC Comics' reprint volumes; Jack Cole *The Plastic Man Archives* (New York: DC Comics, 1999 and 2001).

13 Editor Denny O'Neil allows *Batman* artists to play with the character's iconography, especially his sensuous cape: "We now say that Batman has two hundred suits hanging in the Batcave, so they don't have to look the same" (quoted in Les Daniels, *Batman: The Complete History* [San Francisco: Chronicle, 1999], 159). Nobody has ever drawn more graceful flying figures than 1960s *Green Lantern* artist Gil Kane. His superheroes seemed to float above the page. *Daredevil's* artist through the 1970s was Gene Colan, whose swirling lines created remarkable kinetic effects, within the frame and across the page. Superman's coloration was a function, and a virtue, of the primitive printing in the earliest comic books.

14 Alan Moore and Curt Swan, *Whatever Happened to the Man of Tomorrow?* (New York: DC Comics, 1997), 17 (reprints material originally published in 1986).

15 Jeph Loeb and Tim Sale, *Superman for All Seasons* (New York: DC Comics, 1999).

16 Peter Fritzsche, *Reading Berlin, 1900* (Cambridge: Harvard University Press, 1996), 1.

17 See David M. Henkin, *City Reading: Written Words and Public Spaces in Antebellum New York* (New York: Columbia University Press, 1998); and Fritzsche.

18 Several of his other fantasies shrank him to bug size.

19 Susan Stewart, *On Longing: Narratives of the Miniature, the Gigantic, the Souvenir, the Collection* (Durham: Duke University Press, 1993), 60, 67.

20 *Batman: Mask of the Phantasm* (1993).

21 Stewart, 46.

22 Ibid., 56. For Scott McCloud, the flat colors that until recently defined comics also evoke a child's perception by emphasizing the shapes of objects and reveling in "the wonder of *things.*" Comics present "worlds fairly glowing with that mystery of first encounters. Any wonder then that comics in America has been so reluctant to 'grow up'?" (Scott McCloud, *Understanding Comics: The Invisible Art* [Northhampton, MA: Tundra, 1993], 188–89).

23 Jack (*Starman*) Knight has a poster for the fair on the wall of his Opal City apartment.

24 Stewart, 90.

25 Franco Minganti, "1939: Flying Eyes—Flight, Metropolis, and Icons of Popular Imagination," *Storia Nordamericana* 7.1 (1990): 100.

26 Michel de Certeau, "Walking in the City," translated by Steven Rendall, in *The Practice of Everyday Life* (Berkeley: University of California Press, 1984), 92.

27 Ibid.

28 Le Corbusier, *The City of To-Morrow and Its Planning* (New York: Dover), 86.

29 Cited in Daniels, 164. The screenplay is credited to Sam Hamm and Warren Skaaren.

30 Rick Marschall, Foreword to *Batman Archives* (New York: DC Comics, 1990), 1:5.

31 Tom Gunning, "From the Kaleidoscope to the X-Ray: Urban Spectatorship, Poe, Benjamin, and *Traffic in Souls* (1913)," *Wide Angle* 19.4 (1997): 25–61.

32 Terry Castle, *The Female Thermometer: Eighteenth-Century Culture and the Invention of the Uncanny* (New York: Oxford University Press, 1995), 80.

33 Such writers include Frank Miller, Alan Moore, Howard Chaykin, Paul Dini, Dave Gibbons, and Kurt Busiek, among others.

34 And note that Batman is usually accompanied by his brightly attired "sidekick," Robin.

35 Stan Lee and Steve Ditko, "Where Flies the Beetle . . . ," *Amazing Spider-Man* #21 (February 1965). Reprinted in Stan Lee and Steve Ditko, *The Essential Spider-Man*, vol. 2 (New York: Marvel Comics, 1997).

36 de Certeau, "Walking in the City."

37 The Kingpin, an enemy of both Spiderman and Daredevil, set the standard as an Edward Arnold–style ward boss and gangster well before Luthor's makeover.

38 de Certeau, *The Practice of Everyday Life*, 37.

39 New York is also home to Daredevil, another Marvel hero with enhanced senses.

40 Warren Ellis and Darick Robertson, *Transmetropolitan* #1 (1998), 5.

41 Ibid., 14.

42 Warren Ellis and Darick Robertson, *Transmetropolitan* #2, 2.

43 Warren Ellis and Darick Robertson, *Transmetropolitan* #32 (2000), 5, 6.

44 de Certeau, 103, my emphasis. The City is also the name of the place that the great comic and cartoon hero The Tick has sworn to protect.

45 Motter et al., *The Return of Mr. X* (East Fullerton, CA: Graphitti Designs, 1986).

46 de Certeau, 13.

47 Georg Simmel, "The Metropolis and Mental Life," in *On Individuality and Social Forms*, edited by Donald N. Levine (Chicago: University of Chicago Press, 1971), 339.

48 Ibid., 334.

49 James McCabe, "Imposters," in *Writing New York: A Literary Anthology*, edited by Philip Lopate (New York: Library of America, 1998), 260. (excerpted from James McCabe, *Light and Shadows of New York Life* [1872]).

50 Terry Castle, *Masquerade and Civilization: The Carnivalesque in Eighteenth-Century English Culture and Fiction* (Stanford: Stanford University Press, 1986), 183.

51 Ibid. The internal citation is to Mikhail Bakhtin's *The Dialogic Imagination*, translated by Caryl Emerson and Michael Holquist, edited by Michael Holquist (Austin: University of Texas Press, 1981), 39. The text by Roger Caillois is *Man, Play, and Games*, translated by Meyer Barash (New York: Free Press of Glencoe, 1961).

52 Castle, *Masquerade*, 186.

53 Ibid., 37.

54 Jules Feiffer, *The Great Comic Book Heroes* (New York: Dial, 1965), 18–19.

55 Anne Hollander, *Sex and Suits: The Evolution of Modern Dress* (New York: Alfred A. Knopf, 1994), 7.

56 Zorro, Batman, and the Green Hornet *pretend* to be dandies in their "secret identities," but they're all *still* dandies, right? (especially Zorro and Guy Madison's TV incarnation of the Green Hornet). *Van Williams*

57 Garlick, 19.

58 *Watchman, Squadron Supreme*, and *The Golden Age* come to mind. I should also mention that recent revisions of the Superman mythos have placed new emphasis on his learning how to live with (and live up to) his superhuman powers.

59 Walter Kaufmann, Translator's introduction to Friedrich Nietzsche, *The Gay Science* (New York: Vintage, 1974), 7.

60 Friedrich Nietzsche, "Thus Spoke Zarathustra," in *The Portable Nietzsche*, edited and translated by Walter Kaufmann (New York: Viking, 1954), 153. See also Nietzsche, *Gay Science*.

61 *Is it a bird?* "The ostrich runs faster than the fastest horse, but even he buries his head gravely in the grave earth; even so, the man who has not yet learned to fly. Earth and life seem grave to him; and thus the spirit of gravity wants it. But whoever would become light and a bird must love himself, thus *I* teach" (Nietzsche, "Thus Spoke Zarathustra," 304).

62 Alan Moore, Howard Chaykin, James Robinson, Frank Miller, Alex Ross, Kurt Busiek, Grant Morrison, John Byrne, Neil Gaiman, Walt Simonson, and Todd MacFarlane are only a few of those who have spun out eloquent and varied alternatives.

63 The title refers to the *Elseworlds* titles, which allowed creators free reign to reimagine DC's classic characters outside the constraints of "normal" series continuity.

64 Other than this, however, the series lacked any sense of irony about its own iconography.

65 Alan Moore, "Suddenly, the Supremium Man!" *Supreme: The Return*, #5 (May 2000), 5.

BIBLIOGRAPHY

Books and Articles

Bachelard, Gaston. *The Poetics of Space.* Translated by Maria Jolas. Boston: Beacon, 1964.

Bakhtin, Mikhail. *The Dialogic Imagination,* translated by Caryl Emerson and Michael Holquist, edited by Michael Holquist. Austin: University of Texas Press, 1981.

Balsamo, Anne. *Technologies of the Gendered Body: Reading Cyborg Women.* Durham: Duke University Press, 1995.

Barthes, Roland. *S/Z.* Translated by Richard Miller. New York: Hill and Wang, 1974.

Baudry, Jean-Louis. "Ideological Effects of the Basic Cinematographic Apparatus." In *Film Theory and Criticism,* edited by Marshall Cohen, Gerald Mast, and Leo Braudy, 302–12. 4th ed. New York: Oxford University Press, 1992.

Bellamy, Edward. *Looking Backward.* New York: Penguin, 1982.

Belton, John. *Widescreen Cinema.* Cambridge: Harvard University Press, 1992.

Benjamin, Walter. "Paris: Capital of the Nineteenth Century," translated by Edmund Jephcott. In *Reflections: Essays, Aphorisms, Autobiographical Writings,* edited by Peter Diemetz, 146–62. New York: Shocken, 1986.

——. "The Work of Art in the Age of Mechanical Reproduction," translated by Harry Zohn. In *Illuminations,* edited by Hannah Arendt, 217–51. New York: Schocken, 1969.

Benton, Mike. *The Comic Book in America: An Illustrated History.* Rev. ed. Dallas: Taylor, 1993.

——. *Superhero Comics of the Golden Age.* Dallas: Taylor, 1992.

Bergson, Henri. *Matter and Memory,* translated by Nancy Margaret Paul and W. Scott Palmer. New York: Zone, 1991.

——. *Time and Free Will: An Essay on the Immediate Data of Consciousness,* translated by F. L. Pogson. New York: Humanities, 1971.

Berliner, Paul F. *Thinking in Jazz: The Infinite Art of Improvisation.* Chicago: University of Chicago Press, 1994.

Bliven, Bruce, Jr. *The Wonderful Writing Machine.* New York: Random House, 1954.

Bloom, Harold. *Agon: Towards a Theory of Revisionism.* New York: Oxford University Press, 1982.

Boime, Albert. *The Magisterial Gaze: Manifest Destiny and American Landscape Painting, c. 1830–1865.* Washington, DC: Smithsonian Institution Press, 1991.

Bordwell, David. *On the History of Film Style.* Cambridge: Harvard University Press, 1997.

Boskin, Joseph. *Sambo: The Rise and Demise of an American Jester.* New York: Oxford University Press, 1986.

Brakhage, Stan. *Metaphors on Vision.* 2d ed. New York: Film Culture, 1976.

Braudy, Leo. *The World in a Frame: What We See in Films.* Garden City, NJ: Anchor, 1976.

Bright, Randy. *Disneyland: Inside Story.* New York: Abrams, 1987.

Brooks, Peter. *Body Work: Objects of Desire in Modern Narrative.* Cambridge: Harvard University Press, 1993.

Buck-Morss, Susan. *The Dialectics of Seeing: Walter Benjamin and the Arcades Project.* Cambridge: MIT Press, 1989.

Bukatman, Scott. *Blade Runner.* London: British Film Institute, 1997.

——. "Paralysis in Motion: Jerry Lewis's Life as a Man." In *Comedy/Cinema/Theory,* edited by Andrew S. Horton, 188–205. Berkeley: University of California Press, 1991.

——. *Terminal Identity: The Virtual Subject in Postmodern Science Fiction.* Durham: Duke University Press, 1993.

——. "Terminal Idiocy (the comedian is the message)." *Enfant Terrible! Jerry Lewis in American Film.* Edited by Murray Pomerance. New York: NYU Press, 2002. pp. 181–91.

Buñuel, Luis. *My Last Sigh,* translated by Abigail Israel. New York: Vintage, 1984.

Burke, Edmund. *On the Sublime and the Beautiful.* Charlottesville: Ibis, n.d.

Burns, Ric, and James Sanders. *New York: An Illustrated History.* New York: Knopf, 1999.

Burroughs, William. "The Cut-Up Method of Brion Gysin." *Re/Search* 4.5 (1982): 35–36.

——. "Technology of Writing." In *The Adding Machine: Collected Essays,* 32–37. London: John Calder, 1985.

Caillois, Roger. *Man, Play, and Games,* translated by Meyer Barash. New York: Free Press of Glencoe, 1961.

Castle, Terry. *The Female Thermometer: Eighteenth-Century Culture and the Invention of the Uncanny.* New York: Oxford University Press, 1995.

——. *Masquerade and Civilization: The Carnivalesque in Eighteenth-Century English Culture and Fiction.* Stanford: Stanford University Press, 1986.

Chabon, Michael. *The Amazing Adventures of Kavalier and Clay.* New York: Random House, 2000.

Charity, Tom. *The Right Stuff.* London: British Film Institute, 1997.

Chevalier, Michel. *Society, Manners, and Politics in the United States.* Ithaca: Cornell University Press, 1961.

Chtcheglov, Ivan. "Formulary for a New Urbanism," translated by Ken Knabb. In *Situationist International Anthology,* edited by Ken Knabb, 1–4. Berkeley: Bureau of Public Secrets, 1981.

Clarke, Arthur C. *The Nine Billion Names of God: The Best Short Stories of Arthur C. Clarke.* New York: Signet, 1974.

——. *Profiles of the Future: A Daring Look at Tomorrow's Fantastic World.* New York: Bantam, 1962.

Clover, Carol. *Men, Women, and Chainsaws: Gender in the Modern Horror Film.* Princeton: Princeton University Press, 1992.

Clute, John. Introduction to *Interzone: The Second Anthology,* edited by John Clute, vii–x. New York: St. Martin's, 1987.

Collective, Processed World. "Keep Jane's Fingers Dancing." In *The Processed World Anthology*, edited by Chris Carlsson with Mark Leger, 181. London: Verso, 1990.

Crary, Jonathan. *Techniques of the Observer: On Vision and Modernity in the Nineteenth Century*. Cambridge: MIT Press, 1990.

Csicsery-Ronay, Istvan, Jr. "The Sentimental Futurist: Cybernetics and Art in William Gibson's *Neuromancer*." *Critique* 33.3 (1992): 221–40.

Current, Richard N. *The Typewriter and the Men Who Made It*. Urbana: University of Illinois Press, 1954.

Daniels, Les. *Batman: The Complete History*. San Francisco: Chronicle, 1999.

——. *Superman: The Complete History*. San Francisco: Chronicle, 1998.

Davies, Margery W. *Woman's Place Is at the Typewriter: Office Work and Office Workers, 1870–1930*, Philadelphia: Temple University Press, 1982.

Debord, Guy. "Report on the Construction of Situations and on the International Situationist Tendency's Conditions of Organization and Action," translated by Ken Knabb. In *Situationist International Anthology*, edited by Ken Knabb, 17–25. Berkeley: Bureau of Public Secrets, 1981.

de Cauter, Lieven. "The Panoramic Ecstasy: On World Exhibitions and the Disintegration of Experience." *Theory, Culture and Society* 10 (1993): 1–23.

de Certeau, Michel. *The Practice of Everyday Life*, translated by Steven Rendall. Berkeley: University of California Press, 1984.

Delameter, Jerome. *Dance in the Hollywood Musical*. Studies in Photography and Cinematography, no. 4. Ann Arbor: University of Michigan Press, 1981.

Delany, Samuel R: "Some *Real* Mothers: An Interview with Samuel R. Delany by Takayuki Tatsumi." *Science Fiction Eye* 1.3 (1988): 5–11.

Deleuze, Gilles. *Bergsonism*, translated by Hugh Tomlinson and Barbara Habberjam. New York: Zone, 1991.

——. *Cinema 1: The Movement-Image*, translated by Hugh Tomlinson and Robert Galeta. Minneapolis: University of Minnesota Press, 1989.

——. *Cinema 2: The Time-Image*, translated by Hugh Tomlinson and Robert Galeta. Minneapolis: University of Minnesota Press, 1989.

Dini, Paul, and Chip Kidd. *Batman: Animated*. New York: HarperCollins, 1999.

Douglas, Ann. *Terrible Honesty: Mongrel Manhattan in the 1920s*. New York: Farrar, Straus, Giroux, 1995.

Douglas, Mary. *Natural Symbols: Explorations in Cosmology*. New York: Pantheon, 1970.

——. *Purity and Danger: An Analysis of the Concepts of Pollution and Taboo*. 1966. Reprint, London: Routledge, 1984.

Dyer, Richard. "Entertainment and Utopia." In *Movies and Methods* Vol. 2, ed. Bill Nichols. Berkeley: University of California Press, 1985, 220–32.

——. *Heavenly Bodies: Film Stars and Society*. London: Macmillan, 1986.

——. "Judy Garland and Gay Men." In *Heavenly Bodies: Film Stars and Society*, 141–94. London: Macmillan, 1986.

Eco, Umberto. *Travels in Hyperreality*, translated by William Weaver. New York: Harcourt Brace Jovanovich, 1985.

Eisenstein, Sergei. "The Montage of Film Attractions." In *Eisenstein at Work*, edited by Jay Leyda and Zina Voynow, 17–20. New York: Pantheon, 1982.

Elsaesser, Thomas. "Tales of Sound and Fury: Observations on the Family Melodrama." In *Movies and Methods,* vol 2, edited by Bill Nichols, 165–89. Berkeley: University of California Press, 1985.

Emerson, Ralph Waldo. "Nature." In *Selected Essays, Lectures, and Poems,* edited by Robert D. Richardson, Jr., 13–49. New York: Bantam Books, 1990.

Epstein, Jean. "*Bonjour Cinéma* and Other Writings." *Afterimage* 10 (1981): 8–39.

———. "Magnification and Other Writings." *October* 3 (1976): 9–25.

Feiffer, Jules. *The Great Comic Book Heroes.* New York: Dial, 1965.

Feuer, Jane. *The Hollywood Musical.* 2d ed. Bloomington: Indiana University Press, 1993.

Fielding, Raymond. "Hale's Tours: Ultrarealism in the Pre-1910 Motion Picture." In *Film Before Griffith,* edited by John Fell, 116–30. Berkeley: University of California Press, 1983.

Finch, Christopher. *Special Effects: Creating Movie Magic.* New York: Abbeville, 1984.

Fischer, Lucy. "The Image of Woman as Image: The Optical Politics of *Dames,*" in *Genre: The Musical,* edited by Rick Altman, 70–84. London: Routledge, 1981.

Fisher, Philip. *Still the New World: American Literature in a Culture of Creative Destruction.* Cambridge: Harvard University Press, 1999.

Fishman, Robert. *Urban Utopias in the Twentieth Century: Ebenezer Howard, Frank Lloyd Wright, Le Corbusier.* Cambridge: MIT Press, 1982.

Fitzgerald, F. Scott. "My Lost City." In *The Crack-Up,* edited by Edmund Wilson, 23–33. New York: New Directions, 1945.

Foley, James D. "Interfaces for Advanced Computing." *Scientific American,* October 1987, 126–35.

Foster, Hal. "Armor Fou." *October* 56 (1991): 64–97.

Francaviglia, Richard V. "Main Street USA: A Comparison/Contrast of Streetscapes in Disneyland and Walt Disney World." *Journal of Popular Culture* 15.1 (1981): 141–56.

Franklin, H. Bruce. "America as Science Fiction: 1939." In *Coordinates: Placing Science Fiction and Fantasy,* edited by George Slusser, Erik S. Rabkin, and Robert Scholes, 107–23. Carbondale: Southern Illinois University Press, 1983.

Friedberg, Anne. *Window Shopping: Cinema and the Postmodern.* Berkeley: University of California Press, 1993.

Fritzsche, Peter. *Reading Berlin 1900.* Cambridge: Harvard University Press, 1996.

Furia, Philip. *The Poets of Tin Pan Alley.* New York: Oxford University Press, 1992.

Fussell, Samuel. *Muscle.* New York: Pantheon, 1992.

Garber, Marjorie. *Vested Interests: Cross-Dressing and Cultural Anxiety.* New York: Routledge, 1992.

Garelick, Rhonda K. *Rising Star: Dandyism, Gender, and Performance in the Fin de Siècle.* Princeton, NJ: Princeton University Press, 1998.

Geddes, Norman Bel. *Horizons.* Boston: Little, Brown, 1932.

Gibson, William. "Author's Afterword." In *Neuromancer,* 537–44. 1st electronic ed. New York: Voyager, 1992.

———. *The Cyberspace Trilogy.* 1st electronic ed. New York: Voyager, 1992.

———. "The Gernsback Continuum." In *Burning Chrome,* 23–35. New York: Arbor House, 1986.

———. Introduction to *Neuromancer: The Graphic Novel,* edited by David M. Harris. New York: Epic Comics, 1989.

———. *Neuromancer.* New Ace Science Fiction Specials. New York: Ace, 1984.

Gibson, William, and Bruce Sterling. *The Difference Engine.* London: Gollancz, 1990.

Gillette, King Camp. *The Human Drift*. Boston: New Era, 1894.

Gornick, Vivian. "On the Street: Nobody Watches, Everyone Performs." In *Approaching Eye Level*, 1–29. Boston: Beacon, 1996.

Gunning, Tom. "An Aesthetic of Astonishment: Early Film and the (In)Credulous Spectator." In *Viewing Positions: Ways of Seeing Film*, edited by Linda Williams, 114–33. New Brunswick, NJ: Rutgers University Press, 1994.

——. "The Cinema of Attractions: Early Film, Its Spectator, and the Avant-Garde." In *Early Cinema: Space, Frame, Narrative*, edited by Thomas Elsaesser, 56–62. London: British Film Institute, 1990.

——. "From the Kaleidoscope to the X-Ray: Urban Spectatorship, Poe, Benjamin, and *Traffic in Souls* (1913)." *Wide Angle* 19.4 (1997): 25–61.

——. "Phantom Images and Modern Manifestations: Spirit Photography, Magic Theater, Trick Films, and Photography's Uncanny." In *Fugitive Images: From Photography to Video*, edited by Patrice Petro, 42–71. Bloomington: Indiana University Press, 1995.

——. "An Unseen Energy Swallows Space: The Space in Early Film and Its Relation to American Avant-Garde Film." In *Film Before Griffith*, edited by John Fell, 355–66. Berkeley: University of California Press, 1983.

Hansen, Miriam. *Babel and Babylon: Spectatorship in American Silent Film*. Cambridge: Harvard University Press, 1991.

Harris, Neil. "Great American Fairs and American Cities: The Role of Chicago's Columbian Exhibition." In *Cultural Excursions: Marketing Appetites and Cultural Tastes in Modern America*, 111–31. Chicago: University of Chicago Press, 1990.

——. "Urban Tourism and the Commercial City." In *Inventing Times Square: Commerce and Culture at the Crossroads of the World*, edited by William R. Taylor, 66–82. Baltimore: Johns Hopkins University Press, 1991.

Henkin, David M. *City Reading: Written Words and Public Spaces in Antebellum New York*. New York: Columbia University Press, 1998.

Hine, Thomas. *Populuxe*. New York: Knopf, 1986.

Hoberman, J. *42nd Street*. London: British Film Institute, 1993.

Hoke, Donald R. *Ingenious Yankees: The Rise of the American System of Manufactures in the Private Sector*. New York: Columbia University Press, 1990.

Hollander, Anne. *Sex and Suits: The Evolution of Modern Dress*. New York: Alfred A. Knopf, 1994.

hooks, bell. "Racism and Feminism." In *Ain't I a Woman?* 119–58. Boston: South End, 1981.

Howe, Irving. *World of Our Fathers*. New York: Simon and Schuster, 1976.

Huet, Marie-Hélène. *Monstrous Imagination*. Cambridge: Harvard University Press, 1993.

Huntington, David C. "Church and Luminism: Light for America's Elect." In *American Light: The Luminist Movement, 1850–1875*, edited by John Wilmerding, 155–92. Washington, DC: National Gallery of Art, 1980.

Hyde, Ralph. *Panoramania: The Art and Entertainment of the "All-Embracing" View*. London: Trefoil, 1988.

Jameson, Fredric. *Postmodernism, or the Cultural Logic of Late Capitalism*, Durham: Duke University Press, 1991.

——. "Science Fiction as a Spatial Genre: Generic Discontinuities and the Problem of Figuration in Vonda Mcintyre's *The Exile Waiting*." *Science Fiction Studies* 14.1 (1987): 44–59.

Jay, Martin. *Downcast Eyes: The Denigration of Vision in Twentieth-Century French Thought.* Berkeley: University of California Press, 1994.

Jelavich, Peter. *Berlin Cabaret.* Cambridge: Harvard University Press, 1993.

Jussim, Estelle. "Passionate Observer: The Art of John Pfahl." In *A Distanced Land: The Photographs of John Pfahl,* edited by Cheryl Brutvan. Albuquerque: University of New Mexico Press, 1990.

Kael, Pauline. "West Side Story." In *I Lost It at the Movies,* 127–33. New York: Bantam, 1966.

Kaes, Anton. "Sites of Desire: The Weimar Street Film." In *Film Architecture: From Metropolis to Blade Runner,* edited by Dietrich Neumann, 26–32. Munich: Prestel-Verlag, 1996.

Kant, Immanuel. *Critique of Judgement,* translated by J. H. Bernard. 2d ed. New York: Hafner Press, 1974.

Kaplan, Justin. *Mr. Clemens and Mark Twain.* New York: Simon and Schuster, 1966.

Kasson, John. *Amusing the Million: Coney Island at the Turn of the Century.* New York: Hill and Wang, 1978.

Kaufmann, Walter. Translator's introduction to *The Gay Science,* by Friedrich Nietzsche, 3–26. New York: Vintage, 1974.

Kern, Stephen. *The Culture of Time and Space, 1880–1918.* Cambridge: Harvard University Press, 1983.

King, Margaret. "Disneyland and Walt Disney World: Traditional Values in Futuristic Form." *Journal of Popular Culture* 15.1 (1981): 116–40.

Kirby, Lynne. "Male Hysteria and Early Cinema." *Camera Obscura* 17 (1989): 113–31.

Kittler, Friedrich A. *Discourse Networks, 1800–1900,* translated by Michael Metteer with Chris Cullens. Stanford: Stanford University Press, 1990.

Klein, Alan M. *Little Big Men: Bodybuilding Subculture and Gender Construction.* Albany: State University of New York Press, 1993.

Koolhaas, Rem. *Delirious New York.* New York: Monacelli, 1994.

——. "Regrets?" *Grand Street* 57 (1996).

Kowinski, William. *The Malling of America.* New York: Morrow, 1985.

Kracauer, Siegfried. "The Cult of Distraction." In *The Mass Ornament: Weimar Essays,* edited by Thomas Y. Levin, 323–28. Cambridge: Harvard University Press, 1995.

——. "The Mass Ornament." In *The Mass Ornament: Weimar Essays,* edited by Thomas Y. Levin, 75–86. Cambridge: Harvard University Press, 1995.

Kroker, Arthur, Marilouise Kroker, and David Cook, eds. *Panic Encyclopedia.* New York: St. Martin's, 1989.

Kumar, Krishan. *Utopia and Anti-Utopia in Modern Times.* Oxford: Blackwell, 1987.

Landon, Brooks. *The Aesthetics of Ambivalence: Rethinking Science Fiction Film in the Age of Electronic (Re)Production.* Westport, CT: Greenwood, 1992.

Lang, Jeffrey S., and Patrick Trimble. "Whatever Happened to the Man of Tomorrow? An Examination of the American Monomyth and the Comic Book Superhero." *Journal of Popular Culture* 22.3 (1988): 157–73.

Lant, Antonia. "Haptical Cinema." *October* 74 (1995): 45–73.

Leach, William. "Commercial Aesthetics: Introductory Essay." In *Inventing Times Square: Commerce and Culture at the Crossroads of the World,* edited by William R. Taylor, 234–42. Baltimore: Johns Hopkins University Press, 1991.

——. *Land of Desire: Merchants, Power, and the Rise of a New American Culture.* New York: Vintage, 1993.

Lears, Jackson. *Fables of Abundance: A Cultural History of Advertising in America.* New York: Basic Books, 1994.

——. *No Place of Grace: Antimodernism and the Transformation of American Culture, 1880-1920.* Chicago: University of Chicago Press, 1981.

Le Corbusier, Charles-Edouard. *The City of To-Morrow and Its Planning.* New York: Dover, 1987.

Lefebvre, Henri. *The Production of Space,* translated by Donald Nicholson-Smith. Oxford: Blackwell, 1991.

LeGrice, Malcolm. *Abstract Film and Beyond.* Cambridge: MIT Press, 1977.

Longinus. *Longinus on the Sublime,* translated by W. R. Roberts. Cambridge: Cambridge University Press, 1899.

Lott, Eric. *Love and Theft: Blackface Minstrelsy and the American Working Class.* New York: Oxford University Press, 1995.

MacCannell, Dean. *The Tourist: A New Theory of the Leisure Class.* New York: Schocken, 1989.

MacDonald, Scott. "The City as the Country: The New York City Symphony from Rudy Burckhardt to Spike Lee." *Film Quarterly* 51.2 (1997-98): 2-20.

Manovich, Lev. *The Language of New Media.* Cambridge: MIT Press, 2001.

Marin, Louis. "Frontiers of Utopia: Past and Present." *Critical Inquiry* 19 (1993): 397-420.

——. *Utopics: The Semiological Play of Textual Spaces,* translated by Robert A. Vollrath. Atlantic Highlands, NJ: Humanities, 1984.

Marschall, Rick. Foreword to *Batman Archives,* 1:3-6. New York: DC Comics, 1990.

Marx, Leo. *The Machine in the Garden: Technology and the Pastoral Ideal in America.* New York: Oxford University Press, 1964.

Maslin, Janet. "On the Screen: Images of New York." *New York Times,* May 1, 1998, B1.

Mast, Gerald. *Can't Help Singin': The American Musical on Stage and Screen.* Woodstock, NY: Overlook, 1987.

McCabe, James. "Imposters." In *Writing New York: A Literary Anthology,* edited by Philip Lopate, 260-67. Library of America, 1998.

McCloud, Scott. *Understanding Comics: The Invisible Art.* Northhampton, MA: Tundra, 1993.

McEnery, Paul. "The Candlemaker's Privilege: Grant Morrison Plays God." *Mondo 2000* 11 (1993): 96-101.

McLuhan, Marshall. *Understanding Media.* New York: New American Library, 1964.

McNamara, Brooks. "The Entertainment District at the End of the 1930s." In *Inventing Times Square: Commerce and Culture at the Crossroads of the World,* edited by William R. Taylor, 178-90. Baltimore: Johns Hopkins University Press, 1991.

Meikle, Jeffrey. *Twentieth-Century Limited: Industrial Design in America, 1925-1939.* Philadelphia: Temple University Press, 1979.

Merleau-Ponty, Maurice. *Phenomenology of Perception,* translated by Colin Smith. London: Routledge and Kegan Paul, 1962.

Metz, Christian. *The Imaginary Signifier: Psychoanalysis and the Cinema,* translated by Celia Britton et al. Bloomington: Indiana University Press, 1977.

Michelson, Annette. "Bodies in Space: Film as 'Carnal Knowledge'." *Artforum* 7.6 (1969): 54-63.

Miller, Mark Crispin. "Virtù, Inc." In *Boxed In: The Culture of TV,* 79-94. Evanston: Northwestern University Press, 1988.

Millhauser, Stephen. "The Little Kingdom of J. Franklin Payne." In *Little Kingdoms,* 11-115. New York: Vintage, 1993.

Minganti, Franco. "1939: Flying Eyes—Flight, Metropolis, and Icons of Popular Imagination." *Storia Nordamericana* 7.1 (1990): 93–103.

Modiano, Raimonda. *Coleridge and the Concept of Nature.* Tallahassee: Florida State University Press, 1985.

Monaco, Cynthia. "The Difficult Birth of the Typewriter." *Invention and Technology* 4.1 (spring-summer 1988): 10–21.

Mumford, Lewis. *Technics and Civilization.* New York: Harcourt Brace Jovanovich, 1934.

Naremore, James. *The Films of Vincente Minnelli.* Cambridge: Cambridge University Press, 1993.

Nietzsche, Friedrich. *The Gay Science,* translated by Walter Kaufmann. New York: Vintage, 1974.

———. "Thus Spoke Zarathustra," translated by Walter Kaufmann. In *The Portable Nietzsche,* edited by Walter Kaufmann, 103–439. New York: Vintage, 1959.

Novak, Barbara. *Nature and Culture: American Landscape and Painting, 1825–1875.* Rev. ed. New York: Oxford University Press, 1995.

O'Brien, Geoffrey. *The Phantom Empire.* New York: Norton, 1993.

Porush, David. *The Soft Machine: Cybernetic Fiction.* New York: Methuen, 1985.

Powell, Earl A. "Luminism and the American Sublime." In *American Light: The Luminist Movement, 1850–1875,* edited by John Wilmerding, 69–94. Washington, DC: National Gallery of Art, 1980.

Powers, Richard. *Prisoner's Dilemma.* New York: Collier Books, 1983.

Proust, Marcel. *Swann's Way,* translated by C. K. Moncrieff and Terence Gilmartin. New York: Random House, 1981.

Register, William Wood, Jr. *The Kid of Coney Island: Fred Thompson and the Rise of American Amusements.* Oxford: Oxford University Press, 2001.

———. "New York's Gigantic Toy." In *Inventing Times Square: Commerce and Culture at the Crossroads of the World,* edited by William R. Taylor, 243–70. Baltimore: Johns Hopkins University Press, 1996.

Rifkin, Jeremy. *Time Wars: The Primary Conflict in Human History.* New York: Holt, 1987.

Roberts, Shari. "The Lady in the Tutti-Frutti Hat: Carmen Miranda, a Spectacle of Ethnicity." *Cinema Journal* 32.3 (1993): 3–23.

Rogin, Michael. *Blackface, White Noise: Jewish Immigrants in the Hollywood Melting Pot.* Berkeley: University of California Press, 1996.

Rydell, Robert W. *All the World's a Fair: Visions of Empire at American International Expositions, 1876–1916.* Chicago: University of Chicago Press, 1984.

Sacks, Oliver. "The Lost Mariner." In *The Man Who Mistook His Wife for a Hat,* 22–41. New York: Summit, 1985.

———. "A Matter of Identity." In *The Man Who Mistook His Wife for a Hat,* 103–10. New York: Summit, 1985.

Sanders, James. *Celluloid Skyline: New York and the Movies.* New York: Knopf, 2001.

Schickel, Richard. *The Disney Version.* Rev. ed. New York: Simon and Schuster, 1985.

Schivelbusch, Wolfgang. *Disenchanted Night: The Industrialization of Light in the Nineteenth Century,* translated by Angela Davies. Berkeley: University of California Press, 1988.

———. *The Railway Journey: The Industrialization of Time and Space in the Nineteenth Century.* Berkeley: University of California Press, 1986.

Schwenger, Peter. "Agrippa, or the Apocalyptic Book." In *Flame Wars: The Discourse of Cyberculture,* edited by Mark Dery, 61–70. Durham: Duke University Press, 1994.

Sebald, W. G. *Austerlitz*, translated by Anthea Bell. New York: Random House, 2001.

Segal, Howard P. *Technological Utopianism in American Culture.* Chicago: University of Chicago Press, 1985.

Seltzer, Mark. *Bodies and Machines.* New York: Routledge, 1992.

Shaviro, Steven. *The Cinematic Body.* Minneapolis: University of Minnesota Press, 1993.

Shohat, Ella. "Ethnicities-in-Relation: Toward a Multicultural Reading of American Cinema." In *Unspeakable Images: Ethnicity and the American Cinema,* edited by Lester D. Friedman, 215–50. Urbana: University of Illinois Press, 1991.

Simmel, Georg. "The Metropolis and Mental Life." In *On Individuality and Social Forms,* edited by Donald N. Levine, 324–39. Chicago: University of Chicago Press, 1971.

Singer, Ben. *Melodrama and Modernity: Early Sensational Cinema and Its Contexts.* New York: Columbia University Press, 2001.

Slotkin, Richard. *Regeneration through Violence: The Mythology of the American Frontier, 1600–1860.* Middletown, CT: Wesleyan University Press, 1973.

Smitherman, Geneva. *Black Talk: Words and Phrases from the Hood to the Amen Corner.* Boston: Houghton-Mifflin, 1994.

Snead, James. *White Screens/Black Images: Hollywood from the Dark Side.* New York: Routledge, 1994.

Sobchack, Vivian. *The Address of the Eye: A Phenomenology of Film Experience.* Princeton: Princeton University Press, 1992.

——. "The Virginity of Astronauts: Sex and the Science Fiction Film." In *Alien Zone: Cultural Theory and Contemporary Science Fiction Cinema,* edited by Annette Kuhn, 103–15. London: Verso, 1990.

Spiegelman, Art, and Chip Kidd. *Jack Cole and Plastic Man: Forms Stretched to Their Limits.* New York: Chronicle, 2001.

Spinrad, Norman. "The Neuromantics." *Issac Asimov's Science Fiction Magazine,* May 1986, 180–90.

Stafford, Barbara Maria. *Artful Science: Enlightenment Entertainment and the Eclipse of Visual Education.* Cambridge: MIT Press, 1994.

——. *Body Criticism: Imaging the Unseen in Enlightenment Art and Medicine.* Cambridge: MIT Press, 1991.

Steranko, Jim. *The Steranko History of Comics.* 2 vols. Reading, PA: Supergraphics, 1970–72.

Sterling, Bruce. Preface to *Mirrorshades: The Cyberpunk Anthology,* edited by Bruce Sterling, vii–xiv. New York: Arbor House, 1986.

Stewart, Susan. *On Longing: Narratives of the Miniature, the Gigantic, the Souvenir, the Collection.* Durham: Duke University Press, 1993.

Taylor, John Russell, and Arthur Jackson. *The Hollywood Musical.* New York: McGraw-Hill, 1971.

Theweleit, Klaus. *Male Fantasies,* translated by S. Conway, E. Carter, and C. Turner. 2 vols. Minneapolis: University of Minnesota Press, 1977–78.

Toffler, Alvin. *The Third Wave.* New York: Bantam, 1981.

Toll, Robert C. *Blacking Up: The Minstrel Show in Nineteenth-Century America.* New York: Oxford University Press, 1974.

Trachtenberg, Alan. *The Incorporation of America: Culture and Society in the Gilded Age.* New York: Hill and Wang, 1982.

Virilio, Paul. "Cataract Surgery: Cinema in the Year 2000." In *Alien Zone: Cultural Theory and Contemporary Science Fiction,* edited by Annette Kuhn, 169–74. New York and London: Verso Books, 1990.

———. "The Overexposed City." *ZONE* 1.2 (1984): 15–31.

———. *War and Cinema*, translated by Patrick Camiller. New York: Verso Books, 1989.

Warshow, Robert, "Author's Preface." In *The Immediate Experience: Movies, Comics, Theatre and Other Aspects of Popular Culture*, xxxvii–xliii. Cambridge: Harvard University Press, 2001.

Weiskel, Thomas. *The Romantic Sublime: Studies in the Structure and Psychology of Transcendence.* Baltimore: Johns Hopkins University Press, 1976.

Williams, Rosalind. *Notes on the Underground: An Essay on Technology, Society, and the Imagination.* Cambridge: MIT Press, 1990.

Willis, Carol. "Skyscraper Utopias: Visionary Urbanism in the 1920s." In *Imagining Tomorrow: History, Technology, and the American Future*, edited by Joseph J. Corn, 164–87. Cambridge: MIT Press, 1986.

Wilmerding, John. "The Luminist Movement: Some Reflections." In *American Light: The Luminist Movement, 1850–1875*, edited by John Wilmerding, 97–152. Washington, DC: National Gallery of Art, 1980.

Wilson, Elizabeth. *The Sphinx in the City: Urban Life, the Control of Disorder, and Women.* Berkeley: University of California Press, 1991.

Wilton, Andrew. *Turner and the Sublime.* Chicago: University of Chicago Press, 1980.

Winokur, Mark. "Black Is White/White Is Black: 'Passing' as a Strategy of Racial Compatibility." In *Unspeakable Images: Ethnicity and the American Cinema*, edited by Lester D. Friedman, 190–211. Urbana and Chicago: University of Illinois Press, 1991.

Wolf, Bryan Jay. *Romantic Re-vision: Culture and Consciousness in Nineteenth-Century American Painting and Literature.* Chicago: University of Chicago Press, 1982.

Wollen, Peter. *Singin' in the Rain.* London: British Film Institute, 1993.

Wright, Will. *Sixguns and Society: A Structural Study of the Western.* Berkeley: University of California Press, 1975.

Yaeger, Patricia. "Toward a Female Sublime." In *Gender and Theory: Dialogues on Feminist Criticism*, edited by Linda Kauffman, 191–212. Oxford: Blackwell, 1989.

Žižek, Slavoj. *Welcome to the Desert of the Real!* 2001. Available at <http://imp.lss.wisc.edu/~jddunne/docs/Zizek911.htm>.

Musical Sequences

The Band Wagon (1953)
    Directed by Vincente Minnelli
    Choreographed by Michael Kidd and Fred Astaire
    Sets (musical sequences) by Oliver Smith
    "A Shine on Your Shoes," performed by Fred Astaire and LeRoy Daniels, lyrics and music by Howard Dietz and Arthur Schwartz
    "Dancing in the Dark," performed by Fred Astaire and Cyd Charisse, music by Howard Dietz
    "Girl Hunt Ballet," performed by Fred Astaire and Cyd Charisse, written by Betty Comden and Adolph Green, music by Howard Dietz

Broadway Melody (1929)
    Directed by Harry Beaumont
    Choreographed by Sammy Lee

"Broadway Melody," performed by Charles King

    Lyrics and music by Arthur Freed and Nacio Herb Brown

Broadway Melody of 1938 (1938)

    Directed by Roy Del Ruth

    Choreographed by Dave Gould

    Sets by Merrill Pye

    "Your Broadway and My Broadway," performed by Sophie Tucker

    "Broadway Melody," performed by Eleanor Powell

    Lyrics and music by Arthur Freed and Nacio Herb Brown

The City (1939)

    Directed by Ralph Steiner and Willard van Dyke

    Music by Aaron Copland

Delicious (1931)

    Directed by David Butler

    Music by George Gershwin

42nd Street (1933)

    Directed by Lloyd Bacon

    Choreographed by Busby Berkeley

    Sets by Jack Okey

    "42nd Street," performed by Ruby Keeler and Dick Powell

    Lyrics and music by Al Dubin and Harry Warren

Gold Diggers of 1935 (1935)

    Directed and choreographed by Busby Berkeley

    Sets by Anton Grot

    "Lullaby of Broadway," performed by Wini Shaw

    Lyrics and music by Al Dubin and Harry Warren

Guys and Dolls (1955)

    Directed by Joseph Mankiewicz

    Choreographed by Michael Kidd

    Sets by Oliver Smith

    Music by Frank Loesser

It's Always Fair Weather (1955)

    Directed and choreographed by Gene Kelly and Stanley Donen

    "The Binge," performed by Gene Kelly, Dan Dailey, and Michael Kidd

    Music by André Previn

On the Town (1949)

    Directed and choreographed by Gene Kelly and Stanley Donen

    "New York, New York," performed by Gene Kelly, Frank Sinatra, and Jules Munshin

    Lyrics and music by Betty Comden, Adolph Green, and Leonard Bernstein

Singin' in the Rain (1951)

    Directed and choreographed by Gene Kelly and Stanley Donen

    Choreographic assistance by Carol Haney

    Sets by Randall Duell

    "Singin' in the Rain," performed by Gene Kelly

    Lyrics and music by Arthur Freed and Nacio Herb Brown

Swing Time (1936)

    Directed by George Stevens

    Nightclub set by John Harkrider

Tap (1989)

    Directed and written by Nick Castle

    Choreographed by Henry Le Tang, Gregory Hines, and Dorothy Wasserman

    Prison and Times Square tap numbers performed by Gregory Hines

West Side Story (1961)

    Directed by Robert Wise and Jerome Robbins

    Choreographed by Jerome Robbins

    Production design by Boris Leven

    "The Jet Ballet," performed by the ensemble

    "America," performed by Rita Moreno and George Chikaris

    Lyrics and music by Stephen Sondheim and Leonard Bernstein

Words and Music (1948)

    Directed by Norman Taurog

    Music by Richard Rodgers

    "Slaughter on Tenth Avenue," performed by Gene Kelly and Vera-Ellen

    Choreographed by Gene Kelly

Comics

Busiek, Kurt, Brent Anderson, and Alex Ross. *Astro City: Life in the Big City*. La Jolla: Homage Comics, 1996. Reprints of *Astro City*, nos. 1–6, originally published in 1995–96.

Busiek, Kurt, and Alex Ross. *Marvels*. New York: Marvel Books, 1994. Reprints of Marvels, nos. 0–4, 1999.

Chaykin, Howard. *Power and Glory*. Westlake Village, CA: Malibu Comics Entertainment. Reprints of nos. 1–4, 1994.

Clowes, Daniel. *Pussey!* Seattle: Fantagraphics Books, 1995.

Cole, Jack. *The Plastic Man Archives*. Vol. 1–3. New York: DC Comics, 1999–2002. Reprints of Plastic Man stories from Quality Publishing's *Police Comics*, nos. 1–20 (1941–43).

Dini, Paul, and Alex Ross. *Batman: War on Crime*. New York: DC Comics, 1999.

Eisner, Will. *Will Eisner's The Spirit Archives*, edited by Dale Crain. Vol. 1. New York: DC Comics, 2000. Reprints of stories from June 2 to December 29, 1940.

Ellis, Warren, and Darick Robertson. 2000. *Transmetropolitan*. #32. New York: DC Comics, 2000.

——. *Transmetropolitan: Back on the Street*. New York: DC Comics, 1998. Reprints of the first three issues of the series, beginning in 1997.

——. *Transmetropolitan: The New Scum*. New York: DC Comics, 2000. Reprints of material originally published in 1999.

Golden, Christopher, Tom Sniegoski, and Marshall Rogers. 2000. *Realworlds: Batman*. New York: DC Comics.

Kane, Bob, Bill Finger et al. *Batman Archives*, edited by Dale Crain. Vol. 1. New York: DC Comics, 1990. Reprints material from *Detective Comics* #27–50 (1939–40).

Larsen, Erik, et al. *The World's Greatest Comic Magazine!* Marvel Comics, 2000–2001.

Lee, Stan, and Steve Ditko. *The Essential Spider-Man.* Vol. 2. New York: Marvel Comics, 1997. Reprints *Amazing Spider-Man* #21–43 and Annuals #2–3 (1965–67).

Lee, Stan, and Jack Kirby. *The Essential Fantastic Four.* Vol. 1. New York: Marvel Comics, 1998. Reprints *Fantastic Four* #1–20 and *Fantastic Four Annual* #1 (1961–64).

Loeb, Jeph, and Tim Sale. *A Superman for All Seasons.* New York: DC Comics, 1999.

McCay, Winsor. *Little Nemo, 1905–1914.* Cologne: Taschen, 2000.

Miller, Frank, and Klaus Janson. *Daredevil.* #169. New York: Marvel Comics, 1980.

Miller, Frank, Klaus Janson, and Lynn Varley. *The Dark Knight Returns.* 10th anniversary ed. New York: DC Comics, 1996. Reprints series originally published in 1986.

Moore, Alan, and Dave Gibbons. *Watchmen.* New York: DC Comics, 1987. Reprints the twelve-issue series published in 1986–87.

Moore, Alan, and Gene Ha. *Top 10: Book 1.* La Jolla: America's Best Comics, 2000. Reprints the first six issues of the series, originally published in 1999–2000.

Moore, Alan, and Curt Swan. *Superman: Whatever Happened to the Man of Tomorrow?* New York: DC Comics, 1997. Reprints material originally published in 1986.

Moore, Alan, and various artists. *Supreme.* Image Comics, 1996–98.

——. *Supreme: The Return.* Awesome Entertainment, 1999–2000.

Moore, Alan, J. H. Williams, and Mick Gray. *Promethea: Book 1.* La Jolla: America's Best Comics, 2000. Reprints the first six issues of the series, originally published in 1999–2000.

Morrison, Grant, and Richard Case. *Doom Patrol: Crawling From the Wreckage.* New York: DC Comics, 1992.

Morrison, Grant, and Richard Case (and other artists). *Doom Patrol.* New York: DC Comics 1989–1992.

Motter, Dean, et al. *The Return of Mr. X.* East Fullerton, CA: Graphitti Designs, 1986. Reprints the first four issues, which originally appeared in 1983–84.

Outcault, R. F. *The Yellow Kid.* Northampton, MA: Kitchen Sink Press, 1995.

Robinson, James, and Tony Harris. *Starman.* New York: DC Comics. 1994–present.

Robinson, James, Paul Smith, and Richard Ory. *The Golden Age.* New York: DC Comics, 1995. Reprints the four-issue series published in 1993–94.

Siegel, Jerome, and Jerry Shuster. *Superman: The Action Comics Archives,* edited by Bob Kahan. Vol. 1. New York: DC Comics, 1997. Reprints material from *Action Comics* #1–20 (1938–40).

INDEX

Hart, Lorenz, 168

Hearst, William Randolph, 187, 207, 209

Hertz, Neil, 107

Hine, Lewis, 198, 201

Hine, Thomas, 16–17

Hines, Gregory, 174

Hoberman, Jim, 168

Hoke, Donald R., 36, 229 n.3

Hollander, Anne, 215

Howard, Ebeneezer, 125

Howe, Irving, 148–149

Huet, Marie-Hélène, 55

IMAX, 28, 112

Image Comics, 50, 57–60, 65–66

The Incredible Shrinking Man, 116

Industrialization, 38, 83–84, 106, 113–114; industrialization of language, 34; Industrial Revolution, 101; Machine Age, 45; modernism and, 43–44; trauma of, 53. *See also* Modernity

It's Always Fair Weather, 162–163, 181

Ivan the Terrible, Part 2, 241 n.28. *See also* Eisenstein, Sergei

Jackson, Michael, 134, 139, 142–150, 154–155

James, William, 125

Jameson, Fredric, 34, 43–44, 49, 124

Jay, Martin, 245 n.10

"The Jet Ballet," 179–180. See also *West Side Story*

Jobs, Steven, 25

Johnny Mnemonic, 117

Johnson, Philip, 17

Johnson Heade, Martin, 95

Jolson, Al, 149

Jonze, Spike, 2

Journey to the Far Side of the Sun, 127. *See also* Belson, Jordan

Jussim, Estelle, 239 n.71

Kael, Pauline, 251 n.60

Kaes, Anton, 178–179, 182

Kaleidoscopic perception, 3, 114, 129, 136, 138–139, 158, 175, 241 n.28. *See also* Amusement

park rides; Special effects; Spectacular technologies

Kant, Immanuel, 91–92, 98, 101

Kaplan, Justin, 44

Kasson, John, 163

Katsuhiro, Otomo: *Akira*, 191

Kaufman, Philip, 125, 129; *The Right Stuff*, 125–129

Keane, Margaret, 106

Keeler, Rudy, 168, 176, 178

Kelly, Gene, 144, 181, 183

Kidd, Michael, 174–175, 180–181

Kinesis, 2–3, 9, 28–29, 41–42, 45, 85, 114–115, 121, 129, 141; kinetic urban landscapes, 45; movement-image, 141–142; narrative and, 28; spectatorial kinesis, 95. *See also* Amusement park rides; Dance

King, Margaret, 17, 19, 28

Kirby, Jack, 50, 75–77, 191, 192

Kirby, Lynne, 29

Kittler, Friedrich, 39, 44

Klein, Alan, 51, 55, 59–61, 65–66, 231–232 n.8

Koolhaas, Rem, 163, 166, 186, 189, 214

Kowinski, William, 21, 22

Kracauer, Siegfried, 4, 157, 175–176, 202, 241–242 n.29, 248 n.4

Krazy Kat, 6

Kroker, Arthur, 14, 21

Kubrick, Stanley, xi–xii, 108, 117, 127, 128; *2001: A Space Odyssey*, xi–xii, 82, 91, 93, 95–97, 102, 104, 108, 117–119, 124, 127–128

Landis, John: "Black or White," 144

Landon, Brooks, 91

Lane, Fitz Hugh, 100

Lang, Fritz, 16, 19, 197; *Frau du Mond*, 19; *Metropolis*, 19, 197

Latham Sholes, Christopher, 35–36, 44

Lawrence, D. H., 49, 125

Leach, William, 164–165

Lears, T. J. Jackson, 112–113, 129–130, 165–166, 239 n.78

Leary, Timothy, 26

Lee, Stan: *The Fantastic Four*, 50, 75–76; *Spiderman*, 2, 50, 206–208; *Thor*, 50

Scott Bukatman teaches film studies and visual culture in the
Department of Art and Art History at Stanford University.

Library of Congress Cataloging-in-Publication Data
Bukatman, Scott.
Matters of gravity : special effects and supermen in the 20th century /
Scott Bukatman.
Includes bibliographical references and index.
ISBN 0-8223-3132-2 (cloth : alk. paper)
ISBN 0-8223-3119-5 (pbk. : alk. paper)
1. United States—Civilization—20th century.
2. Popular culture—United States—History—20th century.
3. Body, Human—Social aspects—United States—History—20th century.
4. Metamorphosis—Social aspects—United States—History—20th century.
5. Mass media—Social aspects—United States—History—20th century.
6. Motion pictures—Social aspects—United States—History—20th century.
7. Technology—Social aspects—United States—History—20th century.
I. Title.
E169.1.B933 2003   303.48'3'0973—dc21   2002154087